Drifting

Drifting

Two Weeks on the Hudson

Mike Freeman

excelsior editions

State University of New York Press
Albany, New York

Cover photo courtesy of Dustin Kincaid

Published by State University of New York Press, Albany

© 2011 State University of New York

For information, contact State University of New York Press, Albany, NY
www.sunypress.edu

Excelsior Editions is an imprint of State University of New York Press

Production by Diane Ganeles
Marketing by Michael Campochiaro

Library of Congress Cataloging-in-Publication Data

Freeman, Mike, 1968–
    Drifting : two weeks on the Hudson / Mike Freeman.
        p. cm.
    Includes bibliographical references and index.
    ISBN 978-1-4384-3945-7 (hardcover : alk. paper)
    1. Hudson River (N.Y. and N.J.)—Description and travel.   2. Hudson River Valley (N.Y. and N.J.)—Description and travel.   3. Freeman, Mike, 1968—Travel—Hudson River (N.Y. and N.J.)   I. Title.
    F127.H8F64 2011
    974.7'3—dc22   2011006577

10 9 8 7 6 5 4 3 2 1

Butch: Kid, there's something I think I ought to tell you. I never shot anyone.

Sundance: One hell of a time to tell me. Well, just aim for the center. That way if you miss a little you'll at least hit something.

—From "Butch Cassidy and the Sundance Kid"

Contents

ஃ

Acknowledgments

❧

In addition to the many people who appear in the book, I'm grateful to the following: Professor David Schuyler of Franklin and Marshall College, Jill Lepore of Harvard, Kathy Hattala of the Hudson River Estuary Program, family members near and far, everyone at the SUNY Press, Jeff Simms of the Open Space Institute, Chris Pryslopski of the Hudson River Valley Institute, the staff of Hawthorne Valley Farm in Ghent, NY, Maine's Old Town Canoe Company, and Kate Taylor, Ken Able, Rich Guthrie, David Secor, and Mike Burger, all of whom work for various conservation organizations and agencies. Jerold Pepper of the Adirondack Museum and Helen Vendler of Harvard were both kind and of great help as well.

❧

I am grateful for permission to reprint the following material.

For *The Adventures of Augie March*
The Adventures of Augie March
Saul Bellow
Penguin Group
New York, NY
1999

INTRODUCTION

Prologue

To understand a country it's best to understand its land, to move through it long and slow. Rivers bore through terrain long and slow, and as such a people's relation to their moving water may define them better than anything. Yet as the old Greek reminds us, we never step in the same river twice, and since cultures course through history in similar fashion to flowing water, a float along each may not provide clear definition. Very well. We seek to word the questions in life as much as the answers, for the questions are all we really have.

By 2009, America—a place rigidly defined by many—had become a brew of simmering qualm and wayward identity. Racially, economically, socially, politically, ecologically—the past was aloft. Our wars, moreover, were troublesome, extensions of Vietnam's quick-triggered folly it seemed, though even their frothiest detractors couldn't say why, exactly, they weren't necessary. Yet they had come, and necessary or not, we only knew that a handful of be-turbaned, heavily bearded men had guided us into alien territory, where both hawks and doves defended their positions with more doubt than conviction, knocking our sense of self further askance.

By August of this same year, I was adrift myself, at a time when I should have been firmly grounded. A confluence of rapid events placed me there. I was forty-one and male, tumbling into midlife all in the middle of a greater shift, where twenty-first-century manhood scrambles to redefine itself. In keeping with this, I'd become a father in much the way New Orleans became a lake. One day all was well—sunny, happy, and fine—and then the levies broke, and when the levies break, Robert Plant tells us, you've got to move, and move I did. Not only did I become a father, but a stay-at-home father—a homemaker. I'd been living in Alaska, where I'd worked for ten years gathering field data for fish and wildlife biologists. Like many Northeasterners, I'd abandoned the New England woods of my youth for what the West has always promised—space, time, liberty. I found it in partial portions in Wyoming and California before coming to the remote wilderness I craved in Southeast Alaska. Ensconced, then, in this childhood dream, I met a woman on a visit back home—beautiful, fearsome, Irish, the best and worst kind—with whom I agreed to try and conceive. Four-thousand miles apart, both of us forty, we thought it would take time. Not so. A week after returning to Yakutat, Alaska, I received the news, and back I went, to a place I no longer considered home, a month before Lehman Brothers collapsed in 2008.

The job market was dismal enough, but needing employment more than ever, and that to exceed the salary of my highly qualified, career-engineered, but-now-pregnant partner, would be a trick. I'd had two jobs since college, Invisible Fence installer and Fish and Wildlife technician, meaning I'd buried wire, shocked dogs, and counted fish, nothing compatible with Manhattan's cubicle warrens. Résumés vanished in cyberspace, friends smiled and wished me well. I temped. I contract edited. I day labored, even had a couple magazine articles published. No matter. As the birth approached, both Karen and I recognized that sheaves of diaper changing filled my future, and when the baby came, it was so. I—who had spent a decade running frigid rivers by jet boat, working daily amid brown bears, often alone—was now at home with a baby girl while my partner earned our bread. We only pretend we don't care what people think. I was supposed to be working, and wasn't.

This is America, though, where we make our own way, or so goes the thought. I'd been in Alaska ten years, where they call the lower forty-eight "America." I'd moved back East, the region I'd thought I'd left for good, scarcely feeling connected. I'd published a few essays, and had logged reams of canoe time over the last decade. Having repatriated to the Northeast, I wanted to learn it anew. No better format for that than floating down a river. Dumb luck, moreover, made 2009 the four-hundredth anniversary of Henry Hudson's trip up his "River of Mountains," so the Hudson it would be.

With childcare arranged, I stuffed a couple dry bags with minimal gear, bought the only thing in the world worth owning—an Old Town canoe—and set off for Henderson Lake. Two weeks later, sunbaked and restored, I pulled out in Manhattan. Wind, weather, and tides favored me the whole way, and I cheated a bit. Lake Tear of the Clouds, a pond on Mount Marcy, is the Hudson's highest source, and I skirted several urban portages in Glens Falls by way of the Champlain Feeder Canal, part of New York's spectacular man-dug waterways. In addition, I pulled out in northern Manhattan, not the Battery, saving my brother-in-law a post-twilight pick-up. So be it. My goal was simply to relearn my country. I don't know what I found, but the trip was worth every stroke.

Rivers and the River

America the Beautiful. It's one of the few national bromides I've never dismissed. When Europeans probed the New World, God knows what they actually saw. They must have been stunned. Great chunks of Eurasia had been cultivated for so long that vestal landscapes were likely unknown. Adriaen van der Donck, a Dutchman in mid-seventeenth-century New Netherland, lacked the Puritanical wilderness jitters terrorizing English settlers to his east. Reflecting upon what was then the North River, now the Hudson, he admitted his incompetency "to describe the beauties, the grand and sublime works, wherewith Providence has diversified this land," noting simultaneously—without the irony the identical divergence commands today—the commercial potential locked in that same sublimity. There are "brooks having many fine falls," Van der Donck went on, "which are suitable for every kind of milling work . . . [and] the oak trees are very large; from sixty to seventy feet high without knots, and from two to three fathoms thick." Since Van der Donck's time, this blend of the poet's awe with the shipwright's necessity has wreaked great anxiety in the American soul, as with the advent of heavy industry and an abundance of wild land, our relationship to nature has grown increasingly complex, poising us always between the urge to protect and the need to destroy.

The land, of course, wasn't unknown to human hands, only looking that way to newcomers. Natives regularly burned forest understories to promote game browse, and though less visibly than Europeans, they tilled soil, particularly in what is now eastern America, growing mostly corn, squash, and beans. By and large, though, the land was pure. A healthy Native reciprocity with nature, combined with a lack of industry, kept humans of the Americas far more inclusive in the natural world than the Europeans that came to them. Dimensional lumber, molten ore, industrial tanning solution—these and others were largely unknown to the New World, but the clash came, and when it did, the Natives weren't above their own fractious stirrings. Tribes of the Iroquois and Algonquin—among the first to encounter Europeans—did much to extirpate beavers and other wildlife in order to get their hands on the axes, guns, booze, cloth, and other goods that must have seemed dropped from heaven. Neither Native cultures nor their landscapes were ever the same, a trend that tracked westward. Nature was seen as resource, and accordingly demolished. Murkier currents, however, shadowed the European juggernaut. The natural world's beauties—subtle, soothing, terrifying—stayed the destruction somewhat, and throughout this period to today America the Beautiful has endured.

Not long before our child was born, Karen and I saw Paul Stamets speak in Manhattan. A bearded man in a floppy hat, Stamets looks like he's been studying mushrooms all his life and has. Working the old-growth forests of Washington and Oregon, he's discovered properties in mycelium that could potentially cure many ills, among them bioterrorist threats such as small pox and anthrax. "I'm a patriotic American primarily for one reason," he said. "We still have old-growth forests," a thought that hit hard. From its origin, America has had enough regard for its wilderness to have pulled through two centuries of unfettered industry with large tracts either untouched or on the mend. Much of this has to do with nature's resilience, but much else with the nation's pelagic theology, the need to walk outside and say "My God," and it's for this, if for other things, that we're truly gifted.

Rivers, of course, are endemic to terrain, to life too, and America is rich in rivers. Flowing water runs in great quantities here, thatching us like capillaries, and where it doesn't the big waters—the Missouri, Colorado, Green, Rio Grande—live in our imaginations. From Huckleberry Finn and Shenandoah to "Proud Mary" and David Byrne, from Faulkner's Old Man to Nick Adams' "Big Two-Hearted River" to sad, screeching Ned Beatty in Deliverance, rivers feed American culture as much as they water its land. Like any American male under fifty, I've probably watched Apocalypse Now thirty times, all in my teens. If Do Lung River isn't in America, it dwells in American minds, at least in generations of its boys. My dad watched it too, having recognized the film's theft of Joseph Conrad's Heart of Darkness. "Whenever you're reading a book," he said, "and come across moving water, get your pencil out. A river is never just a river."

Rivers draw people for many reasons. Water, yes, but much else. The Euphrates, the Nile, the Jordan, the Tigris—these and others live in humanity's collective mind because people sat upon their banks and wove a story, stirred by moving water. "I've known rivers," Langston Hughes wrote, "Ancient, dusky rivers / My soul has grown deep like the rivers." Rivers are of water, and water is the source, and scarcely a creature has lived that hasn't pondered its origin. Norman Mclean, then, might speak for all life:

> Eventually, all things merge into one, and a river runs through it. The river was cut by the world's great flood and runs over rocks from the basement of time. On some of the rocks are timeless raindrops. Under the rocks are the words, and some of the words are theirs.
>
> I am haunted by waters.

Oceans receive rivers, and just as all water flows in and out of the sea, all literature seems to flow from one man, Herman Melville, who delved origin like no one else. At *Moby Dick's* outset, he fingers water as the source of human wonder:

> There now is your insular city of the Manhattoes, belted round by wharves as Indian isles by coral reefs—commerce surrounds it with her surf. Right and left, the streets take you waterward. Its extreme down-town is the battery, where that noble mole is washed by waves, and cooled by breezes which a few hours previous were out of sight of land. Look at the crowds of water-gazers there.
>
> Circumambulate the city of a dreamy Sabbath afternoon. Go from Corlears Hook to Coenties Slip, and from thence, by Whitehall, northward. What do you see?—Posted like silent sentinels all around the town, stand thousands upon thousands of mortal men fixed in ocean reveries. Some leaning against the spiles; some seated upon the pier-heads; some looking over the bulwarks of ships from China; some high-aloft in the rigging, as if striving to get a still better seaward peep. But these are all landsmen; of

week days pent up in lath and plaster—tied to counters,
nailed to benches, clinched to desks. How then is this?
Are the green fields gone? What do they here?"

What they did there was contemplate, for even as it relaxes,
water terrifies, reveals as it dissembles. We come to it for answers, if
not as mad as Ahab, then certainly with the same questions.

Physically and mythically, some rivers are bigger than others. I
pushed a canoe into Henderson Lake having scant knowledge of the
Hudson beyond a general understanding that it has swayed much of
American history. Melville, after all, wasn't describing the ocean, but
where the Hudson and Atlantic push into one another. Though he
set his book in far-flung whaling grounds, he drew much from Hudson
imagery, knowing this river infused the American character. Nearly
a third of the Revolution's battles, after all, were fought inside this
watershed, and from Henry Hudson to the steamship to Finch Pruyn
to Thomas Cole to Pete Seeger, the Hudson is fogged with import.

Many people take this all the way, dubbing the Hudson "America's River," a tag I can't quite apply. The Mississippi, for instance, is
certainly a prime competitor, and as words make up much of what we
are, nothing eclipses Abe Lincoln's news after the Battle of Vicksburg.
"The Father of Waters again moves unvexed to the sea," he wrote,
communicating far more than a Northern victory.

Personally, as well, it's difficult to live outside your own experience. "We love the things we love for what they are," Robert Frost
ends his tribute to an ephemeral New England rivulet, "Hyla Brook."
I grew up near the Hudson in Connecticut, but hardly went near it.
People didn't do that in the 1970s. As a kid, I once thumbed a *Mad*
magazine. They'd sketched Evel Knievel swimming the Hudson, saying for his greatest stunt he should cross it. His gasping face lay amid
trash and poison barrels and dead, three-eyed fish, telling all. Karen's
mother, too, grew up in Glens Falls, and scarcely knows the river that
defines it. In the mid twentieth century, she said, no one went there,
or barely mentioned it. As in Houston, where they say the refinery
stench smells like money, if befouling the Hudson was contingent to
a strong economy, then that was good enough. I spent my time on
other waters, hunting, fishing, and trapping with my father at a family
cabin in Pennsylvania's Endless Mountains. I know myself and my dad
and the world-at-large, then, through the creeks and springlets there,

some no wider than a human leg. These creeks are more salient to me than the Mississippi, which I've only seen from a couple bridges. Myth, though, is hard to escape, and there it is, the Hudson, a boulder among pebbles. I had one sense of this. We crossed the Hudson countless times on our way to Pennsylvania, over the New-burgh-Beacon Bridge, the only time I ever saw it. Once, alone with my father, he looked upstream, where summer twilight streaked the wide, breezy water. It almost looked clean. "You can really see why he thought he'd found it," he said. I didn't know what he meant, but even before I asked, his inflection had said enough. This river was more than a filthy canal.

Over time, the Hudson seeped into me, as it does consciously or not to most Americans. If I can't call it America's river, it certainly is an emblematic register of our past, present, and future, given its four-hundred-year settlement. From trappers' first contact with Natives to its primacy in the Revolution to connections with whaling, logging, and the Erie Canal, the Hudson is vital to understanding both Colonial and early American history, not to mention it as the locus for much of the nation's artistic origins and the birth of the frontier myth. Following the Civil War, as well, this textured account doesn't stop. Hard industry rose and fell here in the form of brickyards and paper mills, quarry blasting and iron mongering, General Electric and General Motors, and it contributed to the early computer revolution with IBM's Poughkeepsie operation. Stemming from this, and central to present-day tribulations, is the discord between modern convenience and environmental destruction, and the Hudson represents nothing if not this friction's topography.

Racial unrest, too, pervades the Hudson, which saw a conten-tious event in 1987 Newburgh, as well as slavery and points along the Underground Railroad. Presidents have been reared in the Hud-son Valley, agriculture has flourished and waned, risen again, while a nuclear plant still operates twenty-four miles from New York City. The Hudson saw the surge of ethnic political machines in the nineteenth century, the first federally mandated Environmental Impact Statement at Storm King Mountain, and Benedict Arnold's West Point trea-son, where today's officers prepare for the country's divisive wars. The river, then, is a place to sift the American experience, and to do it by canoe was more luck than I could ask. Having spent five months with a daughter at my side, I convinced myself the trip wouldn't be much over her life span. Soon after, I strapped the new canoe to my brother-in-law's minivan then drove with him up the Taconic Parkway, over to I-87, and on into the Adirondacks, intermittently feeling that the free life had never left me.

Dimensions

The Hudson is often described as two rivers, tidal and nontidal, but to a canoeist it's three. Long ago, from the retreat of the Wisconsin Ice Sheet through to industrialization, the two-part river would have held. It's raised in the Adirondacks, though exactly where is in question. Lake Tear of the Clouds—over forty feet up Mount Marcy—is its highest source, drained by Feldspar Brook, a tumbling, bouldery affair feeding the Opalescent, a yards-wide stream. To the west, Henderson Lake is another candidate. A concrete governor retards its drainage, which spills into Sanford Lake, a marshy stretch flowing through abandoned iron pits. The current picks up, widens, coursing through cedar and hemlock, paper birch and sugar maple, where it eventually joins the Opalescent. Part One begins here, the river as river. Lasting about a hundred miles, it has long stretches of whitewater, particularly rough in the Hudson Gorge, a fourteen-mile enclosure cut through steep, bluish rock. As rivers do, Part One changes along the way—accumulating volume, losing gradient, shifting direction—but maintains a strong current until just past the Sacandaga confluence near Corinth, where Part Two begins.

Prior to Industrial Man, this section must have been seamless with Part One, but between Corinth and Troy, maybe fifty miles, over a dozen dams have been erected, most with shifting purposes. Glens Falls started as a sawyer's mill in the nineteenth century before converting to hydropower. Other dams ran paper mills and textile factories but have been switched to power as well. The Champlain Feeder Canal, which saved me several portages, was constructed primarily to divert water to the Champlain Canal, keeping summer commerce open.

Part Two earned the Hudson its noxious infamy. General Electric takes the brunt of the blame and perhaps should, but industries from paper to forging to leathery to fabric-making used the Hudson as a septic for over a century. Sewage pipes, too, fouled it the length of the river, along with other industries, but the bulk of the slime came from Corinth through Troy. That it doesn't today is testament to the nation's shifting priorities, as ecological health slowly displaces fiscal monomania as the ruling ethic. Whether or not industry and healthy ecosystems can be wed is an urgent matter, and much of it is being bandied about now in Part Two.

Below Troy is the Hudson to which people generally refer. Smooth, wide, and tidal, the river here is a revolving sphere of oceanic and terrestrial influence. Like all transitional zones, it's a highly fertile place—ecologically, commercially, metaphorically. It's also slow. In its upper reaches, the Hudson drops elevation quick, averaging sixty-four feet per mile in the first fifty miles. In Part Three, the 153-mile estuary, the bed is almost flat, descending just five feet from Troy's Federal Dam to Manhattan, all below sea level. As with so much in America's northern half, ice is the culprit. Though it's difficult to tell today, the Hudson is an old fjord, having been cut by glaciers long ago.

All rivers change from source point to endpoint, but some more than others. In the Hudson, the fjord is unrecognizable from the wadeable gurgles coming out of Henderson Lake. This stretch, nearly half the river's 315-mile length, is progressively more ocean than river, and is where the Native name Muhheakantuck derives, Mohican for "river that flows both ways." As with all tidal rivers, then, Part Three about-faces four times a day and flows in the opposite direction. Saltwater can reach as high as Poughkeepsie during droughts, whereas spring and fall floods push it as low as West Point. The brackish zone, where saltwater blends with fresh, is the most productive in any estuary, providing plankton blooms for successive pegs in the food chain.

Part Three widens considerably, stretching to three and a half miles at Haverstraw Bay before funneling to a mile as it pushes by Manhattan. Functionally, the river ends at the Narrows, where it meets New York Harbor, but technically doesn't stop until the Abyssal Plain halfway to Bermuda, where its finest sediments are deposited, dust some billion years old from Precambrian Adirondack bedrock. This powder drifts over spectacular depths—a ribbonish, submarine gorge known as the Hudson Canyon. Once again, ice is the reason. During the last glacial age, ocean levels fell far below their current depths, about four hundred feet, exposing much of the continental shelf. This left rivers 130 more miles to run, and the Hudson cut quite a furrow, with the canyon diving from 9,000 to 15,000 feet. When the ice fell back, something called isostatic rebound raised the land. The oceans, too, advanced, flooding these former river mouths. "Drowned rivers" they're called, and the Hudson is among the largest, but it begins where most rivers do, high in the hills.

PART I

๛

MOUNTAINS AND WILD

My Land, Your Land

I didn't plan the trip, at least thoroughly. Not blessed with organizational skills, neither do I fetishize the latest gear, looking upon such people the way Bill Bryson did in A Walk in the Woods. Beware "Equipment Man," Bryson warned, and I do. Besides, floating a river isn't hiking. You put a boat in and pull it out. Flow goes one way, making getting lost a trick. Gear-wise, this was New York in August. I tossed a sweater in if the mountains cooled down, but otherwise needed only my tent and sleeping bag, a gizmo called a Leatherman—good for anything shy of brain surgery—a few shreds of clothing, a headlamp, filter and bottle, life jacket, three paddles, the boat, two tarps, and a hundred feet of rope. I packed a small fire bag—two butanes, wax starters, cedar shavings—just in case, but didn't plan on making fires and never needed one.

Food, of course, was necessary, though I'm not one for camp stoves. The extra weight along with the nasty fuel aren't worth an MRE. Coffee, too, is for suckers. There may be something that I hate more than people who need coffee, but I've yet to meet it, though that excludes the New York Yankees, who at the time were rolling along famously. "I have begat Great Evil," quoth the Lord, "and called it 'Jeter.' "

Meals wouldn't be a worry. The first fifty miles looked absent of diner-sized towns, but after that lunch wouldn't be a problem. For other sustenance I packed a hundred energy bars. Certain insects feed their young by catching prey, eating it, then regurgitating the mash to squishy offspring, a process called trophallaxis. I'd be astonished if energy bars weren't made the same way, where workers masticate high-caloric foodstuffs, climb the rafters, then hurl the new product to the floor. No matter. They're light to pack, filling to eat, and fuss-free, the perfect camp food.

In terms of logistics, there wasn't much. The river would be what it would be. Finding out it was tidal for half its length, for instance, was a help, but it would have been tidal regardless. The Hudson Gorge, too, was apparently rough, and I called a rafting guide a few days beforehand, simply to see if it was passable in an open boat. "You'll go swimming," he said, "but people do it." Good enough. Beyond that, it was a matter of getting dropped off, paddling, and getting picked up. I budgeted a month's time and took a crude map. As far as camping permission went, I'd find public sites if I could and free-form when I couldn't. Most people wouldn't know if I snuck a tent in after dusk, and some wouldn't care if I did. As for the others, well, who doesn't like a good chasing? *Olly olly oxen free*, we shouted as children, and secretly yearn to do so again.

I packed two books, *Moby Dick* and *The Adventures of Augie March*, both dog-eared. *Augie* contains my life's philosophy:

> I had no eye, ear, or interest for anything else—that is, for usual, second-order, oatmeal, mere-phenomenal, snarled-shoelace-carfare-laundry-ticket plainness, unspecified dismalness, unknown captivities; the life of despair-harness, or the life of organization-habits which is meant to supplant accidents with calm abiding. Well, now, who can really expect the daily facts to go, toil or prisons to go, oatmeal and laundry tickets and all the rest, and insist that all moments be raised to the greatest importance, demand that everyone breathe the pointy, star furnished air at its highest difficulty, abolish all brick, vaultlike rooms, all dreariness, and live like prophets or gods? Why, everybody knows this triumphant life can only be periodic. So there's a schism about it, some saying only this triumphant life is real and others that only the daily facts are. For me, there was no debate, and I made speed into the former.

I was interested in what the trip had to say, then, not its oatmeal. My brother-in-law—a jolly Brit ever sporting a pink Izod—drove me up the old mining road toward Tahawus, helped carry the canoe into Henderson Lake, then said goodbye, leaving only the star-furnished air.

Like all terrain, the Adirondacks have their own quirks physiologically, but that isn't what sets them apart. Americans have a contentious relationship with land, particularly the rift between public and private. To understand this, it's best to understand the Adirondacks, no easy doing. Whatever our land ethics are now, whatever they might become, they started in this bizarre range of Upstate New York, mostly to protect the Hudson's coveted wellsprings, and from within that legislative wrangle came our national wilderness problem.

Growing up in the Northeast, then moving West, isolated this public-private tension. "No Trespassing" rules the East. Public land exists, but primarily in small-acreage parks, often a half-day's drive away. To access most open space, you need permission, forcing a relationship that can never be reciprocated, as nothing you offer will quite compensate for using someone's land.

To many Westerners—who live amid public land—land allocation is the only thing Easterners got right. For developers, public tracts have "no trespassing" qualities of their own. As Willie Nelson points out, after all, cowboys are special, with their own brand of misery, and "kill it, drill it, fill it, then put up an Arby's" seems the governing ethos that brought them there. Westerners fume at the amount of public land with which they're saddled, claiming that it denies them economic opportunity. This is tricky. As with any emotional debate, both sides have validity while neither has an ear for irony. I usually side with the Lorax, leaning toward any position that leaves land unscathed, but it's foolish to pretend that developers have no point. This is the friction between wilderness and industry, scraping our guts, and it's been hashed out best in the Adirondacks, even while the hashing hasn't stopped.

A Westerner's primary devil is GOVERNMENT. If there's evil in the world, the government plotted it, and as public land is government land, a state park is Satan's hideaway. National Forests, then, which comprise much of the West, are the Ninth Circle, where nature is left alone, leaving little room to make money (unless you're a miner, rancher, or logger, exceptions notably absent from hillbilly diatribe), and a National Park is beyond description.

I flew a lot in Alaska, performing aerial salmon surveys across the Tongass National Forest. The pilots—sunburnt go-getters from the Pacific Northwest—were like most Westerners. Few had been more than twenty miles east of their hometown, their rancor for that particular compass point running thus deep. Flying with these guys, transecting government land to do government fish counts, it usually wasn't long before the grousing commenced. "What's the sense of all this land if you can't put up a house?" Flying over the ample clear-cuts only perked them up a little. "At least somebody made money."

Loath to rile the man flying the plane, I kept quiet, learning something besides. This country wasn't my country. These people came up differently. Nurture, too, wasn't all of it. Having hunted, fished, and trapped my whole life, I had exploitation urges of my own, which out West soaked up much of the local disdain for parameter. A chainsaw, for one, is a problematic implement to one who loves trees, like myself, but when the saw fires up pictures himself bounding along every mountainside in sight, making a golf-green the world over. Such desires suffuse our bloodstream, and in the West, where all that public land dangles temptation while mandating restraint, it's easy to understand why people reared there have a different view than those hemmed from birth by private deeds.

The irony of the pilots, of course, is that they're as awed by Creation as anyone. These guys wouldn't be up there if they flew over Big Box plazas and bowling alleys all day. Wildness pulls them as much as it pulls a coterie of Sierra Clubbers to mountain flowers, who if they don't have raging tree-cutter genes of their own, at least understand that resources must be extracted. These are the reciprocating ironies, and wilderness is their spawning ground. Though you won't hear this from regional extremists on either side, things have come to at least philosophical satisfaction in the Adirondacks, and they did so prior to any region in the country.

The Adirondack Park is enormous. Called "The Blue Line" for the boundary color on the original map, it's larger than Yellowstone, Yosemite, and the Grand Canyon combined, being the size of New Hampshire. Densely forested, it contains about 30,000 miles of flowing water and a lakes-per-acre ratio to rival Minnesota. With a mountain range that once eclipsed the Himalayas, the peaks now stand at a modest if venerable height. That few outside the Northeast don't know this isn't surprising, yet not many in New York City itself—four hours by car—know it either.

If past is prologue, this isn't shocking. Native Americans certainly used these mountains, but likely as transient hunting grounds. Evidence of permanence exists—notably at Chaz and Cranberry Lake—but it's scant. More probably the range was used for summer and autumn harvests—deer, beaver, berries, and nuts, particularly beech, acorns, and the now-vanished chestnut. Indications point to eight thousand years of such activity, and by the time Henry Hudson arrived, these peoples had been long solidified as Algonquins and Iroquois, each consisting of several tribes, akin to the Western concept of "nation." They both used the mountains, and neither had a good word for the other. The name "Adirondacks" itself, like many eastern place names, is bastardized from a Native tongue. However, from early French Jesuit accounts through to the highly regarded *A History of the Adirondacks*, by Alfred L. Donaldson, the term is an Iroquoian cut-up for Algonquins, meaning "tree-eaters." The Iroquois built cabins, or longhouses, while the Algonquins lived in the forest, a habit, it seems, looked down upon by their nemesis. It's a wonder how many names share this lineage. Today we speak with reverence for the Anastasi, the quasi-urban culture that seemingly vanished into desert sand. The name itself recalls the wisdom of ancients, as well as the ruin of wisdom, and we feel bound to something sacred when it's spoken. It turns out that it's a Navajo pejorative for these same people, as if Americans were reverentially known to future cultures as "The Honkeys."

According to Donaldson, both the Algonquin and Iroquois called these temporary grounds "The Dismal Wilderness," a name with compacted meaning. Since both peoples laid claim here, this is where they clashed most, leaving untold numbers of dead, though there's probably more to it. These mountains are forbidding turf in all seasons. Black flies make spring a masochist's delight, it can snow in summer, and autumn often takes the year off. Brush is dense, wet, and buggy, and in the frequent cloud cover the mountains aren't available as landmarks. Getting lost, then, isn't difficult. Indians are by no means without irony, and it's not hard to see a bit of sarcasm in the label "Dismal Wilderness."

When whites arrived they took the term to heart. Henry Hudson, though English, was under Dutch contract when he sailed upriver. His boat was called the *Halv Maen*, or *Half Moon*. The Dutch were master's-of-the-sea at this point, 1609, and inveterate traders. Beaver hides were their chief desire here, though no Dutchman penetrated the mountains to get them, rather relying on the Algonquin and Iroquois. Empires juggled North America from Holland to France to England to Spain, wars raged, settlers plodded ever westward, and still the strange mountains between Albany and Montreal were largely a myth, being skirted by the bulk of expansionists. The headwaters of the Columbia were discovered two centuries prior to Lake Tear of the Clouds, and Stanley presumed he'd found Livingstone along the Nile the year before. For two hundred years before that, as war, politics, and disease diminished Native presence, the Adirondacks became the province of trappers, miners, loggers, and misanthropes. This bunch, though, left their mark, and by the 1870s, when people began pouring out of the stifling city for fresh air, they found in these mountains what they sought.

Arguments abound as to whom the Adirondack Park can be traced, to what source this blend of conservation and exploitation is owed. Like the source of a river, this is difficult to determine. Was conservation the original impetus, or economics?

Conceptually, the need for nature as a place people could commune with whatever spirits they wished, there are any number of American sources. Henry Thoreau is chief among them. Like the Beatles, we elide him when considering the Greats, but there he is, on the most ordinary of days, radiating, "If you would know the flavor of huckleberries, ask the cow-boy or the partridge. It is a vulgar error to suppose that you have tasted huckleberries who have never plucked them." The Hudson River School gets a nod, binding nature with providence, as does Ralph Waldo Emerson, who helped found the Philosopher's Camp in 1858 on Follensby Pond, now in the Adirondack Park. Emerson and Thoreau were deeply submersed in Romantic thought. The former's scholarly loft fused well with Thoreau's primitive pith, providing Americans a wilderness creed that stands as firm now as any church's. Emily Dickinson, too, as the greatest poets will, sensed the changes of her time generations before they were popularly accepted. American attitudes toward nature pivoted sharply in the mid-nineteenth century, and Dickinson picked it up mid-rotation:

A Field of Stubble, lying sere
Beneath the second Sun—
Its Toils to Brindled People thrust—
Its Triumphs—to the Bin—
Accosted by a timid Bird
Irresolute of Alms—
Is often seen—but seldom felt,
On our New England Farms—

Life had been brutally thrust upon the earliest Americans, and they had been brutal in kind. Yet they succeeded, their posterity now having leisure to stand apart from toil and notice a bird in the field. Wilderness was rapidly becoming something other than the detested menace that it had been for over two centuries, and in a rare marriage, this emotional turn had a pragmatic match.

For those who feel that science—or the head—propels human endeavor, George Perkins Marsh is probably the Adirondack Park's prime mover. Perkins possessed an omnivorous mind, being a leading philologist as well as the author of *Man and Nature*, considered by many the preamble of environmentalism. Recently, in his popular *Collapse*, Jared Diamond warned to temper resource extraction, noting that it's toppled many dynasties. Easter Island, the Mayans, even the Anastasi—all were doomed by poor land management. Marsh has him beat by more than a century, noticing in Europe that deforestation had led to crippling aridity along the Mediterranean rim.

The book came out in 1864, when minds like Charles Darwin and Alfred Russel Wallace were finishing what Nicolai Copernicus had started four centuries prior, kicking humanity from the universe's center to the general swirl of cosmic dust. What Marsh's divine beliefs were I'm not sure, but in practical terms he rightly blends the religion and science of his day. In the preface to *Man and Nature*, he ascribes to humanity "a power of a higher order than any of the other forms of animated life, which, like him, are nourished at the table of bounteous nature." Marsh put human beings level with all life, but separates us too, though for different reasons than the old Great Chain of Being model. Unchecked, we're lethal, a destroying angel to ourselves and everything else. Whether God or natural selection made us as such is irrelevant to Marsh, it only matters that we're different. A Vermonter, he saw what we'd done to New England forests, having razed nearly every standing stick by his time, and he cautioned that we'd end up like the desiccated wastes of the Old World. He pointed to the Hudson canals running too low for commerce in the summer, as well as the river itself for log drives, and at least a few people took note, including Verplanck Colvin.

Born in New York, Colvin spent a great deal of time in the Adirondacks from 1865 onward—mapping, surveying, charting, absorbing. He was often alone, sleeping beneath a canoe or ledge, soaking in the woods the way he noticed the mosses around him soaking up rain. Much madness is divinest sense, Dickinson tells us, and wilderness is where it resides. Solitude in nature bleeds something into you. It may not be the language of God, but it feels like it. Fortunately, Colvin kept his wits quite a while, locating the Hudson's highest source—which he called Lake Tear in a journal note—and imposing Marsh's observations upon the timber-stripped hillsides around him. The Hudson would dry up, he knew, if steps weren't taken.

As both the official New York State Surveyor and an impassioned man, Colvin spent roughly a quarter century agitating state officials to create a park preserve. Along with other voices, he succeeded, and in 1885 a toothless but important Adirondack Forest Preserve was approved, nominally protecting seven hundred thousand acres of state land. Timber companies kept lopping chunks off the new reservation, allowing them to cut, but severe droughts a couple years later brought commerce and logging to a halt, and Colvin was finally vindicated, having insisted for over two decades that an intact forest was crucial to maintaining consistent water flow. In 1894, then, nearly three million acres were protected beneath the poetic aegis of "forever wild," words condensed from the original law that have since become a phrase of perpetual contention.

As much as he adored nature, Colvin had a foot in two paradigms. To the assembly came hordes of what we today call environmentalists, though more hunter-heavy than now, along with others craving wild land. Though Frederick Law Olmstead created Central Park in 1859—rightly knowing urban denizens would grow anywhere from lunatic to lethargic without open space—many people needed more. When the railroad surged into the mountains, people other than miners and loggers came to the Adirondacks, breathing easy in the woods. Here they recuperated, but were as mortified as Colvin by what logging had done, providing America its first concentrated environmental movement. Hunters and woodsmen, guides and the guided, fishermen and recreationalists, artists and poets, all assailed the assembly for preservation.

In the end, though, industry decided it, and Colvin, as Marsh before him, didn't mind accommodating. Lumber and paper companies yarded millions of board feet from the mountains every year, mostly spruce, and tanneries ransacked the region's hemlocks, whose bark contains a particularly fine tannin for leather making. Mining, too, sucked its share. Pits just below Henderson Lake—itself named for an original prospector who died nearby—needed heat to smelt, taking all the trees they could to provide charcoal. Furthermore, the assembly well knew that without the canal system, New York wouldn't be the empire state it had rapidly become. With barge traffic suspended by ever-diminishing summer waters, untold treasures would be lost. Neither Colvin nor Marsh were strict primitivists, and provisions were made for timber harvesting and other growth potential. Since its origin, the park has expanded in size and scope, cheered on by voices like Bob Marshall and Teddy Roosevelt, whose respective wilderness lusts echo far and wide. Championed thus, the park now includes roughly seven million acres.

These are different acres though. National Parks can scarcely be trod upon, and National Forests, while open to big-gun extractionists such as miners and tree-fellers, aren't often available as commercial or living space. The Bureau of Land Management (BLM), moreover, which tends more acreage out West than all others, is known even to ardent government-haters as the Bureau of Logging and Mining (BLM). What makes the Adirondack Park unique, and a showcase for why humans have such difficulty with compromise while maintaining a capacity for it, is its mixed ownership. The state owns a little less than an acre for every one of private land. Most private tracts are deeded to timber companies, while the rest is an admix of farms, second homes, one active mining claim (garnet), prisons, and the villages of the park's 130,000 permanent residents. New York, then, and its park, are a microcosm of the great East-West divide, with the bulk of city-types clamoring for preservation while the residents—though in marvel of the land's natural gifts—favor development. They do, after all, live there, and need to make a living. In crafting legislation, there is much pulling of hair and gnashing of teeth, violence has been threatened and occasionally enacted, but with New York, Boston, Philadelphia, Buffalo, and Hartford all within a day's drive, genuine wilderness exists here that accommodates limited development. No one is ever entirely happy, nor anyone entirely miffed, and this park—however flawed many think it—may be the most workable model going forward, abiding America's schizophrenic cravings for both economic growth and the ineffable properties of wilderness.

For its part, the Hudson's recent reclamation from industrial ooze began before anyone knew what polychlorinated biphenyls (PCBs) were. Whether it started with Henry Thoreau or the Hudson School painters or George Perkins Marsh or Verplanck Colvin or captains-of-industry is irrelevant in terms of result. The Hudson's headwaters down through its first third have been protected for over a century, predating any synthetic damage to the lower stretches. The clean rivers and wild forests available there now are owed to this conglomerate of interests, along with the capacity for compromise. I owe them too.

The Maturity of Idols

Woods. Karen and I had gone to Vermont since I'd moved, but never made it out of Burlington, and we'd spent a couple days at my family's Pennsylvania cabin, walking country roads, growing accustomed to one another and the creature gaining within her. Her family has a similar place in the Adirondacks, and we'd spent two days there in August. It was the first time I'd been, and even the carpeting forests couldn't conceal the glacial scarring. The U-shaped valleys, the lacerated bedrock, kettle ponds, shorn mountain tops—it was like visiting Southeast Alaska twenty thousand years from now, a place currently stripped raw by ice. Other than these brief interludes, however, it had been mostly Queens, and the scantly foliated, splenetic-frenetic tempo of urban life.

Henderson Lake runs cigar-shaped, north-south, two fingers jutting from its eastern shore. A creek spills out one of these through a concrete sluice where the canoe launch lies. Having shaken my brother-in-law's hand, I shouldered the dry bags then walked back to the launch, bristling as I tied a bag to the cross beam. The West had affected me. I'd anticipated bureaucracy as the trip's doom, and on cue a park ranger came out of the forest, chatting up two hikers. Permits. I'd never checked, certain the state required a myriad. Here I was, then, the paddle not even wet, and Roscoe P. Coaltrain had my number.

New York City is everything haters of paperwork despise. It's difficult to cross a street without completing ten forms. Want a job jackhammering? "Deeze is union jobs, fella. Fill out deeze paypah's heh and wait tree years, 'den fill'em out again, see?" The streets are awash with bureaucratic oatmeal, and I simply assumed the Hudson would be no different, demanding a qualifying exam for each mile floated. I smiled at the ranger as he finished with the other two, then lashed the second bag, priming my considerable well of premeditated ignorance.

I couldn't sell a life raft to a drowning man, but have soft-shoed my way out of many a minor legal scrape. Look stupid, be humble. Like Billy D. Williams and Colt 45, it works every time. The two people thanked the ranger and headed toward the car lot, leaving me to the robust lad beneath the stiff green ball cap. Lay it on me, brother. What section of what paragraph have I trespassed against this time? Sixteen-foot-four-inch canoe in sixteen-foot-two-inch waters? He wriggled his shoulders, adjusting his rucksack.

"Staying out a couple days?" he said, smiling.

You smug bastard. Out with it.

"I am."

"Have a great time. It's a beautiful lake. Just try to stay in the designated campsites."

He walked off. No permit check, no snooping, no nothing. "I'm Free!" Roger Daltrey declared, as did I, though in a far more perplexed tone.

I'm not one for good omens—bad, yes—but this was unmistakable, and the luck never wavered. From the Adirondacks to Manhattan, through three hundred miles, bureaucrats never molested me, badged or otherwise. I passed police boats and Coast Guard vessels, receiving only gassy wakes and puzzled looks. As a youngster, I lived in Wyoming for a stretch, volunteering on a federal fish hatchery. A warden cited me for not signing the state conservation stamp while duck hunting, a trifle on par with flashing the First Lady, given his chilly condescension. At least in its wilderness, then, New York has the buckaroos beat a mile. I picked up the paddle and slid the canoe forward, warm water shrouding my feet.

Birds are a solace to me. I've read they move through air, the realm between heaven and earth, and sensing agency, we observe. Perhaps, but I do know that my emotionally taciturn father effulges whenever there's birdlife about. In all my memory, I follow him through forests and meadows, attend him on porches, sit by him on summer stream banks, easy dusk, watching warblers dimple the midge bloom. I never go birding as defined by the binoculared crazies, but suburb or mountaintop, benchside or streamside, I'm looking. Yakutat funnels migrants between ocean and ice by the tens of thousands, channeling every manner of passerine, shorebird, raptor, and waterfowl through flooded verdancy. Walk outside in June and be amazed. The Five Boroughs are a bit different. I saw a broad-winged hawk on Park Avenue, a common yellowthroat outside Grand Central, several cardinals and a downy woodpecker in our Sunnyside neighborhood, and a black-throated green warbler flittering in ailanthus branches by the Fifth Avenue Library. You're nearly embarrassed that such paucity after such wealth matters, but it does.

I launched four hours before sunset. Having looked at the trail-side map, the public spots would be easy to find, and I moved the paddle side to side, unhurried. Out ahead, the finger opened to narrow lake, crowded with timber—hemlock, maple, and birch. A warm breeze fingered the water, bringing the tannicky vapor of rotting coni-fer. Across the lake, a veery called in solemn declension, followed by a happier yellowthroat nearby. The chickadees I could see, a trio off to the right, gamboling in a paper birch. Others whom I couldn't identify chipped and twitted in the bankside canopy. Coming into the larger lake, a glacier-sheared pass loomed to the north, while to the south lay a gentler gap, where at water's edge corrugated sand bars marked an inlet. Closer, a pair of common loons drifted fifty yards off the bow, then dove, and a kingfisher dropped from a hemlock limb, plunking the surface. Close your eyes, let your body glide over dark water, and soon whether you came to remember or forget is lost.

The breeze blew south to north, and I turned with it after crossing to the west bank. Wind-formed trees spoke to the trials of open water growth. Roots wrapped around exposed rock, while trunks twisted over water, gasping for sunlight. Common to mountain lakes, this one had more than one inlet, and I could hear a rolling creek as I approached the north end where two people bathed. They weren't the only human sign. Long ago and not long ago, successfully and unsuccessfully, people had come here for money. A rusted ring-bolt sprouted from exposed bedrock, likely a log boom, and along the shore, pointed stumps dotted the incline while fresh peeled sticks glowed in dark water—beavers, our first love, and the inadvertent lodestar of the New World.

A friend of mine, a high school chum gone California surfer, has a theory. Human intelligence began with negotiation, when two apish hominids each had something the other wanted. Beforehand, much beating and boulder tossing would have ensued, with one booty-laden combatant limping away while the other lay dead, jungle justice served. Now, however, the two links in question had simultaneously had enough, giving birth to haggling. Desires were communicated, demands compromised, and a settlement agreed upon. Fifty pounds of mammoth meat to you, seventy of mastodon to me. This required savvy, and language, and dissembling facial expressions belying the howling purity that said, "I'm going to kill you, then take your stuff." Commerce, then, may have catalyzed our outsized gray matter. I don't know, but can plausibly state that furs were likely the first traded commodity. Cold kills, and furs keep us warm. While this remains true, their utility has waned from those earliest days, and when seventeenth-century Dutch merchants sailed up the Hudson, their trip paralleled a quirky trend in European fashion.

History is tough to define. It can be personal or remote, relevant or academic, maddeningly clear or maddeningly opaque. Accounts are absent, unreliable, bloated, or simply false, and piecing together precisely what happened and why is often impossible. Fact is difficult to pry from myth, and if we're being honest, the two probably exist as a single species called "History." As all creatures do, moreover, this one evolves, and its cultural role can transform quickly. One such shift happened centuries ago, here in the Adirondacks, and its echo shifted me in turn.

Like many white kids, I revered Indians, mimicking what I thought they were throughout childhood forests, and I had an archetype in mind. This Indian was a man, young but not a kid. Mostly naked, he was alone—bow and arrow, buckskin quiver—moving fast or slow, but mostly just sitting, watching. On prairies and hillsides, in oak groves and saguaro stands, riverside and the littoral, I saw him clearly. He wasn't in Nature, he was Nature. Nature didn't exist. It was everything. One. His purpose was food, not killing, and nothing to excess. We didn't kill animals, he knew, they gave themselves to us, and to compromise this was to compromise all. I adored him, My Indian, not in the cutesy-pie English sense, but in the French—*adorer*, to worship.

Like any myth, variable amounts of fact birthed it, and culture filled in what imagination didn't. Without question, Natives far more compatibly approached living with creaturely life than the strangers who came to them, though ritual guided each. From coast to coast, Natives believed that to forego custom in killing was to offend that animal's spiritual entity. Breaking this covenant would eventually lead to that species no longer providing itself to human beings. I hunted and fished with my pop, and this ethos drew me from an early age. Flannery O'Connor once said that everything important that happens to us happens before we're twenty, simply meaning that beyond that we're ossified. Ethics, paradigms, iconography—all these form when we're sopping wet, unable to find much purchase once we harden. If a belief, though, can no longer form, it can certainly shatter.

My idealized Indian decayed more than shattered, but the effect has been the same. Like all childish beacons—from the Easter Bunny to George Washington—experience undid my Romanticism. Having grown up in Connecticut, it would make sense that I'd never met an Indian, and in fact never did until I was nineteen, working with a half-Mohawk at a moving company. This guy smoked cigarettes, drank filthily, and was rip-roaring funny, a T&A joke for every occasion, but he neither looked nor acted like the seamless fusion with Nature I expected. I knew the comparison matched a pre-Contact, post-Contact model, I just didn't expect to meet a normal guy.

Next to fall were the great Western buffalo jumps. As a kid, I'd read that plains tribes drove the herds to certain bluffs prior to acquiring horses from the Spaniards, stampeding up to several hundred off at a time. Women waited below, not wasting a single sinew. Artists rendered these rituals beautifully, and I studied every brush stroke, marveling over such efficiency with nothing but knives, muscle, and will. Later, not long after I'd worked with the Mohawk, I drove across country, spending time in Nebraska. The prairie's subtleties aren't visible at seventy-five miles per hour, and I intermittently ducked off I-80, finding a bluff along the way. This was August, grueling heat, and even with a heavily biased imagination I couldn't fathom 250 buffalo lumped on the plain, much of the muscle jellied by gravity, without at least modest spoilage. Every scrap but the bones, we were taught, was utilized. At Head-Smashed-In Buffalo Jump in Alberta, the bones are thirty feet deep. Bones rot slow. Gelatinous muscle doesn't, and I'll never be convinced that every last fiber was used.

The erosion accelerated from there, peeling myth off in strips. Here Rousseau threw a long shadow, whose Noble Savage notions stained my thoughts, as it did much of the nation's. Seventies' schools, working against institutionalized white preeminence, taught Rousseau's model even if they never mentioned his name. Fascinated with the cultures greeting colonial Europeans, Rousseau intimated that these were a uniform breed, peaceful by nature, violent only when wronged. They lived in unison with God's work, not at odds, and were a model of what Westerners were—and could be again—before the Fall. This fell straight to me. Indians were figments, something on a page. As a child—even an adolescent—I scarcely knew they existed in the present day. In such a state, in such a cultural atmosphere, I'd crafted the image I needed of Perfect Man. Perfection, though, dies hard, and my conjured Native was no exception. Reading didn't help, nor did living a decade in a Native community.

That Natives were violent prior to contact isn't disputed. Cherokees roughed up everyone in their path, and in their own tongue, "Mohawk" translates as "people-eaters." There's a natural jetty north of Yakutat, too, called Tsimshian Point, not for the culture that thrived there, but for the Tsimshian trespasser whom the Tlingits gutted and left on the rocks. Violence I understood. *Lord of the Flies* was assigned to me at fourteen, plump within O'Connor's molding age, and I've never stopped believing that civility and culture are anything but a veneer, shrouding humanity's catholic savagery. If Indians had a cruel streak independent of white encroachment, I could handle that. It was their relationship with Nature that I needed to be inviolable, but Calvin Martin corroded that need.

Martin studied Native cultures thoroughly, particularly their spiritual relations with animal life. *The Way of the Human Being* focuses on the fur trade, when Dutch, English, and French merchants offered the Natives products they'd never seen. Iron pots, tools, textiles, weaponry—these were too much, and immemorial traditions collapsed, as it was mostly Native trappers that performed the ensuing holocaust.

Though all furs were welcome, beaver was the prize. Swedish military officers wore a felt hat, which Europe took to like catnip, and beaver pelts, when shorn, produce terrific felt. The Indians, then, had stuff, the whites too, and the haggling commenced. The Dutch controlled what is now Manhattan, while the English had lesser ports to the east. Up north, the French ruled the St. Lawrence. It's estimated that sixty million beavers populated the Hudson watershed when the *Halv Maen* arrived. Though the last was trapped in 1880, they were effectively extinct before the Revolution. The Natives—Iroquois and

Algonquin, always battling—split this feat in halves, feeding fur to whichever whites offered the better bargain.

With the animals around Manhattan gone, Natives branched into every watershed. Greed drove them, not sacred bonds, and rather than granting beavers the reciprocal homage their former trust mandated, they lost themselves to avarice. Tragically, small pox and booze ravaged tribes throughout this period, and some members were certain that the Beaver spirit was exacting revenge. However it happened, though, flintlocks, duffel, iron cookware, and other items largely drove the slaughter, as too many Natives sniffed the good life, forsaking tradition for material wealth. Doug George-Kanentiio, a Mohawk from the Akwesasne Territory along the St. Lawrence River, told *Spirit of Change* magazine in 2009 of this trend's continuance:

> In our tradition we have in our creation story an important part about the twins, one twin of the good mind and one twin of the bad mind. . . . These twins are always present. Smuggling of tobacco and other narcotics, and gambling—whatever commands a profit—has created a narco-culture at Akwesasne. Our good, traditional Iroquois values of humility, compassion, simplicity, generosity, and communal service have been replaced by greed, intimidation, violence, and death.

This parallels difficulties during the fur trade, and it's complicated. For one, the Indians weren't trading for rubies and gold. This stuff had practical value, and particularly with the firearms, they'd never compete with either the whites or their ancestral enemies without them. The booze and disease, too, must be calculated, along with white ambition. "Decimate" means to kill one out of ten. Tribes lost that many times over to pathogens, and drink crippled the remnants. Having not been there, it's difficult to say, but it's not a stretch to assume that many saw the end at hand and threw custom to the wind. Still, motives are many, and it turned out My Perfect Indian wasn't a monolith of abstract goodness, but a vast group of diverse human beings as subject to greed as anyone. Native beliefs, their ceremonies, the wisdom that kept them in balance with Nature were no less true or effective, but they were as vulnerable to human avidity as anyone.

Long before Martin concluded this, Alexis de Tocqueville observed it not long after it happened:

> The Europeans introduced amongst the savages of North America fire-arms, ardent spirits, and iron: they taught them to exchange for manufactured stuffs, the rough garments which had previously satisfied their untutored simplicity. Having acquired new tastes, without the arts by which they could be gratified, the Indians were obliged to have recourse to the workmanship of the whites; but in return for their productions the savage had nothing to offer except the rich furs which still abounded in the woods. Hence the chase became necessary, not merely to provide for his sustenance, but in order to procure the only objects of barter which he could furnish to Europe. Whilst the wants of the natives were thus increasing, their resources continued to diminish.

My Indian, then, came to Yakutat knocked down but swinging. The town is coastal, a fishing community, seven hundred residents cut-off from the road system. Paradise. Here I met Tlingits, real Indians, and as far as these things go ones in closer proximity to their original environment—and therefore traditions—than most modern tribes. Martin and de Tocqueville were white men. What did they know?

Second chances, though, don't always pay out. Alaskan Natives are quite different than those down South. With one exception, Alaskan tribes don't live on reservations, which provide sovereignty within defined bounds, but a process cutting tribes off from their traditional lands and ways. Alaskans, conversely, forfeited prescribed turf for the right to exist on their original lands, though these tracts were open to whites as well. In addition, the environment is in much better shape there than elsewhere, allowing Natives a closer relationship with the land than Mohegans in Connecticut, say, for whom a casino seems to be the sole consolation. The Tlingits, then, are fairly intact culturally, primarily because they live where they've always lived, doing what they've always done. The methods, though, have changed.

Cruise ships sail up Disenchantment Bay across from Yakutat all summer, the passengers observing the glaciers there. Seals pup here, hauling out on ice to do so. It's thought that the intruding cruise ships have led to the seals' waning numbers, which in part they have, and yet this isn't all. While I have no scientific study in support, I do have ten years of observation, along with human calculus, and sometimes that's enough. Seals are a millennia-long Tlingit food and spiritual wellspring. Formerly, however, they were followed up into Disenchantment by canoe and hunted with harpoons, a much trickier enterprise than with motorboats and firearms. Many fishermen in town carry rifles, and any seal that pops its head up is a brave one. In the logic of self-interest, this is understandable. Seals eat salmon. Salmon are easier caught in a net than on the fin. Seals, therefore, plunder nets, along with fishermen's paychecks. By federal law, only Natives can shoot seals, provided it's for sustenance. Most bullets, then, comes from Native rifles, and if a seal should sink out there, well, this is the stuff of life. Cruise ships play their part, but the cannonades don't help much, and while many of these seals are eaten, many aren't.

People are tricky though. The Tlingit are like any set—a mix. Some adhere to tradition as best they can—quite well in many cases—while others have adopted Western recklessness when it comes to killing wildlife (sea otters, for instance, are chased around with 90-hp skiffs until exhausted, then shot). This may have always been true, this blend of respect and bloodlust, but rifles and combustion engines have facilitated attrition, and when I saw it firsthand, my Noble Savage shed his last decrepit flakes and became human—flawed and decent, lusty and reserved—just like me and mine.

Je sens mon couer, et je connais les hommes. Rousseau didn't get it all wrong. "I feel my heart, and I know other men"—history's shadow branch, and one of its most effective. I tied up at the inlet, a tumbler coming out of elevation through boulders and hemlock. Cedar waxwings rousted the air, a dozen or more, their glassy forms intercepting adult caddis high off the water. I was sure a brook trout or two would haunt the little delta, but found it bare. The two campers, kids nearly, might have been squatting given all their gear. They said I could stay, but looked relieved when I paddled the shoreline back toward the Hudson.

Trapping changes you. I've trapped mink and muskrats with my father for thirty years, and can't remember what a day in the woods was like beforehand. Your mind populates terrain, envisioning furbearers where you'd guess their habits would put them. Red fox mouse in hip-high grass, beavers look for poplar to fell, and marten follow swamp-side timber, seeking voles. You're attracted to transitions—forest-to-meadow, water-to-land, plateau-to-incline. Prey is here, and their predators too.

This was mink country. I shy from words like totem, but if my father and I have one, mink would be it. Washed-out roots tangled the shoreline. Blueberries and fern cover sheltered rodent life. Trout and dace swam the lake and crayfish hid beneath broken rocks along the shore. A green frog leapt in the lake as I paddled by. Their food was here. The mink must be too.

My fancy found him, a big buck, ghosting in and out of the lake, loping the edge. There, where the boulder forces him in, that's where to set, and there, under that root complex. *Je sens mon coeur, et je connais les hommes.* We don't trap for money, my father and I. Inexplicably, we do it for love of the animal, to understand them, to reach back, groping for some scrap, some sense, of that old way, when Man and Nature weren't distinct. However I exaggerated it, American Indians were among the last to experience that immersion, and trapping allows a toe in this water.

Paddling along, still looking to shore, a genuine brown flash dipped into a rotting stump, then out. Mink. Female. Working the water's edge, she was now curious over the odd creature in the long green shape. Henderson is remote enough that a mink wouldn't retreat upon sighting a human. She reared up, scenting, darting in and out of the hollow stump. I drifted by, watching her resume the hunt, where she wended in and out of the water back toward the campers.

She wasn't the only furbearer. The beaver sign picked up as I worked toward the south end, all of it fresh. The inlet is gentler here. Beavers have flooded the brush for generations, and only dwarfed trees survive on mucky ground. I paddled up the creek a bit, then beached. A sedge wren scrambled from a grass tuft. Trickling water indicated a dam. Walking up a silted rivulet, I came to it, the peeled sticks woven high, a smooth run down the middle where beavers funneled through. *Savez votre couer.* I bent low, getting beneath the dam's sight line, then peered over. I've trapped enough beavers to know a well-kept secret. Deep maroon, lush and fatty, their flesh makes fantastic meat dishes, and everything about the tail is true—roast it, peel it, cut it into greasy chunks, then add to stew. The pelts, too, are ample, making the warmest clothing.

Indians took beavers with steel traps, but also tore the dams, clubbing animals as they floundered in mud. This isn't beyond me. I revere wildlife, but humans are a tangled breed, and we'd do well to know this. Having sighted me, a beaver stilled itself in the small pond, only the head visible. Reading will tell you much of the fur trade. The Dutch dominated at first, inciting Natives to bring hides to the Hudson for duffel and iron, alcohol and firearms. Men like William Johnson, an Irishman in the Adirondacks, were pivotal go-betweens. The French competed from the north, and the English from the east, eventually winning New Amsterdam in 1664. Other treasure would have brought them, but it was the beaver's plush fur that first established European empires, all for a Swedish lieutenant's deft chapeau. This induced the inevitable wars that followed, and Native Americans—confused by this presence, decimated, awed by its durable goods—fed whites what they wanted with their own rapine, helping exterminate beavers east of the Mississippi, and from there nearly west of it. They turned, the Indians—abandoned the custom so often ascribed to them—seeping into every Hudson drainage for what now amounted to stuff, not food or spirit. To determine why, it's best to leave the books behind.

I could enjoy this beaver now, soak it in as it floated. Our toils have abated, and Dickinson's bird is now my own. Sweet afflatus. The beaver lilted, unsure of what I'd do as a raven chortled behind us. If circumstances were different, if I was hungrier, or simply eager for trade, I'd turn too. We all would, hewed by the right conditions. I stood. The beaver plunged, thwacking its tail. It knew my heart, too, the buried part, that said all along, "I'll roast you, you son-of-a-bitch, and have that pretty hide too."

The sun was gone, dipped below the western ridge. I'd passed a public site before the inlet and paddled back, pitching the tent in purple-blue light.

Tenting Tonight

It took a bit for the quiet to chase the horns and sirens, the diesel boom, the midnight teenage bravado from my ears. As night sucked the last light off the paper birches, the thrushes wound down their chorusing. These were the woods, lovely, dark, and deep, and I was back in them.

I'm a sucker for the old songs. Civil War old. Well after Appomattox, a Confederate colonel said the rebels matched the Yankees in every way but one. "If we'd have had their songs," he said, "they would have licked our boots." Well said. From "John Brown's Body" to "Father Abram" to "Rally Round the Flag," the Union had some beauties, and I sang them to Shannon from the start, who flared into mute, toothless laughter. One of her favorites was "Tenting Tonight," sung in easy lamentation, slightly understating the gravity of bivouacked soldiers too long in the fight:

> Tenting to tonight, tenting tonight, tenting on the old
> campground . . .
> We are tenting tonight, we are tenting tonight, tenting
> on the old campground.
> Many are the hearts that are weary tonight, wishing for
> the war to cease . . .
> Many are the hearts that are weary tonight, hoping for
> songs of peace.

We don't understand how fun singing is until there's an infant about. Each line is carried as long as you like, and both Shannon and I delighted in the process. There on Henderson, I hummed a verse or two while standing among the dark and mosquitoes, listening to a fox yip as distant lightning illuminated the hollows.

I didn't know what this trip would bring. It wasn't a lark—the publisher gave it purpose—but larking, I knew, wasn't absent, as legs have always been my engine, quite a collision with the home life. Plucked from Alaska and dropped in Queens, straight in the lap of pregnancy. Delight didn't evade me, not a jot, but more than one river runs through us. "Marriage has joy," my mother once said, "but it's not joy. It's attrition." This is common. We want home, kinship, and rooted love, but God and death and the thousand unknowns lie just over that ridge (along with vagrant sexual possibility, if candor suits us), and our feet grow itchy. The lightning drew near, the thunder louder. In the flashes, ripples cut the lake—a beaver, awaiting the wind and rain.

It came, plump and slow, followed by drizzle. I ambled up the hill, then crawled in the tent. Southeast Alaska receives 150 inches a year, and the sound of rain-on-tarp filtered in like fond old music, along with something new. That kid had been stuck to my hip for five months. Crying or giggling, compliant or feisty, asleep or engaged, I reveled in her. Even this, though, had complications.

While living in California I flew to Jersey once to see a high school buddy marry. Bunches of the old squad were there, and I hopped a ride back to my sister's with one of the first to fall. He'd married Tenley, an Ohioan, as aggressively passive as the region that made her. Pregnant, she slept soundly in back while Paul drove, with their first child awaiting at Paul's parents'. Paul had gone into sales, but had a knockabout's bone. Two kids, loving wife, high-paid work. Life was well with him and I knew it, but I also knew something else.

"Things are in order?" I asked.

"Oh yeah. Everything's fine."

He drove, then looked over a shoulder. Tenley snores like a kitten. He turned back.

"Sometimes I just wish I was a freakin' lumberjack though."

Quiet Is the Word

Whoever makes Snickers bars ran a series of ads too ingenious to last. They were here, then as quickly gone. Too bad, for they ferreted one of the least discussed yet most glaring angsts among us.

Though treated as one, manhood is no joke. I was born in 1968, in lock-step with feminism. My mother was a rager. She drilled it into me that along with being superfluous louts, men were violent, boorish, and cruel. In her worst fits, she may have meant ten percent of this, but history supports at least that. Feminism had to happen, but as with most passionate leaps forward, it over-bounded. Most women presently acknowledge that the 1970s dream of Super Woman performing a dozen juggling acts of child-rearing and corporate prowess was a stretch. Today, then, while debate persists over what role females should have in the world, in the lives they live most women can make choices without incurring the old wraths. Professionals aren't scorned by traditional homemakers as were feminist pioneers of the sixties, and stay-at-homes are no longer chastised by professionals as happened in the seventies and eighties.

If women, though, are feeling their way toward equity, men are groping with alien apathy, every bit the ennui that Betty Friedan phrased for pent-up housewives in the fifties with the line, "Is this it?" Unfortunately, technology has coincided with women's rights to belittle manhood beyond any salvation from a feminist corrective. This is a problem. Manhood is elemental. Mores and technology can shape us, but we'll only change so much. After an evolution's worth of gleeful barbarism, men have been on the ten thousand–year wane, eroded by civilization, a spiritual vagabondage picked up by the Snickers troupe.

Throughout the series, manhood is both character and theme. Five guys—a Viking, Henry VIII, a Hawaiian chief, Caesar, and

Genghis Khan—are on the road, driving a beat-up economy car. Despite their get-ups, these are five work-a-day schmoe's whose elemental manhood—violent, expansive, jovial, explicit, monstrous, magnificent—is pinioned by modernity in such a way that fantasy is its only valve. They fumble through modern life, then, in search of the old mythos. In the best installment, the five drive in silence. The Viking is at the wheel, while Henry rides shotgun. The rest are crammed in back. Henry smacks his lips on a drumstick, a merry foil to the others' malaise.

"When I was a king," he quips, "a troupe of minstrels bid me good cheer whilst I dined."

The Viking rolls his eyes, the others groan, except the Hawaiian. This is Henry, he knows, and Henry expects things. Reverent of the Englishman's need for the old life, the islander saves him, belting out a verse of "Greensleeves," to which the others supply the hearty refrain:

> Greensleeves await, My Dear!
> O Greensleeves await!

Henry is restored, as are they all.

This is silly, of course, but devilishly so. Manliness—once the lion-tamer in the human circus—has been banished to the clown car. It's gotten so that eating potato chips and watching football is a respected pursuit, and scarcely a TV show goes by without some innocuous tub-a-lard latched to a woman of great character and astonishing good looks.

The brilliance of the Snickers crew is to parody parody. We make fun of the old days, deprecating what remains largely unchanged in men—aggression, sexual caprice, and a preference for male friendship. Programs such as *The Man Show*, or the flood of buddy movies that follow a directionless fop as he's finally brought to heel by a grownup woman—make cartoons of manliness. While this can be funny, it's peripheral. The boozing and wenching are incidental, with the best parts—competition, restlessness, motion, physicality—now buried beneath a mile of ice. This isn't healthy, but social tectonics are tough to reverse.

The nineteenth century. This was the peak. Room to roam, Indians to fight, fur to trap. Fields to lay flat and plow. Sweat, sweat,

sweat. Rules didn't apply, and paperwork had yet to drown a single soul. Maps were full of blanks, even the Adirondacks. Tools, too, weren't digital or hydraulic as they are now, but companionable to human muscle, not its master, and nowhere is this more evident than an ax. Old practice logging made a mess of things, but it lodged a nation, and if you're talking manhood and tree-felling, you're talking the upper Hudson.

It's nothing to break a tent down and stuff it in a bag. The canoe was loaded at first light, with a mother merganser and her adolescent clutch the only ripples on windless water. I needed water myself. Having passed another inlet the night before, I paddled north. Below, submerged logs lay rotting, the ends sawed clean. I looked up the hillside. The spruce, the yellow birch, the hemlock, the maple, the beech, the creatures they house—fungal, animal, vegetal. It's tough not to slip into pantheistic glee out here, but equally tough to fight other urges.

Those drowned logs sealed it. Loggers had been here. The dam, the old cable eyes, sunken timber—Henderson was likely a banking ground, one of many in the Hudson watershed. The dams had two purposes—to hold logs back and control flow for their release. From autumn through winter, men cut timber and piled it on frozen lakes. They returned in spring, riding the logs a hundred miles or more to the mills. At each lake, wood was corralled by a boom—cabled timbers penning the payload. As the wood released, men winched—or "kedged"—what logs remained toward the dam. The drives lasted into the fifties. Today, conservation is the ruling word, a thought most people abide, but out on such places as Henderson, that word can be challenged. Primitive voices yearn for something else, when you could walk into this timber with a cant hook and ax, nothing to say you couldn't swath every mountain.

Not far into the inlet, I tied to a withered birch and walked the creek aways. Filtering in a riffle, I noticed an old stove rusting in a depression. Flakes of iron barely hung on. Somebody had a cabin here, but this and a few leaf-stuffed jars were all that remained. Tire tracks cut the forest floor, with forty-year-old trees pushed through each rut. Skidder activity is hard to mistake. Timber had been cut up this draw with chainsaws, maybe a feller-buncher, then mechanically skidded to the lake. The end was the same as the old days, but the means—and the men—quite different.

The Dutch West India Company built the first Hudson mills. *Kill* is Dutch for stream, and the watershed is strewn with names like Wall Kill and Roelif Jansen Kill. The Saw Kill, long since buried on Manhattan, is thought to be the Hudson's first mill site, built around 1623. Early operations were called "mud mills," a single blade powered by a running stream. With the nearby timber felled and planked, the sawyers moved on. Glens Falls had such a mill. Like all mills before it, it would have died quick. The expanse of the Hudson helped a little, as drives were made, but they were cumbersome affairs, masses of bound logs difficult to control. For marketing purposes, mills weren't feasible in the mountains, and it looked like the Adirondack forests—still the Dismal Wilderness—would be spared.

Strange what invention will do. In 1813, with tree-cutters about to leave the mountains alone, Alanson and Norman Fox were cutting timber on the Schroon River, a major Hudson tributary around Warrensburg. This would have been the last cut, as binding the large rafts didn't turn the desired profit. Perhaps out of frustration, the two simply heaved single logs into the Schroon, racing to catch them in a boom further downstream. It worked. Sad news for Adirondack forests, happy news for American mythology.

Contrary to modern belief, hippies didn't conjure up environmentalism in a hookah. American conservation, in fact, travels through Rachel Carson, Aldo Leopold, and Henry Thoreau to second-generation colonists, who noticed the devastation they'd wreaked. In 1646, a generation after the Mayflower, Portsmouth, Rhode Island instituted deer harvest regulations, and other colonies fell in line. Concerning timber, even with a continent of uncut growth before them, some sought restraint. Fresh from Europe, the Earl of Bellomont—New York's governor from 1698–1701—recommended limiting tree harvests to mast cuts for ships, even then planting five seedlings for every tree taken. Environmentalism, then, is old, and as with the Adirondack Park, it has more to do with economics and industry than granola. There's only so much out there, and if you take it all, it's gone for good.

Jones Ordway was not the Earl of Bellomont. Nor was he a hippie. He was a guy who cut a boat-load of trees, having sense enough to see money in front of him and the drive to gather it up. Not long after the Fox brothers sent their logs downriver, Ordway did the same, erecting a "gang mill" in Glens Falls. He and other operators put thousands of lumbermen to work, and the logs kept coming for a century and a half, peaking in 1872. These were the great log drives, which spread throughout the Northeast and Upper Midwest. Having floated through the scene of the first drives, I can't tell you much, only that those guys were nuts, and that I envied them the whole way down.

Green, Green, Green. Everyone nowadays is Green. The hippies may not have started environmentalism, but they got the modern ball rolling, though you wouldn't know that from today's advertising. I'm Green, you're Green, we're all Green together. Simply to do business, corporations big and small have to at least feign environmental concern, and to be UnGreen is nearly on par with cannibalism these days. Looking back to the lumber camps of the nineteenth century, then, it's nearly impossible to grasp how such destruction could have occurred. Still, if we burrow into our flesh deep enough, we see it. Manhood only changes so much.

They didn't cut in summer. Wood worms are active in heat, and running sap additionally affects quality. Labor, too, was short. Most lumberjacks had seasonal jobs, farming or milling all summer while a few worked as fishing guides. Come fall, though, it was off to the woods.

Lucky for maples and oaks, hardwood doesn't float. This left the conifers. Most of the white pines had been taken for ship building, leaving spruce. Crosscut saws didn't arrive until the 1890s. Prior to this, men used axes. Work was seven days a week, dawn to dusk. The Adirondacks get cold fast and early, and the weather worked in conjunction with the labor to crimp most men with rheumatism by age thirty-five.

Once the trees were down, they were cut into thirteen-foot lengths, a practice for which no one can account. William Fox, Norman's son and a lumberjack himself, wrote *The History of the Lumber Industry in the State of New York*, in which he simply said, "The reason for adopting this odd length is unknown." The actual length in the woods was thirteen feet, four inches. During the drive, ends were mashed into the bottom and banks enough to jam with grit. Once at the mills, either end was "butted" two inches to avoid blade damage.

The standard Hudson log was nineteen inches at the base, and a thirteen-foot-four-inch by nineteen-inch piece of wood was known as a "market."

Markets were stacked on slopes. On flatter terrain, oxen were used, though as ground gained pitch, horses replaced them. Stacking on gradient ensured an easier time come winter, when the logs were piled on sleds for the banking grounds.

Until the railroads arrived after the Civil War, the hardwoods were left standing, and as maples alone make up a quarter of Adirondack timber, this is no small amount. Despite this inadvertent select-cutting, though, spruce was abundant, and the drying limbs and unmarketable wood left in their stead were terrific kindling. Sparks from coal-fed engines descended on the tinder, or "slash," and many mountainsides went up this way. Clear-cuts existed, but were limited to the charcoal needs of mine forges. Just below Henderson Lake, in fact—right on the Hudson—the remains of an old mining village stand. Tanneries, too, used hemlock bark, which contained the preferred leather-making tannin until 1890 when chemical salts arrived. Once felled, a tree was stripped, leaving the wood for future wildfires. The Prattsville Tannery alone ate up six thousand cords of hemlock bark a year—six million feet of tree. Ironically, hemlocks weren't spared when the salts arrived. In 1844, Friedrich Keller invented the pulp grinder in Germany. Soon after, pulp mills dotted the Hudson, with some still operating today. Now the wood was needed and the bark discarded. In the 1920s, log drives changed to reflect this market, as the soon-to-be-liquefied wood was cut to four-foot lengths to avoid log jams.

By far, though, the Glens Falls mills chewed up the most timber, feeding New York City its firewood and lumber. By late January, enough snow had accumulated to move the market stacks, lubricating skids far better than rock and soil. This is where "bobsled" derives, taken from *toboggan*, an Algonquin word. "Sprinkler wagons" held sixty barrels of water and followed an empty sled on the first run, wetting the tracks, as ice facilitated travel even further. Men again worked through the week, frequently "bobbing" by torchlight. Draft horses took the brunt, hauling tons of lumber up slopes and down, piling it on the banks and ice of frozen lakes, often dying. Men didn't fare better. Many were smashed on tree trunks or halved beneath skids before proper braking was found, and even then, machinery is only good when it works. Axes claimed fingers, toes, and occasionally lives all autumn, wayward tree falls pulped the inattentive, bobbing crushed still more, and the spring drives found new ways to kill each season, yet men returned every year until they were too cramped to do so.

This part isn't hard to see. I'll leave women out of it. At an early age, my father told me a successful marriage is this: The woman loves the man a little and understands him completely, whereas the man loves the woman unconditionally and doesn't even try to understand her. Rough-cut, to be sure, but wise words. Women, then, may have similar drives, but I'll stick to men. We love grueling work. Nasty, bitter, hard-driving, body-bruising labor, all day, the sort that's increasingly effective the more you huff and puff, cursing all the while. I had a friend in Alaska who once worked a North Dakotan oil rig. One day, some guy hung high on a girder, trying to cinch a bolt. Failing, he swore profusely. "Come on, Vern," the foreman shouted up. "Out think that bolt!" The camaraderie, the physicality, the brutishness of it all, not to mention the break from women for a while. We crave it, particularly when young. If you're a man, join all the environmental organizations you like. Love Mary Oliver. Refract those gorgeous words of hers and make them your own, then bound through the nearest forest kinsman to every living creature you see, but don't lie to yourself. Perch atop that concrete sluice on Henderson Lake. Imagine it's spring. High water. Put a boot on that first log, from all those hillsides you helped clear last fall, stacking spruce, bobbing all winter beneath Northern Lights, whores and whiskey at the end, no one to tell you otherwise. It's time. Kick it free. Now another. Then a third. The payload's out. Goddamn, boys. I'm going on a river drive.

That's how they started. Just a few logs, set free. Scarcely a Hudson tributary didn't have a log-and-mortar dam just up from the confluence. Across from the town of North River there's "The Mouse," a dark swirl on white rock. When spring freshets hit the mouse's tail, word went upriver quick.

The "Big Boom"—a massive chain of logs strung across the "Big Bend," where the Hudson cuts east a few miles above Glens Falls—was the end point. Here logs were sorted by owner and sent in more controlled fashion to their respective mill. "Kerfs" were stamped on logs at the banking grounds, much like cattle branding out West. One such kerf, for Job A. Wilcox of the Luzerne Warren County Log,

Timber, and Lumber Company, read simply "JOB," a fitting mark for the happy hell suffered by the river-drivers.

Initially, it was harum-scarum. Kerfs didn't exist, and competing mills enacted every manner of skullduggery to harness more logs for themselves. This went on for decades, until Lyman A. Beeman, of Finch, Pruyn, and Company called for a truce in 1862. Others cooperated, kerfs were applied, and logs were driven as one until the Big Boom.

Like all human labor, there was a hierarchy. Many men didn't ride the river at all, standing in coves or on islands to steer logs from troublesome snags. Others—the true drivers—hopped a log and rode, prodding other markets along as they did. In men, pride often trumps pragmatism. Real guys floated a single log, whereas others lashed two together. Such rafts were called "cooters," which may be where that derogation for vagina derives. Today, in Western rodeos, you see a descendant of this. Female contestants rope goats rather than calves, and if one cowpoke wants to rile another, he calls him a "goat-roper." I'd imagine "cooter" had similar meaning in the lumber camps. Such jousting is undoubtedly an affront to women the world over, but snuffing it is a losing endeavor. When two guys get into it, out come the vagina slurs. Lumberman, cowboy, or accountant, it's in the grain.

"The Hudson was bad at Ord Falls below Newcomb," recalled Yankee John Galusha of Minerva, "bad again just above the mouth of the Indian, and very bad on the big bend below Blue Ledge, near the Deer Den." "More than a few drivers," added another, "lost their lives trying to save a comrade marooned in midstream or floundering in the torrents." You read these words and they mean something, but they mean a lot more when you see where these guys did what they did. I went through there in a canoe during the hottest stretch of the year, wearing a PFD. Nothing impeded me, let alone a million jumbling logs just after ice-out, a century and a half before Gore-Tex, satellite phones, and antibiotics, even a decent map of the surrounding land. A cooter indeed.

As skilled as they were, rookies were out there, veterans made mistakes, and sometimes just a snot-pile of logs stacked up. There's genuine whitewater in the Hudson Gorge and elsewhere, and how a box of matches gets through unscathed is beyond me. Rolling through rapids on a thirteen-foot piece of wood, these guys jolted loose what they could as logs banged off boulders and each other. Jams occurred with frequency, though, which brought the boatmen out.

They worked in threes—a sternman, a bowman, and an oarsman. Approaching from below, they searched out the "key" log, or the one holding everything up. If found, the three left the boat, trying to pry this key—and therefore the jam—loose.

"In some instances," said one, "the boat crews resorted to a charge of dynamite, but, more often, they relied on their brawn and dexterity." However it happened, once the key log gave, the Devil took the hindmost for the boat, where the oarsman earned his money. Logs came stumbling out of the jam, and anything but a posthaste stroke for shore resulted in unspeakable sorrow. Even if you came out of the splintered boat in good shape, it was near-freezing water, and hypothermia claimed more than a few guys. They slept in lean-tos, ate flapjacks and salt pork by the sackful, and didn't have much thought beyond the task at hand. Boys to some, maybe, but not to me, and not to most modern men, not if you got them drunk enough.

Logging wasn't the only enviable field. Anthony Lane, a film reviewer for *The New Yorker*, reviewed *Master and Commander*, starring Russell Crowe as Lucky Jack Aubrey, a British naval captain during the Napoleonic years. It's a terrific film, nothing but booming cannonades and clanging swordplay. Lane plops himself down where his readers will be—on subways, at corner bistros, doctor's waiting rooms, cozy divans, and climate-controlled office space, weeviling into our collective conscious, where well-captained sailors weather fierce gales, hunt phantom Frenchmen, and sing grog-sopped ditties in choral *bonhomie*. Despite the perils and privations, Lane writes, "We feel ourselves to be in good company with these men, and strangely jealous of their packed and salted lives." Their packed and salted lives. Amen.

Much has watered those lives down since. Ironically, it started at the log drives' peak, in 1873, the year after 213,800,000 board feet went into the Big Boom. Jones Ordway requested to build a canal to access more logs. Shockingly, he was denied. Harold K. Hochschild, in his *Lumberjacks and Rivermen in the Central Adirondacks, 1850–1950*, put it this way: "By 1873 when Ordway's dam and canal plans were blocked, the Adirondacks were no longer a frontier land where the lumberman, the trapper or the sportsman could be a law unto himself. The long arm of regulation was reaching up from the south."

Technology, as well, has contributed. In terms of lumbering, saws replaced axes, chainsaws replaced saws, and now there's the feller-buncher, hydraulically shearing trees at ground level before stripping everything not millable. One guy operates it, moving levers in a heated cab. By nearly every measure this is good. Men live longer, and though feller-bunching sounds hideous, properly managed it's actually much easier on a forest floor than a hundred guys with axes and oxen. This is the crux. Unregulated and unmapped, working with tools and not for machines, we live free and rugged, but without regulation, we're sunk. As the Earl of Bellomont saw, no restraint means it will all be gone, yet we look back to who we were prior to GPS, zoning laws, and combustion engines, and we mourn.

"Who were these drivers?" asks a diorama at the Adirondack Museum in Blue Mountain Lake. "Few remember. For many a lad, to be a riverman and go downriver with the drive was his greatest ambition. To follow these brave souls who broke the log jams, 'tailed' the drive, manned the sorting booms—and often drowned in the process—was the desire of every small boy. Many a man prided himself on his ability to ride a log in the whitewater, and many a village suddenly became a loud and busy metropolis and often a violent one when the drivers came to town. No longer does the long wood crowd the piers and booms. No longer do the banks of our streams echo to the shouts of men in red shirts and caulked shoes. Quiet is the word."

As a kid, my parents took my sisters and me to the Danbury Fair in Connecticut, since replaced by a mall. There was cotton candy and carousels, but what I remember were the lumberjack shows. Guys competed with crosscut saws, ax throwing, tree scaling, wood chopping, even log rolling. In retrospect, it was Buffalo Bill's Wild West Show. With the buffalo killed and the Indians treatied off, what was there to do but don a bit of rouge and put on a pageant? Most of these guys were in their fifties, making them old enough to have worked the Hudson's last drives, the pulp ones anyway. Less than ten at the time, not knowing what clowns they'd become, all I could do was romantically intuit what fantastic lives these men led, so unlike the well-laundered regimen of my suburban father that even at eight I could sense was a diminished thing.

I'm not alone. My dad kept an oil painting of a mountain man in his corporate office until he retired, and the week he looks forward to most—even in his seventies—is the week we spend trapping. I was soon to marry, too, which entails a father-in-law. The specimen assigned to me is Emmett, a good guy and an interesting one. Reared in White Plains, New York, he had three kids by his twenty-ninth birthday, Karen among them. "I don't think he ever wanted to be what he was," she said. "If I had to guess, he wanted to be a poet and farmer." She then told a story.

At age fifty-five, having sloshed around the boozy bric-a-brac of high finance for thirty years, Emmett retired from one company with the intent of joining another. First, though, he and Karen's mom, Carol, went to Europe. While in Spain, she returned home. Emmett bought a bike, pedaling north. He wound up in Ireland, where his parents were from, ending the trip at the edge of a cliff at sunset. Twilight passed, and well after dark he found his way to a phone.

"I think I just found the meaning of life," he told Carol.

"That's nice, dear. Now why don't you come home and find a job."

Bow your heads for Emmett and for all, then, for the Viking hordes and King Henry too. Quiet is the word.

Where the Wild Things Were

Thank God for the quiet, though, as due to the slumber of old-style manliness, there's still quiet to be had, with increasing amounts of it in the Northeast. What an odd turn.

The dam chute at Henderson was a bit dodgy, forcing an up-and-over across gravel. The Hudson here is swift and heavily rocked, and I walked more than paddled, skirting around waterfalls a couple times. A flat of mossed-over masonry girded a bank in one shaded stretch, part of the mine site I guessed, or an old tannery. One hand on a gunnel, I negotiated boulders and frothy water, only slipping once, coming up soaked but happy, relieved of the morning heat.

I waded by the Adirondack Village, where for over a century men pulled iron out of the mountain. These were exploited immigrants, smelting ore for downriver foundries—structuring buildings, forming cannons, concocting World War II–era smokescreens with titanium oxide. The wreckage of the miners' cedar-shake houses refed the forest, now all engrossing. Expense more than anything killed the pits. Even today, the Adirondacks remain an engineering challenge, and the rails took their long, back-breaking time punching through to Tahawus, the region's name. At a certain point I thought to get out and look the cadaver over, but one tree-ruined structure had a thin column of smoke snaking through a collapsed roof, and I'm too old to stumble upon a pack of dilated hill folk huddled over a meth cooker.

This landscape shouldn't have seemed strange, but did. I grew up in the southern reaches of the North Woods, and while each draw—let alone watershed and state—has its own texture, these forests were close enough to my upbringing that they should have felt more familiar. Ten years, though, is a long stretch away, and it took some time to reaffiliate.

Sanford Lake lies below the mine site. In fact, a more recent mining effort exists on Sanford's east bank. It's not a lake, just a slow stretch, maybe forty yards wide. The water lilies were in bloom, and I floated among creamy, yellow centers studded with white pedals. After a day of eating reconstituted barf bars, they looked like fried eggs. The sun took the lake in full. A dozen Canada geese clung to the opposite shore, while a pair of trumpeter swans herded four signets downstream before all took up in cacophonous commotion, kicking the creek for take-off

Rafters use the terms "river-right" and "river-left" to denote a specific bank, always with the idea that you're facing downstream. Even if facing upstream, therefore, "river-left' is on your right. The road to Henderson, then, lay somewhere through the recovering forest on river-right, with an occasional car engine ruffling the quiet. On river-left, the woods opened entirely, with banks of blasted rock obscuring whatever lay beyond. I came to the answer soon enough, a collapsed road that had crushed the several culverts the miners installed. Hauling the canoe over the sapling-carpeted pass, I left it on the other side, walking east to see the damage done.

Westerners scoff at Eastern forests. In many ways they're right. Size-wise, the stoutest oak is no Doug fir. Traveling east to west, you hear this all the time. Alaska is full of Oregonians. I laughed with one who had been to Maine, where at a diner he'd asked a driver with a load of pulp trunks what he'd been doing.

"Logging," the guy said

"Logging? You mean pruning."

For all their differences, though, forests the world over do share one thing—resilience. If our transglobal, across-the-millennia, collective butchering of them hasn't proved anything else, it has affirmed the toughness of certain ecologies, and the Northeastern American forests are no exception. Timber was cut for everything—planks, beams, shingles, scaffolding, forge fuel, house fuel, rail ties, rifle stocks, kitchenware, coopering, wagon making, ship making, tool handles, gallows—everything. While coal and oil today cause anyone with the slightest ecological sensibility perpetual apoplexy, they can be rightfully deemed the savior of the world's trees. Without the advent of fossil fuels and plastics, not a withered shrub would be left standing, and as Europeans hit the East Coast first, those woods fared worst.

This upper Hudson mine site is particularly bruised. Not only were the trees cleared, but black powder and heavy equipment disrupted soil and bedrock. Activity peaked around World War II, lingering into the seventies. An old ore chute rusts along with a couple tin-roofed buildings, and a deep lake sits amid dune-like mounds, the water as clear as any you'll see. My pop grew up around Philadelphia. He said the rivers running out of anthracite country were clear to the point you could count pebbles on the bottom of ten-foot-deep pools, yet scarcely a slug lived in them. Mining unleashes a heavy metal concentrate from bedrock while chemically processing the ore, a combination poisoning everything. Standing atop a dune, looking over the man-dug lake, I half expected to walk down there and catch trout until my arms fell off, yet I wouldn't have stuck a toe in that water.

I ambled down to the flat. Fine sand marbled the gravel, marking the crush of industry that desiccated this patch of former damp forest, the kind that still surrounds the damaged bowl. Verplanck Colvin likely tramped this same ground while nearing the Hudson's origins, his feet mired in sawdust and fire-ash where my own were rapidly drying out in desert-scape. If I walked a mile east, I'd regain forest floor, sponging into the cool mosses that Colvin knew were central to stabilizing the Hudson's flow, fibers so absorbent that Iroquois and Algonquin mothers used them for diapers. Such contrast could be depressing, but there's always more to see.

The scratch-and-blast nature of open pit mining here was nothing like the mountaintop removal strategies currently metamorphosing Appalachia, but the geography has been noticeably changed, with hillsides turned flat and dried slag replacing forest. This was no moonscape however. In Alaska, it's alders that colonize the gravel left by retreating glaciers, whereas here—restoring our own glaciation—it's willow and paper birch. Throughout the site, thin white trunks bunch sporadically, grouped with the smaller willow as well as various grasses. These copses provide shade, which in time will hold moisture for other species. In addition, state and federal agencies have worked with Kronos, the company mining here until 1978, to experiment with habitat restoration, mixing the mine waste with pulp sludge and birch chips from a local mill in the hope these nutrients will stimulate growth. I didn't notice this fifteen-acre guinea pig, but didn't have to. Nature was replenishing itself. Birch seedlings had purchased across the site, along with grass and willow, which in turn had brought other life.

Up high, a kestrel's sickle wings, framed in cloudless sky, orchestrated the thermals, dipping close enough to reveal its mottled chest. Perching on an old power pole, it joined another. The smallest falcon, kestrels primarily prey on large insects, but take mice and small birds. Sure enough, grasshoppers hummed in the gravel while sparrows hopscotched from one birch to the next.

Walking back out, I'd missed something before. Clumps of fur, some as wide as a hockey puck, mingled with twisted tubes of the same in a tight circle. Coyote scat, cluttered on the gravel road. As with the hawks, coyotes wouldn't be using the site were the creatures they eat not there too—deer fawns, snowshoe hares, voles, and mice. I stooped, picking up a segment. Rodent hair and hollow deer-hair shafts. The land will never be what it was, but something similar is returning.

I didn't see a fisher on the Hudson, nor a pine marten, bobcat, moose, black bear, or coyote, but that doesn't mean they weren't there, and if the trees aren't the same size or even species as the old Dismal Wilderness, growth has returned enough for these animals to thrive. Some think cougars have even crept back, and the Adirondacks have long been eyed for gray wolf reintroduction. In terms of what has returned, I saw twenty-five bald eagles on the float, which alone speaks to the Hudson's recovery. It wasn't always so.

The last moose was shot in 1861, the last cougar in 1890, with wolves hunted out around the same time. Adirondack beavers were mostly gone by 1800. Pine marten and fisher need broad tracts of unbroken forest. More through axes than traps, then, these melted into Canada and the most removed parts of Maine. Deer, too—hunted for sport and market—grew scarce. All through these mountains, animals took their lumps, dwindling to shadow or disappearing altogether. That's changing, and like any shift, it's laced with unforeseen consequences.

Environmentalism started with the same zealotry as the industrial stampede it combated. Ground down by generations of manufacture, advertising, consumerism, suburbanization, urban decay, technological whirlwinds, pollution, and everything else separating warm-blooded, air-breathing creatures from their habitat, people set up an extremism of their own. Suddenly, anything human-derived was evil. This rancor served a purpose, but it's since evolved, now realizing that things like mines are probably necessary. Such philosophy forsakes hammering ecosystems back to their pre-Columbian state, rather letting them adjust to human infringement largely on their own while doing what we can to lessen our current impacts. This means junking most of the "Humans Out!" aspirations of preceding environmental thinkers. My brother-in-law and I missed the Henderson turn when he dropped me off, which had us stumble across the SUNY (State University of New York) Environmental Science and Forestry School. A Stacy McNulty directed us where we needed to go, whom I later called about the Tahawus titanium site, asking if the original forest might return. She doubted it, but wasn't outraged. McNulty looked about ten years younger than me. My generation is tainted with environmental absolutism, whereas the ones beneath us seem to see the world-as-it-is.

"Forests are changing all the time from natural and human disturbances," she said, noting two things rarely acknowledged by my generation—that humans are a part of ecology and that ecosystems are not static entities. This doesn't mean dumping mine waste into waterways is a good idea, but simply that—like children—landscapes eventually morph whether you want them to or not. "The soil and rock at the Tahawus site," she went on, "has been moved and modified into those big piles of tailings, creating a very different environment for a tree seedling than the moist, dark, intact forest. It will take many decades of rebuilding soils and the fungal associations within them to create suitable conditions for the forest to grow back, but even then, it will probably be a different forest." One, in other words, that's modified itself to the alterations we've come to rely on. Like it or not, we need the earth's resources, and while our past wantonness has nearly done us in, early environmental fervor checked it. As it has matured, though, at least the dream of détente between the human and natural worlds is alive, something already taking shape in the Adirondacks.

Moose sign is simple. Watersheds around Yakutat are choked with it, enough so that even a week within them would make anyone fluent. Nibbled willow buds, cherry-sized droppings, the pungent musk, the opposing crescent hoof prints routing out the river mud. To read, moose sign is as easy as it comes.

Below Sanford, I paddled through prime habitat—sun-drenched willow swamp on either bank, plenty of open water created by beavers. I'd seen moose in upper New England while living in Vermont, and heard they were returning to the Adirondacks. Tracks are the proof, and there they were, mud-clouded foot-stomps pocking a silty stretch. This bodes well. Plugged with bogs, wallows, and willow flats, moose once ran thick in these mountains, and there's little to say they can't again. Moose, too, would be a draw for other creatures, two of whose controversy has preceded any future return.

I spent my first twenty-five years in Connecticut. Wolves once roamed there, cougars too. Though there's only been one recorded wolf attack in North America—near Yakutat, coincidentally, quite recently—they have competed with humans for food throughout our relationship. Wolves hunt deer, moose, and other human-favored game, as well as preying on livestock. A big cougar will kill an adult deer every three days, and their growing numbers out West have produced a handful of human deaths. The return East of wolves and cougars, then, wouldn't be celebrated by everyone.

None of this matters to a suburbanite. It can't. The association of violence and wildlife often doesn't register, though that may be changing. Until quite recently, suburbs had been drained of nearly everything wild. Apart from garbage-toppling raccoons, there wasn't much that could bother somebody, let alone threaten them. Living without that ancient, Olduvai fear, then, desensitizes people, leaving them vulnerable to Walt Disney. Disney is an easy target for this stuff, but they earned it. Generations of Americans have grown up thinking Thumper and Bambi bask in a world of bottomless ruth, devoid of every violence except our own. We love those movies and always will, but what rubbish. Living in the cities and suburbs, however, you really have no reason to believe otherwise, and when people elsewhere make claims that certain animals are dangerous, or need to be hunted, you tighten with fury. I was one of these people once, and still can be, though no longer unalloyingly so.

My Alaskan job was simple. Count fish. There were nuances, but the day's mandate always read "Count fish." They're counted from planes and boats, with nets and on foot. One fish, two fish, red fish, blue fish. It was heaven. Go out it in the woods, often alone, and we'll give you money.

Things happen afield. I'd felt fear before, but nothing like what predators arouse—fang-gnashing, claw-ripping, torn-throat fear, something largely unavailable these days. Sharks give it to you, if you're foolish enough to surf where seals are pupping. Lions and tigers do too, should you fancy villages in India or Africa. Crocodiles, maybe, if you want to swim the Nile, but in North America, on *terra firma*, brown bears are our chief terror, and have largely been boxed into parks. Alaska, though, teems with them, and it doesn't take long before that moribund fear revives.

Many days I wouldn't see a bear. Many others I would. Most sightings were distant and fleeting. Some incidents were tight, while a handful were paralyzing. Bears in Alaska don't maul people much, but they do. Every year I was there, one or two people died, while a dozen or so were attacked and lived. With all the people and bears in the woods, these are long odds, but combined with what lay at the end of them—being mutilated by an enormous animal—they're enough to bring the fear back.

Prior to my stint in brown bear country, I didn't understand the fervor with which people opposed Nature, and I was highly indignant toward the hurt our not-so-distant ancestors put on mountain lions, bears, and wolves. One year in Yakutat, however, bears were particularly nasty. There were lots of them, and a poor berry year combined with a poor fish year to make them mean. By November, I'd had enough. Alongside this, hunters had a great year, downing bears everywhere, and off-the-books shootings ramped-up considerably. The next season, activity fell off. The Connecticut man in me lamented, cursing rednecks up and down, but the Neanderthal in me rejoiced, a phenomenon that may be stirring across the country.

Wolves were released in Yellowstone in the nineties, where they've blossomed, filtering out of the park to environmentalist glee. In others, though, they've provoked biblical fury. I still side with the wolves, but now understand the fury, as well as the resistance to cougar reestablishment in places as urban as fringe Los Angeles. The old fear is back, and after a million years of flinging spears, poison, fire, and bullets into the sources of it, many people aren't enthused to see it return. I've felt it myself, having pointed rifles at bears within fifteen yards, ready to empty a chamber into any one of them quite joyfully. I normally hold such creatures in mystical solemnity, but they're scary, and while the grizzly's tragic Lower 48 story saddens me, I've come to understand why people mowed them down whenever they could.

Biology's official word is that cougars don't currently exist in the Northeast, including the Adirondacks, irking locals everywhere. Pennsylvania's Endless Mountains are about a hundred miles south of the Adirondacks. My dad and I ask the same farmers for trapping permission every season, and the same guy comes by to fill the cabin's oil heater. One year, cougars were all the farmers talked about, guys who spend every day on the same piece of ground. Two we trust said they'd seen lions. That night, I kept the oil guy company in the basement as he fidgeted with the burner. Nearly everyone hunts deer here, and with the season a week off, I brought it up.

"Ready for deer season?" I asked, holding a flashlight over a bramble of copper piping.

He steadied a tin to catch any wayward diesel.

"You bet. Don't expect much though."

"Why's that?"

He raised his head.

"Not much around. Game Commission doesn't know a thing. They say it's natural cycles, but it's coyotes and lions. I was driving a couple weeks ago with my kids. This thing looked down on us from a ledge, long, rope-tail. 'You guys see that mountain lion?' I asked. My son says, 'That wasn't a mountain lion, dad. It was a cougar.'"

If biologists don't project a reciprocal disdain for local input, they've learned to cover it up. I asked Scott Van Arsdale, a biologist with New York's Department of Environmental Conservation (DEC) about cougars. "Oh yeah," he said. "Our favorite is when someone says they found a lion with a state radio-collar on its neck. We're certain there aren't animals out there, but if there are, we haven't tagged them." He didn't believe lions had come back, which Howard Quigley corroborated. Quigley works for Panthera, one of the niftier outfits operating today, dedicated to saving the world's wild cats, which mostly means preserving their habitat. Africa, the Americas, Asia, Europe, Australia—everywhere. Quigley studies lions in Montana, but keeps tabs on them elsewhere.

"There's no bodies in the Adirondacks," he said over the phone. "If they were there, you'd see road kills. They're moving back into North Dakota for instance, where people hardly ever see a live one, but up to a couple hundred have been road-killed there in one year." That cinched it for me, but local legends persist from New York to New Hampshire to Maine to Pennsylvania.

If cougars, though, are something of an Adirondack boogeyman, wolves are absent even in rumor, though not all would have it that way. Simply having a conversation about wolf reintroduction would have been laughable a few decades ago, but despite strip malls and subdivisions, Northeastern forests have recovered remarkably, creating habitat not only for wolf conversations, but the actual reemergence of other species, most notably the fisher.

The fisher has long been regarded a deep-woods mammal. *Mustelids*, or weasels, fishers are twice as big as a dachshund. Nimble hunters, they're one of a few species to target porcupines, racing in circles, attacking the quill-less face. Fishers once thrived down to Maryland, but logging and trapping chased them into Canada and what remained of the New England outback, where they barely hung on. Ironically, timber companies reintroduced them to the Adirondacks to curb porcupines, who kill young trees by eating their bark.

While in Vermont, I saw a fisher a few miles from Massachusetts, and had heard they were heading south. When I came back from Alaska, I was astonished to learn how far they'd gone. Karen grew up in South Salem, New York, in Westchester County, maybe forty-five miles from the city. South Salem has the Pound Ridge Reservation, five thousand wooded acres. Fishers live there now, where a few miles over and thirty years before in Connecticut, I only dreamt of them. While the Northeast, then, remains a swirl of congestion, population growth is down and preservation up, with animals like fishers, foxes, bobcats, and maybe cougars making their own adjustments. If this brings joy to some, however, it doesn't to all.

I installed Invisible Fencing in Vermont and New Hampshire for two years. Most people hated fishers. Fishers can—and do—kill house cats, which for many condemns them outright. To some, if they can kill a cat, could a child be next? Such loathing has spread south. Karen and I visited Rhode Island a month after the float. I took Shannon to a wildlife preserve, knowing the state allowed trappers four fishers a year, meaning they run thick. After delighting in questions about the fall warbler migration, I watched the tender old lady volunteering at the desk turn sour when I asked about fishers.

"Not too fond of that animal around here."

"Oh," I muttered.

"Very dangerous," she said.

The old fear is back, then, and if all ten pounds of the fisher will provoke it, woe to the mountain lions and wolves should they return.

For my own part, I was pleased as punch. I passed under Route 28N at Newcomb, knowing this would be the last human sign for at least a day. The river is flanked by marsh here, with beaver lodges scattered about. Acres of thatched plant life abound, and two immature wood ducks paddled into the lilies, while closer to the boat a drake and hen mallard flushed, starting a dozen others. Four painted turtles hopped off an old beaver lodge, and cedar waxwings wallowed in dun life. I looked back. A car made its way over the river, while ahead, the current renarrowed, pinched by hemlocks.

I camped a couple miles below the bridge, long past the last cottage. Elevation dropped again, though this time the water was navigable. It had been some time since I'd canoed such conditions, but these first riffs were friendly enough. The forests, too, began laying on old, familiar hands. Yellow birch twined up through the hemlock, and the first, faint blush on green leaves gave the sugar maples away. No oak yet, but they'd come, as would the ash, and beech and white birch were everywhere. Black cherry I knew to be out there, along with a dozen or more species I couldn't name. It turned that quick. I'd been back East for a year, but all that time it seemed exotic, a distance that closed in a rush. Feeling at home again, I looked to the banks for a camp.

Wanting the morning to start easy, I felt my way through a last rapid, slipping around boulders, into eddies, always eyeing for a less obstructed path. I pulled up on river-left, where for at least the first half-mile, a calm, flat stretch would begin the following day.

Dusk had died by the time the tent was up, and I ambled to the river in the last light. The current had worn the soil from under the hemlock above me, while at its base, compacted tubes of fish scales marked an otter toilet. Sliding down the bank, I flopped in the filter tube and began pumping. A stone moved a few yards down. I turned. A snapping turtle, its shell the size of a chair back, walked from the undercut bank, plunking into the river. It's funny what we think of when we think of wilderness. The usual names crop up. Wolf. Cougar. Lynx. Wolverine. These are the sensitive ones, those who don't abide human contact. Such animals have been cast in myth, pariahs and idols alike, but what of the ones that never left? Their resolve should warrant a mythology of its own, but doesn't. Snapping turtles live to seventy years and are among the toughest creatures out there, yet whoever thinks of them? They're everywhere, and have avoided both our reverence and disdain because of it.

Tomorrow I'd hit the Hudson Gorge. I didn't know what that meant, but was just then looking up at a belittling smear of stars. The gorge would be what it would be, and I'd either make it or I wouldn't.

In the meantime, I soaked up the woods. No lights, no industrial chatter. In the surrounding forest, creatures were restoring themselves year by year, and others—the wolf and cougar—might return. A fish slashed an insect mid-river, while overhead, framed in starlight, a pair of mergansers whistled downstream, late for somewhere. Beyond that there was only moving water, along with the sense of life all around.

My parents never took me to church. Why would they? Wilderness has spawned every religion. Just don't stay out there too long. Verplanck Colvin did, and died a madman. He largely saved the Adirondacks, but too much time alone here affected him. Deteriorating in his later years, he finally succumbed to lunacy. Merriweather Lewis didn't wait that long. Decades before, he trekked from St. Louis to the Columbia and back before a single privy had been erected out there. Indians, grizzlies, wolves, bison. Enough birdlife to blanket the sun, and always the rivers, running. A couple years after returning, he put a bullet through his head. No one knows why, but spend enough time in the woods and it isn't hard to see.

The East is alive after all, I thought, and growing wilder by increments. I was glad of it, but crawled into my bag, content that this wilderness is available, though with an exit. We belonged here once, seamless and savage, but don't now, and have never recovered from that weaning.

The Country Behind

Christ in the Kingdom we love putting country behind us, don't we? Over the next two days the river melted away. From Newcomb to Lake Luzerne, maybe sixty miles, the Hudson rips along from rapid to pool, rapid to pool, unencumbered by concrete, not yet affected by the tide. Gravity powered, mountain fed. Cloudless days, too, these, and I simply basked in the sun, pulling one stroke after another.

Such deference in our time for indigenous peoples, first peoples; family life, home life, rootedness, and all the rest, but what word for the wayfarers, the world's rovers, and peripatetics? Who would we be, what would we be, without this bunch? They brought us out of the trees and up through the deserts, across the narrow straight and over the numbing steppes, northward into ice and mountains, and ever east to jungle and tundra, high peaks and river bottoms, across the frigid tide flat before the sea closed back, leading to more tundra, mountains, steppes, and jungle, all the while leaving others behind to raise up a brood. The itch to move, the need to settle—a useful divergence when overrunning a planet, but a hellish cleavage when contained in a single soul. "How do you stop," old Elton sings, "when your feet say go?" Maybe I had it right. Wandering in full stride, I was additionally heading home, though it never felt that way. Movement lends itself to immortality—if you can stay in motion, maybe just a little longer, the Reaper won't have you. I've had a happy, fortunate life throughout, and scarcely remember better days than these.

Breaking camp, I pushed off, a tad jumpier than the day before. The river widens a bit, and in many stretches the pitch is visible. The mountains, too, close in, forcing rich vibrations as the water tumbles through. At the outset, the rapids were more enjoyment than anxiety, but even in the longer pools, where the water catches its breath, the next rush could be heard.

Canoes have made marvelous strides. Though the blueprint hasn't changed much from the original, the material has. The boats were employed by many Native American tribes—"canoe" itself is Carib-derived—but the form we generally think of when we picture a canoe is of Eastern origin, which is to say Algonquin. They made theirs from wooden ribbing and birch bark, quick-rotting stuff. Mine was Royalex, which won't rot for ten thousand years. In rapids, you slide over rocks that would perforate an aluminum craft and tear birch bark models in half. Your hind end takes a beating, but the boat makes marginal paddlers look good. I'm caught here. Once, in Vermont, I poked around for another job. Mad River Canoe had its factory in Waitsfield, so I parked and got out, hoping to stumble on an opening. I didn't make it ten yards. The stench reeked of poisoned water, death. I left, satisfied that I wouldn't contribute to such befoulment, but put me in one of those things and I swear I'm half otter. It's complicated being human.

The Hudson here isn't all whitewater. In one stretch, I eased into something like Lake Sanford, though it tumbled behind and ahead. There couldn't be a dam, I knew, so natural rock must hold it up. With the sun climbing, I pulled into a small tributary. Silt choked the mouth, and muskrat tracks marred its muddy banks.

My father introduced me to trapping through muskrats. Each summer he'd take me to creeks and marshes, studying. After a while, reading their sign is reflexive. Clay-colored pellets littered the little delta, tipping an active colony. Sweeping bank grass aside, a mat of green rushes lay half in the water—a feed bed. Beavers, too, were active, drowning a few acres of riparian forest. Gray, branchless trunks stood above the willow and alder shrubs, testament to the older woodlands. A yellowthroat called, buried in foliage, while down valley, gravity turned the silent water to din.

I don't know what officially starts the Hudson Gorge. Two weeks before, I'd come across an *Adirondack Life* article covering its whitewater rafting. Karen's family calls her mother "The Clipper," as she's constantly clipping magazine and newspaper stories for people who might be interested. Whenever we see her, a stack of tidbits is sure to come forth. They're spot-on. My impression of the Hudson had been as a flat-water ditch from start to finish, but the article claimed that the upper portion is one of the nation's top ten whitewater rivers. That may or may not be, but regardless, the gorge is a daisy.

I was looking for the Indian River. The article featured outfitters who put in at the Indian's Abanakee Dam. To support the industry, each shop pays to have the dam released on designated days, raising the river to raftable levels, though for me, what days didn't matter. I wouldn't have time to camp while the river went down, and besides, high water makes some rivers easier.

From a crude map, I thought I'd reached the Indian. It turns out it was the Cedar, but I only knew that because of the jumbo packs of Skittles awaiting me a couple miles below. These were rafters, seven boats' worth, held in place by guides where the Indian meets the Hudson. They were a mile off, but probably visible from outer space, bedecked in matching helmets and rain gear. One boat was purple, one red, another yellow, and so on. I paddled until a quarter-mile of gentle rapids lay between us, but never reached them. A last pack of green candies shot out and all filed downriver, guides shouting instructions. I wondered what they thought of me. Having just convinced seventy people to uncork a C-note for an experience only trained expertise could provide, here comes Mr. Dingleberry in his jolly green canoe.

For several reasons, I took out at the Indian. For their sake and mine, I didn't want to get tangled in a hopscotch affair with the rafters. This was partly egotistical. There was a good chance I'd flip, and who wants to be rescued? Mostly, though, I needed to scan the river. Choking down a couple energy bars, I climbed a tree. The guides have a gurney here, as they do at intervals throughout the gorge. This one is tacked to a white pine, also the best tree for scouting. Even from height, however, I couldn't see much, but the dam had obviously been released. The rafters wouldn't be there if it hadn't, and the Indian, though smaller, was pumping every bit the volume of the Hudson.

What I did see was whitewater and green mountains. Whitewater is truly white, energy wracking into rock. This, too, was the first look of a gorge. The sun caught one incline, while the other remained in shadow. The roar muted everything. As for the water, I have no eye for picking a path and never will. Flow is less on the inside of a bend, but more water allows greater error, and as the lumberjacks knew, the deeper the current, the more rocks will be covered. Other than that, I look water over only to determine if I have a shot. The rest is decided midstream.

Canoeing has taught me two things. Take what the river gives you. As a kid, I had several rigid rules, but with experience learned to use them as guidelines, then not at all. For a long time, I never pushed off rocks or logs. Canoes balance well as long as you do, and should you put a paddle on a stump to gain a little *oomph*, there's a chance the purchase will give, possibly tipping the boat. Now, I simply judge the risk and use or don't use leverage from there. If the river gives you a sturdy stump to take a twenty yard glide, then by all means.

Secondly, there's time until there's not. This isn't anything you don't learn by almost getting in car accidents or losing your balance at height. I just happened to learn it in a canoe. I don't know this, but assume most people capsize when something unanticipated arises and they gauge there's no time to recover, but you only can't recover when you're swimming.

The first set went well. A bit nervous, I maneuvered to the deepest cut and began picking routes four eddies long. I didn't always maintain a perfect lay, water splashed over the side, but for the most part all was fine. For a bailer, I'd cut the bottom off a half-gallon milk jug and tied it to the seat. A soloist's weight drains water sternward, and I reached behind to bail. Another set went as peacefully, then another. I scraped a few rocks, misjudged certain waves, let the boat turn uncomfortably a time or two, but nothing critical. A half-hour passed this way, and with it several miles.

The gorge is something to see. Deeper cuts exist out West, but like anywhere, this place has its own appeal. Banks of bedrock slope into the river, and the North Woods have colonized every patch that isn't cliff. It's impossible not to feel that you're in deep wild here, and I never shucked the sense that I was seeing what trappers, loggers, and Natives had seen. Stumbling down one car-sized boulder to scout a rapid, a bear dropping lay at the base, a stray hair or two threaded into seeds and vegetable fiber. I was sure cougars weren't there, but every mountainside looked like it might house one, as they once did. Mostly, though, I paid attention to the river, keeping at it, growing more confident with each rapid.

A boat only holds so much water. That's another canoeing tidbit. I'm not sure confidence alone produced my one spill, but I've always said I'd have made a fantastic Major League pitcher if only I had more talent. So on the diamond, so on the river—you reach a certain level and truth will out. The water grew louder, rougher. I sized-up a long stretch, the ugliest. Things had gone well enough, though, so why not?

Funny how our minds work. With much on hand, the brain still manages to flush out every manner of thought. Bailing the last dribbles, I put in, standing for a last look. Troughs lay between each wave, and once I hit the main rift, the water would be white and nothing else. I cheated to river-right then sat, steering between two boulders.

Karen is far from trouble when it comes to shopping. I've dated some beauties in that regard, and Great Sorrows upon my many friends who suffer similar tortures. Edge left, four workable eddies, right there, just like skiing moguls. Still, she has her weaknesses. Bed, Bath, and Beyond, for God's sake. What Devil concocted that man-sump? Jesus, that's a big boulder. A man could leave a piece of himself on a rock like that. Are the Sox playing the Yanks this week? They are. Crap. This year has Empire written all over it. You can feel it. Hideki Matsui—Japanese for "Beelzebub." Bow's cockeyed. Little water in, nothing to fret. Was that a Myrtle's warbler? Don't look. Christ. More water, straighten out. Why do Irish guys talk about their mothers so much? They're worse than Southerners. Hedge left. Now. Do people really love? What does that mean? Such feeling in the beginning, but where does it go on a Tuesday night, baby crying in your arms? Cut right. More. Back paddle once. Twice. Now drive. I'd never felt rage before. How does she do that? Such strength, such weakness, none of it predictable. What did Sammy Malone say? How many do you have to sleep with before you understand just one? *Bon mot*, Mayday. Yikes, that's a lot of water. This set's worse than the rest. Heavy boat, paddle deep. Two rocks, no time. Hit that one, you'll carom. Bingo. Now that one. Ouch. More water. *These are the times of dreamy quietude, when beholding the tranquil beauty and brilliancy of the ocean's skin, one forgets the tiger heart that pants beneath it.* No one can touch you, Herm. You're too good. You too, Dickinson. *Faith slips—and laughs, and rallies . . . Plucks at a twig of Evidence.* A twig of evidence. Are you kidding? You were sent. I'm sure of it. Look for an out here. This water has to go. Nothing, only waves. Dig right. Hard. Harder.

Is Shannon crawling yet? Speaking? Blown away the Ivies with her *Hamlet* dissertation? Of course she has. She's her old man's kid, isn't she? Jesus. I'm a father. Dad. The start or the end? In my end is my beginning. Great Christ, this is heavy chop. Too much water, get to shore. No shore to get to. How many friends divorced now? Family? Is that possible? What happens? These troughs are too big, and that rock hurt. What became of that Montreal girl? Such soft eyes, and it's true about blondes, isn't it? Hot damn. Best we never connected though. Simple thing, loving a statue. That bird. There. Overhead. Unquestionably a Myrtle's. Christ. I'm taking a bath. No more time. This boat's sunk.

When a canoe is carried overland it's called a portage, pronounced *portedge*. Unfortunately, select Americans retain the French pronunciation, and little makes me queasier than to hear some git describe his or her trip and the horrid *poeur'tazh* they had to make. There is, however, a delightful exception. When a boat flips, separating paddler and craft from their own volition, this can rightfully be called a *poeur'tazh*, as in "Sacre Bleu, mes amis! C'est une portage tres magnifique!"

Too much water came in the boat. Any bit of fluid makes a craft sluggish, and while a canoe can take buckets, choppy water puts in much. Prolonged lengths of such stuff are a challenge, and I simply didn't have the talent to keep it out here.

For a time, the boat stayed upright, where I undulated rapids like a surfer. I'd purchased canoe floats before the trip, triangular balloons to stuff in the bow and stern. My gear bags—tight to the yoke and cross-beam—never moved. Bouncing through some turbulence, the stern disappeared. Later I'd learn that the balloon popped. I hung onto the paddle and watched the second oar—the immediate reserve—float from its nook and drift free. A third paddle was tied with the bags. Legs dangling, I one-handed a gunnel. Life jackets really do keep you up. Prior to this trip, I'd never cared for one, thinking them for pessimists, but fatherhood changes things.

Nothing is stronger than water. It wasn't long before it ripped the boat from my hand. Occasionally, I saw the bow tip up or the hull roll over. My legs dragged over boulders, and rearing up a time or two I could see this wouldn't end anytime soon. I didn't want to leave the boat. It might crack, or the gear become lost. Dying was a remote outcome, but having to walk fifteen miles after a night in the dark would be more ignominy than I could bear. If I could just catch up, I might kick the boat into an eddy. The river shot me between two cabin-sized boulders, then churned. Bubbles and froth. Bubbles and froth. I kicked free, but the process repeated downstream, then again. The boat was on its own.

The Hudson is narrow here, which along with the pitch accounts for its temperament. As difficult as it is to get a boat to shore, it's not much to latch yourself to a rock. I did this, hearing plastic scrape over stone.

Luck, however, was mine. Thirty yards down, the canoe perched midstream on two boulders. It lay on its side, and from what I could tell, was sound. Hopping rocks, I came parallel. After confirming its integrity, I sat on a boulder, gauging the difficulty of getting it to shore. It wouldn't be hard. Heading upstream, I entered, stroking easy until in line with the boat. From there, I drifted right into it, slipping around the upstream catch to wind up between the two rocks. The stern was downstream, but squarely on the boulder, and I simply lifted the bow to turn everything over. The water dumped out, and I turned it again, suspending it on the boulders while the current passed beneath. In their lee, the two rocks created a calm. I slid the boat in, cocked it toward shore, then dipped in myself, kicking off a boulder. The stern caught between two bank rocks, and I hand-over-handed along the gunnel as the canoe pivoted, reaching shore well before the craft was free. The boat secure, I rested, watching blood seep from numerous ankle scrapes while the river rolled. A better boater could have had it, but I was lucky. I only lost a paddle.

That was the worst of it. The dry bags worked. The rapids, too, eased, and I put in, making it to the long-awaited pool. Emptying the boat, I turned it over and ate five energy bars. There were rapids to go, plenty of them, but I'd learned. Twice I lined along sets similar to the one that swamped me, a process involving using the stern line to guide the boat while walking the shore. The rest of it was a sun-filled joy. Coming around a hairpin, I was surprised to see two families on a sandy beach. This is the Blue Ledge, where a trail access winds up on river-left across from a bluish, limestone cliff. The families were occupied with lunch, maybe dinner, but one mother sat upon a waterside rock, toeing the river, blue sun dress stuck to her body.

"We don't see many canoes. Where you heading?"

"I'm trying for Manhattan."

She laughed.

"Going to do it, huh? Good for you. I hope you make it."

"Thanks. Enjoy the day."

"You, too."

I drifted by, nodding to the others, then squeezed through a rough patch below, praising our loving Lord for sun dresses.

The west bank mountains made a shell game of the sun, and several times I sized up campsites from the water. The day, though, kept going, the river leveled out, and a couple miles passed before I realized the heavy stuff was behind me. Apart from a couple cabins, North River's Barton Mine facility is the first building you see after Newcomb. The Barton is the last active Adirondack mine, a garnet operation. Mostly it's used as an abrasive for sandpaper. They make a mess of things up on the slopes—Karen's family cabin abuts mine property—but as with Tahawus, the healing is in process. It won't be what it was before, but it will be something, and sandpaper isn't optional. It's complicated being human.

A mile later I took out in North River. Weary of barf bars, I couldn't keep Café Sarah in North Creek out of mind. Karen and I ate there the summer before, and armies would war for their breakfast burrito. I couldn't remember how far apart the towns were, and the map didn't list North River. Tying to a willow, I climbed to the road.

North River is like mountain villages everywhere. Much to do if you love the woods, not much if you love money. The Barton supplies about sixty jobs, and servicing second homes makes up much else. Other than that, tap some maples and boil syrup. You're on your own.

On the road, there's a tourist pull-off. Among other things, a series of plaques describes the logging industry, including The Mouse across the river, the large, black swirl on off-white stone which let the bosses know when the river was high enough. A guy and his wife were taking a kayak off a Subaru. I asked about North Creek. Five miles. Good enough. I'd make it.

Though nothing like the gorge, plenty of whitewater exists between North River and Lake Luzerne, including a patch just off The Mouse. As I worked through, I caught sight of two kids—teenagers—sitting among the stones on river-right. The shaggy-headed one passed something to the other, who put it to his lips. Seventeen, summer winding down, reefing-up on a river bank, right up there with baseball and apple pie nowadays. Dog days, boys. Enjoy.

Five miles, no effort. The river broadens here, runs smooth. Not a deep stretch, I'd imagine that most summers you see more dry rock than current, and I drifted over, happy for the heavy rains days before. The first ash trees are here, until very recently the only wood sought for baseball bats. Something called the emerald ash borer—an Asian import—has swept through America's stock, threatening it with a similar doom to the elm and chestnut. Bat makers have switched to maple. Ash are in the olive family, tall, with deep-grooved bark and elongated leaves. Birds love them. My father first pointed out a red-eyed vireo nest in one. "There," he said. "See? Up high. Listen to the chicks." I paddled along, picking out ashes, wondering if Shannon would ever see one.

Islands are river gypsies' friends. Road and railroad parallel the Hudson the rest of the way. It's difficult to tell where permissible camp sites might be, but islands are normally fair game. At the top of North Creek I came on one. The sun nearly down, I pitched the tent beneath a stand of out-sized white pine, paper birch among them. At the island's north tip there's a hemlock stand. A bird hopped in branches framed by the sun's last light. Kinglet, maybe a chickadee. I treaded softly, angling to undermine the glare. The bird jumped up and gave a profile, perfect light. Chestnut-sided warbler. I'd never seen one. No doubt about this though, like looking at a painting—chestnut stob accenting black and white barring, a splash of yellow in the mix.

Later, after lying in the tent, something just shy of rigor mortis set in. I didn't realize what a beating I'd taken. Maybe it was the river, maybe age. Who knew, but egos heal much. The Hudson Gorge. I know the Colorado River is a damn sight rougher. I know John Wesley Powell fought at Shiloh. I know he lost an arm there, and that he rafted the Colorado in a slap-together dory. I know all this, and now knew that by comparison the Hudson's worst is little more than a pony ride, but what did it matter? Forty-one and still doing it, I thought. Colorado-Schmolorado. Little Wesley wore his mother's underwear.

Sarah's was all that memory had promised, North Creek too. Hippies have melded with rednecks here, birthing something different, the greenneck maybe. Guys that look like Country Joe McDonald take shots of wheat grass and run chainsaws. Women split wood and pray for peace. Gore Mountain, a nearby ski resort, likely imported the youthful idealism, but it's gone native. A local wind farm has been proposed, opposed by second home owners worried of their view. The younger set, though, mountain man and Bohemian alike, seem to like the idea. There's a wine bar mixing hillbillies with deer-shooting earth muffins, and such hybrid vigor has produced a creative energy that other town's lack. Sarah's is an example. In keeping with Stacy McNulty's generation, the clientele had an optimism about them, wild for environmental upkeep but with a pragmatist's governance. I don't live there, and am sure a small town's petty underbelly thrives, but as a passerby I couldn't have been more at ease.

I ordered my burrito and sat on a stool, reading the local events handout. Theater and art, music, bluegrass to chamber, in and about town. The burrito came, and then was gone, dream-like. Outside, I found The Last Pay Phone in America to call Karen. The coin feed was broken. Collect it was. What a guy. All was well, and I walked back to the boat. I could've eaten fifty of those burritos.

If some days are a little rough, others are easy. This one was sunshine and warm water, free-flowing, easy current. The soreness shook off quickly, and I passed through Riparius, scarcely a hamlet, below which the rails crowd river-right. A marble quarry must have been upstream. Great white blocks lay in water here, drill holes bored alongside like worm burrows. I wondered if a single wreck produced such loss. Regardless, anyone with a wet saw, generator, and piles of ambition could tile a palace with this stuff.

One stretch was particularly suited to trout. Quick water, many rocks. I pulled over to filter. Fine sand bedded scattered boulders here, and a mink had worked between them. Tracks girded the rock edges, dipping beneath grass clumps. Insects came off the river, waxwings working them, but a trout never rose. Fish were here though. An osprey perched downstream on a dead pine, eyes to the current.

More river, more pleasure, more sun. The mountains eased, leveling to hills. Oak dotted the banks now, and the yellow birch backed off, while the first farm came in sight, a lone silo risen over trees. At a place called The Glen, the river dips beneath Route 28. A couple kids fished on river-right, but the left bank was clear and I pulled out. I loved such bridges as a teenager. The water here looked deep enough. Take a breath and step off the rail. Fly for a moment. Swim ashore, find your buddies, crack a beer. Days the memory never kills.

Junkus grew thick here, verdant, reedy, bunched around a spring. I waded in and dunked my head. Turning back, a green frog froze in the reeds. I edged forward, lowered my hand. Its head slid between my fingers, placid eyes belying the fear. I let go. I wasn't the only one here. A water snake waggled out of the reeds, vanishing upriver. What hell runs under our every step? That snake was after the frog, the two burning up another act of life's combustion, terror and hunger. The Believer in us says no, it's love, but what is love, but hunger and a little terror too?

Back in the river, I passed the Shroon, where the Fox brothers let America's first log drive go on a whim. Not far below that, many islands lay, and with the sun down, I picked out a long, broad one, heavily wooded, pitching the tent in the center before going back to pull the canoe on the bank. The berm was ten feet high, and with the boat halfway up, I saw headlights across the narrow river cut. It was a pickup, sirens on top, state insignia on the door. Despite being on an island, I froze. The lights eased by, and I tugged the boat up and roped it to a hemlock.

An old fire-ring rested near the tent, along with the twisted remains of an aluminum canoe. Mushrooms proliferated, coaxed by the rains. Fast to the tent, some purple-black thing grew, looking like quick death. My eyes sank and I slipped into the bag, listening to a pair of hermit thrushes trill down to silence.

Portals

The cops didn't take the boat, and by mid-afternoon I'd hoped to reach the Sacandaga, one of the Hudson's largest tributaries. Hill country lingers up here, but the river changes, molding more to the broad, slow-channel flow typifying the Hudson further south. I knew dams were ahead, just not where.

Whether it's the water or bottom is unclear, but the river here turns black. It's pure, but darker than above, where all is river-blue. Drifting beneath the mounting sun in such stuff, it's tough not to hum a little Doobie Brothers, "Old Black Water," while conjuring other climes than this. Weeping willow, even cottonwood, swoon across sandy banks, and you half expect to see Jim and Huck tillering alongside, the pair ghosting our every waterway.

Shadowing the right bank, I paddled a deep cut while pushing off grass hummocks. A female cardinal startled from a wild rose tangle, while further down, a gray squirrel fled in a rattle of leaves before skitching up a pin oak. Silent and quick, tight to the bank, I couldn't be seen, and the trio of white-taileds didn't see me either.

Deer are a great interest. More than cougars, more than black bears, more than even the dreaded fisher, white-tailed deer have tested America's renewed bond with Nature. After *Bambi* sanctified them, deer have since swarmed into suburbs, causing car wrecks and spreading Lyme disease, but above all munching every Japanese maple bud they can find. Long a sanctuary from hunters, many suburbs—from Chicago to Boston, Charlotte to Minneapolis—have either opened restricted harvest methods or hired "deer assassins," nocturnal marksmen rifling dozens of animals at a sitting. Once a symbol of vulnerable nature, deer have become outcasts.

Brushing the briers on river-right, I simply steered when the first one emerged, then eased the paddle to the bank, creating enough friction to stop. A second animal issued from wild grape, a fawn, then another doe. They all stood, hock-deep. Above, an alder flycatcher fluttered back and forth from a cottonwood, taking midges. The lead doe looked across the water, while the other gazed downstream, one ear slapping flies. Sipping from the Hudson, the fawn then nuzzled an elder's flank, jumping back in jest, but it was the one that saw me. One doe leapt ashore. The other jumped in the river. The fawn started for the bank, then spun, plunging. The shore-bounder never reemerged, while the baby bleated until reaching the swimmer. On shore, each shook dry, then dipped beneath the bank brush. Such a scene fit the site. I didn't know it yet, but Lake Luzerne was ahead, where one Hudson stops and another begins, though not before a final stroke of the mountain river.

The current creeps into town. I was certain a dam lay ahead. Houses line river-left, while the opposite shore offers public camping. A sign tells of a canoe portage. The water didn't show anything ominous, so I eased by, hugging river-right. Water became audible, then louder, though I figured with the rain, flow was only topping the dam, and I'd get as close as I could to shorten the carry. Two people, man and woman, barbecued on the rumpled bank ledge.

"Hi," I said.

Smoke drenched the griller, while the woman, seated in a lawn chair, thumbed a paperback.

"Hi," she said. "Where'd you start?"

"Henderson Lake, near Newcomb."

"How long's that?"

"Maybe eighty miles."

I smelled like eighty miles.

"What's up ahead?" I asked.

"Nothing you want to mess with. That's our land back there. Use it all you want, though it's technically off limits."

"Thank you."

The guy put down his tongs and came over.

"Someone died down there a couple weeks ago. It happens. Tried to swim it without a life jacket."

"Oh. Well, thanks again. I won't leave a mark."

They smiled.

"No worries," the woman said. "Good luck."

I paddled back, hauling out at the portage. Two trips. I put the bags on my back. A trail headed downriver, crossing the couple's access before climbing a ridge. I scaled this and found the noise's source, Rockwell Falls. Excluding the headwaters, it's the Hudson's narrowest point, maybe twenty yards across. The water funnels through a drop, forcing a jumble of spout and spray. Up ahead, cars crossed a suspension bridge, and I laid the bags beneath a ledge before returning for the boat, maybe a quarter-mile. In the right conditions, plastic canoes can be dragged, but not here. I laid the yoke across my shoulders and started walking. Reaching the bags, I shucked the boat, listening to it thump the ferns flat. I took some water, then admired the cataract. Such sights were common in the Hudson and Mohawk Valleys, but industry changed that.

The rest of the carry would be easy, a road-crossing then a straight drop to the river. Not bad. That determined, I crossed the bridge and found Papa's Ice Cream, a fifties-style parlor with a deck upstream of the falls. Sitting outside, I listened to water mingle with small town chatter, then spotted a red-eyed vireo shuffling along a maple branch. I couldn't imagine ever being angry here.

Not normally one for sweets, I had a vanilla shake. Then another. Then two more. Days of sun suck the sugar right out of you. I paid the bill and walked out, calling Karen. Shannon cooed on her knee. She was all we talked about. Karen and I were learning each other day to day, largely through our roles as parents. We were better as three than two, I knew, but just then didn't see harm in that, and I walked back to the river, shored up in the thought of three.

Below the bridge, people of every size, age, and body shape laid out on towels to enjoy the day, river lizards basking on ledges, listening to boom-boxes, drinking beer. Just below, the Sacandaga poured in from the west, and tubers came pouring out with it, bobbing along with Budweiser and laughter. Like the Indian, the Sacandaga is dammed, an effective flood control to prevent catastrophes like the 1913 flood, which nearly carried off the state. This dam additionally releases for summer recreation, allowing some fun for the heat-weary and income for the locals. Controversy exists, but not much. Of all the environmental horrors this valley has seen, pumping a bit of water so kids can have a bob isn't among them.

The river bends east here, sharp, and with it an equally abrupt change in its properties, purpose, and history. This is the second Hudson, the shortest stretch, though the longest in terms of canoe-miles-per-effort. It has current, but dams have slowed it to almost nothing, hence its name, Lake Moreau. Cigar-shaped, I couldn't tell from the map where it begins or ends, but in relation to the water's nature, it starts at Lake Luzerne and ends at Glens Falls. I'd made more than twenty-five miles a day, but that number would shrink fast right here.

Something else marks the change. A memorial. Not a statue, but a ruin, the foundation of an old paper plant where the falls' last energies scrape the base. A third of it is made of stacked limestone, while the rest is cement, about thirty feet high. The town is noted for it. Near here, in 1869, Albrecht Pagenstecher set up the first pulp grinder on Wells Creek with imported German technology, refashioning both the paper industry and the upriver log drives. Mills sprouted up and down the Hudson, including this one, built in 1878 by Charles Rockwell.

Little fouls a river like paper production. Along with textiles, it destroyed Eastern rivers for generations, and yet where would we be without them? "Always have a poet in your pocket," John Adams said, yet until the digital age this was only possible through the toxic processing of wood fiber.

Looking over the Rockwell foundings, you can fathom the sludge they generated while recalling Melville's pasty, withered women toiling within similar cells:

> At rows of blank-looking counters sat rows of blank-looking girls, with blank, white folders in their blank hands, all blankly folding blank paper . . .
>
> Not a syllable was breathed. Nothing was heard but the low, steady, overruling hum of the iron animals. The human voice was banished from the spot. Machinery—that vaunted slave of humanity—here stood menially served by human beings, who served mutely and cringingly as the slave serves the Sultan. The girls did not so much seem

accessory wheels to the general machinery as mere cogs to the wheels.

Such scenes haunt other countries now, but the residue remains, with the Hudson drenched in it. From Lake Luzerne to Yonkers, its banks are studded with the tombs of America's fagged-out industrial chutzpah, and like any graveyard, a thousand questions seep from the stones.

PART II

☙

COGS AND WHEELS

Pink Flamingos

From the Sacandaga to Corinth, the Hudson is a riviera, or as my father would call it, a redneck riviera. Plastic bull frogs and pink flamingos, motor boats and party barges, bottle rockets and Budweiser. These are the times that try men's souls.

Fortunately, we have a word for it, and it's no mystery where it came from, for among the many gifts that Jews have bestowed, Yiddish tops them. *Tchotchke*. Cheap, tawdry, bawdish crap. Above Corinth, Lake Moreau is a wadi of cultural *tchotchke*. My tolerance is ample, but there is a threshold. Normally flayed by guilt and good conscious in the oubliettes of my soul, my WASPy haughtiness only bears so much. "Manchester, England, England," sing our friends from *Hair*, "across the Atlantic Sea." Indeed, and Father Winthrop did not erect Our Shining City to see it besmirched by goateed ying-yangs yodeling away on jet skis, yet there they were, tattoos and all.

The tin-tin begins where the current stops, or at least appears to stop. Cigarette boats turn doughnuts in the remnants of flow where tubers tumble in conflicting wakes, while upon the many lakeside gazebos the motley refuse sod themselves from plastic cups.

The river here, such as it is, runs a hundred yards wide, as still as any lake to the eye. Clouds had crept in, and I only realized the sun's absence by the lack of sweat. Motor chop is nothing like nature chop, but it must be honored. Wakes are taken on the quarter. Finding the right bank, I hugged it, only to sense my snobbery do what it normally does, ease quietly away, for I shared far more with these people than not.

These were second homes, cottages, little different from the Endless Mountain retreat where my own people summer. The ambience and activities were largely the same, and though the yayhoo variable seemed to run much stronger here, creeping affiliation soon outpaced my knee-jerk contempt. Summer on the water, fleeing the snakepit workaday. This is a broad stitch of American life, so ugly it's beautiful, and the Hudson has much to do with it, now and otherwise.

Downriver, from Newburgh to Peekskill, the Hudson Highlands were a great respite from the clammy Manhattan sties of early nineteenth-century New Yorkers. These considerable peaks—alive with Revolutionary ghosts—bank the Hudson, and when Robert Fulton commercialized the steamboat with a trip from Manhattan to Albany in 1807, it coincided with the first dose of disposable income for the nation's upper class. They made good on it, deluging the Highlands and Catskills to the fruitless horror of the region's early promoters, including Thomas Cole, who probably more than any other extolled the meditative properties of the Hudson Valley.

Cole fathered what became the Hudson River School of painting, which wed theology with the American landscape, particularly that of the ethereal Highlands. Viewers awed, and enough people steamed up the Hudson, tramping its banks, so that coupled with the industries colonizing the valley, Cole soon lamented the pull of his own work, shifting themes. Commissioned in the 1830s by Coxsackie merchant Luman Reed, Cole crafted *The Course of Empire*, five paintings progressing from nature unbound to human decadence and doom. This theme runs through to today. If it's changed at all, it's only by degree of urgency. As in any human endeavor, however, deep complications exist. In this case, they stem from how we choose to recreate in nature, something you contemplate all through Lake Moreau.

If we go out in it, we disrupt it, and yet if we don't go out in it, we abandon it, which is a way of saying we abandon ourselves. If not everyone wants to live among wilderness, most people understand its cleansing effects. If Cole noticed the damage done to the Highlands when most of the continent remained undeveloped, he'd immolate himself today. Summer people, day-trippers, and others increase each year, further impacting our dwindling open space. In the Hudson and Adirondacks, moreover, ecological recovery has had the ironic effect of increasing tourism and second home development. The Adirondacks add about a thousand second homes a year, the Hudson Valley a like number. If people don't want to live here, they want to spend time, and no matter how lightly we may choose to do so, we leave a considerable stamp. Seven to ten million people visit the Adirondacks a year, and even if each only took a short walk, listening to birds, all those footfalls make a mark. If Othello killed what he loved, we do too.

And yet. There's always an "and yet" with our kind. If we legislate ourselves out of the woods—restrict visitation, disallow second homes, curb use more than we already have—people won't experience them, and lacking that sensual influx will no longer care what happens to wilderness, or city parks for that matter. Yakutat is an example. Everyone in town makes fun of sport fishermen, or "sporties." They come in great packs spring through fall, crowding the rivers, flailing monofilament. There are more every year, eroding banks with foot traffic and taxing fish populations. Yet without the experiences these people imbibe, Yakutat would be far more prone to resource exploitation than it already is. When I left, a mining company had put in claims to scour the Forelands for several minerals. "All that water is great for mining!" beamed a company report. All that water is great for other things too, though, and the sportie multitude—endowed with cash and influence—will have their say come the miners' days in court.

Accustomed to letting the river do the work, the still water took some getting used to, as did other things. Retirees puttered on barges while water-skiers back-and-forthed boat wakes. Heavily mulleted men careened about on jet skis, wispy moustaches collecting spray, and if I passed one more grinning dime-store frog I'd have punted it across the offending lawn.

Most of me doesn't understand this. Quiet is what I seek. Solitude. Revision. The vibrations of God. I find them, too, or think I do, in dark, silent waters, or the paint of a redstart's wing. These people don't come here for what I've come for, and yet I know myself better than that. My Alaskan work required much time in a jet boat, a sled propelled by a converted motor enabling it to navigate tight, shallow rivers. Yee-hah is all you can say in one of these things. I made myself feel better by saying it was simply a job, but that was dishonest. Hit that turn just right. Feel her slide. Zip between that sweeper and stob, right there, now gun it. Listen to her open up, all cylinders. Moose! River-right! Out of the way, Fat Man, I'm coming through! From the start, I've told Karen that I'd wanted to leave Alaska for a long time, and she's been kind enough to pretend she believes me.

Hypocrisy used to bother me, but I waltz with it now. It's who we are and what we are, and we may as well dance. I paddled through Lake Moreau's recreaters, disgusted only with our common denominator, along with the knowledge that if they didn't enjoy this place however they enjoyed it, it might be put to more sinister uses, as so much of the Hudson has been before it. Crowding up from Ossining and Mamaroneck and all the other downstate towns, these people leave pieces of themselves with each visit here, and would no sooner see it tarnished than I would. Each cottage has its stories, and families bring their kids here to watch them grow.

"I contain multitudes," Walt Whitman said, and we do. If jet skis drive me nuts, I check myself by looking back to those fish-chocked Alaskan rivers, one hand on the tiller in a fierce southeast blow. Nobody can make that turn. Nobody but me.

We contain multitudes.

The Gospel of Dean Wormer

Paul brought Jesus to Corinth, and Corinth brought Hell to me. If not Hell, then certainly the International Paper Company, whose dam requires the first grueling portage.

Corinth is the first sizeable town you see. The day wasn't over, but that was coming, and there was now no mistaking a dam ahead. Not knowing what that entailed, I docked at a public beach on river-right to gain some local knowledge, but only found a trio of tubby drunkards.

Animal House. To men across my generation, this is hallowed scripture. Along with *Caddyshack*, we set our lives to it. If Greeks guided themselves to Apollo and Zeus, ancient Hebrews to Yahweh, then Modern American Man has Otter and Flounder, Carl and Judge Smails. I've yet to come across a situation that doesn't warrant a quote from at least one of these films, and men everywhere agree. My Colorado sister, now happily married, took the same minefield path to romance as me. It's a tough world out there, and limbs can be lost. Once, after the latest "The Next 'The One' " failed to materialize, she resolved never again to date a man who could line-for-line *Caddyshack*. "Good enough," I said. "You're down to three Amish guys and the Yanomamö People. Happy hunting." She recanted, and now waxes blissfully with one of the Belushi/Chase faithful.

Pulling into the public boat launch, I tied to a cleat, planning on asking the beach's lifeguard about a portage, but would quickly about-face. Three guys who probably add a decimal point to the national health care deficit waddled up the floating pier to have a look. The planks creaked and bobbed with each cow step. They drank from red plastic cups, and their frothy breath matched their stumbly gaits.

"Hey-hey," one said, scratching his belly beneath the Black Sabbath logo on his faded t-shirt. Acne constellated a cat-fur moustache, and as he leaned over, I prayed only that the dock rail would hold.

"Doin' a little canoe'n?" he went on.

"I am."

He turned to a buddy, whose hour in the sun that day was an hour too long.

"Hey, don't your cousin have one of these?"

"Yeah, Frankie's got one. Got it for two hundred bucks, too."

"How much you pay for this one?" Black Sabbath went on.

"More than two hundred," I said.

The cousin lapped a patch of foam from his lip.

"Yeah, Frankie's a dealer."

I needed an out. A bridge crosses the river here. Beyond it, a cordon of buoys tells of the dam. On river-left, a sign hangs from a tree above a patch of gravel on the wooded bank. I couldn't read it at that distance, but guessed "portage" was the gist.

"Well, I have to go," I said. "I picked the wrong side. My wife's waiting for me down there and I'm already late."

The guy that hadn't spoke yet liked this. I don't think he was thirty-five, but the purple worms of a dandy gin blossom already tailored his nose.

"Freakin' bitches," he said. "They're all the same, eh?"

I smiled, then nodded as I untied. Wedging the paddle between two planks, I pushed off. Black Sabbath was a last word man.

"Alright, Dude. Have a good one."

Who doesn't think of Dean Wormer at such times, the ignoble Noble of Faber University?

"Fat, drunk, and stupid is no way to go through life, son."

I thought this, but only tipped my paddle before turning downriver, stroking for my phantom wife, wishing—for the first time, I realized—that Karen would be there.

Short carries are enjoyable. Long ones—anything over a mile—aren't. The trail here is wide and well maintained, but the tract steep and long. The sign, though, said .7 miles, which didn't seem bad. I yarded the canoe up to a dirt parking area, then went back for the bags. Trailers and ranch houses cluster along the forested slope upstream of here—remnant kin, I assume, of the town's former pulp culture.

Downstream it's only woods. I put the bags on my back and followed what I could of the signs.

A power line cuts through the hilltop, and the two trails on the other side make locating the portage a bit tricky. So do deer flies. Anyone who chooses not to believe in God has my blessing, but I defy these to trek the Northeastern woods in summer for even a hundred yards then deny the existence of Satan. He inhabits the deer fly, a black-orange–eyed, triangular-winged menace that repeatedly bounces off your face and head with a ground-gear buzz. Their bite can hurt, but it's the perpetual harassment that makes the devil in them, and with both hands occupied, you simply gnash your teeth and bear it. As I continued downslope along a trail I wasn't sure was right, the flies accumulated. A rolling stone may gather no moss, but it'll be covered in deer flies.

Through the hemlock canopy, the dam sounded like what it is, an immense waterfall. I hadn't heard such percussion since the gorge. By the sound, I was right on top of it, yet the trail kept going, then some more, and still further. It's wide, though studded with rocks, and the blisters I'd picked up below Henderson—along with the scrapes in the gorge—made each step a gingerly one. As the day darkened beneath the hemlocks, I hadn't forgotten the canoe. Blisters and deer flies aside, then, I picked up the pace, cursing the slatternly mothers of whoever painted .7 miles on that sign. Like Forrest Gump, I'm not a smart a man, but I know what .7 miles is.

Eventually, the trail ends. You come out on the river, the water moving again, and look upstream. It's not the world's largest dam, but standing below even that, you'll forget whatever environmental reservations you may have of such structures, and marvel at what people can do. Across the river lies the paper plant for which this dam was built, a brick structure sprouting several now-smokeless chimneys. Looming above, water spills over the concrete cliff in a singular white sheet. I worked with a New Jersey guy in Alaska for a while. Real Jersey. Teaneck. We were out in a field camp for a few weeks tagging salmon smolt with two born-and-raised Alaskans. They didn't understand why anyone would go to New York. "Go," Jersey said. "You'll walk beneath those buildings and look up, as awed as you are by any canyon or mountain chain."

The dam covers what used to be the largest natural drop on the Hudson, originally called Hadley's Falls. A torrent in spring and fall, water scarcely trickled over in summer. Despite this, early engineers saw the potential. At what was known as Jessup's Landing, lumberjacks portaged logs around it, but mill owners wanted the river's power and took it. Woolen mills filched a little at first, but a crib dam—covering a portion of the river—went up in 1880, buttressing another Pagenstecher pulp operation. After the 1913 flood ruined the crib, a concrete replacement was put across, which stands today.

International Paper bought the Hudson River Pulp Company in 1898, the largest of its seventeen Hudson mills. Immigrant labor filled it up, and Corinth experienced the early twentieth century's grueling labor disputes, as management contended with workforces across the nation in a seismic dialectic. A 1910 strike in Corinth was a workers' success, while a five-year holdout starting in 1921 failed.

"Strike-breakers were brought in," Rachel Clothier, Corinth's museum director, told me. "They didn't know what they were getting into, of course, just thought they were coming to do a job, but those were violent times. Garages were set on fire, there were fights, and International Paper posted three machine guns on their grounds. For at least a couple generations, older families still knew who was related to the strike-breakers and who wasn't. Everyone thought that to the company it was just a matter of more money. Those weren't good times."

I could talk to people like Clothier all day. Stocks and bonds be damned, the wealth of nations is locked in neighborhood curators. Just lift a latch and learn.

By the sixties, Corinth was a corporate town, with most of its population employed at the mill, sometimes three generations working together. Employees gave themselves to the company, and the company in large measure gave back—beefing up schools, public works, and paid-for festivities. Such symbiotics ruled twentieth-century America. Opinions on these relationships vary, as they favored certain towns far more than others, but the end was always the same. After gradually dwindling, International Paper succumbed to economic pressures and enticing offers abroad, leaving Corinth in 2002, making it one more town with a broken-windowed riverside mill, along with a scantly employed, vestigial population.

I hustled back for the boat, taking another glance at the sign, which actually reads "1.7 miles." Feeling foolish, I threw the paddle and life jacket in the bottom, wrapped the bowline around my hands and put it over my shoulder, the best way to drag a canoe. The rocks were mostly on the downhill side, where the uphill portion was dirt. I put my head down and barely raised it the rest of the way, at last reaching the bags. I couldn't say what smelled worse—aged pulp or my own armpits.

Some daylight remained. I loaded up and headed downstream, where the current slows again to lake. Unlike above, I paddled through silent forest, primarily maple and hemlock, camping a couple miles below the dam. It was black beneath the canopy, and I pitched the tent by headlamp, though light lingered over the river. A bald eagle coasted above it, its white head drawing the last bits of day. It turned, cackling atop an evergreen downstream. Closer, a brown creeper hopped about a gray birch grown over the river, wrenching clefts of bark for a twilight pillbug. It tacked round the trunk, then hopped off, disappearing into forest. I followed, and didn't wake for ten hours.

Borders

More dams, more still water. Stroke, stroke, stroke, hump when you have to—slow going, but pretty country for all that. Below Corinth, Moreau Lake State Park abuts the river, making a tranquil paddle. A few campers had set up in isolated spots, but other than that it was clear, nothing but deep woods and deep water. I passed a canoe, a father and son fishing the opposite shore. Over many years, my old man rowed my sisters and me countless miles around the lake before our cottage, trolling. Chain pickerel were the prize, a small pike with a duck-bill mouth and razor teeth. When we pulled one up, my dad's hands ran with blood as he worked the hooks free. He'd lay the fish in water, scarlet petals blooming, rocking it back to life.

At a sharp northeastern bend, the river picks up County Road 24, a quiet byway, with the Spiers Falls Dam not long after, another hydro plant. No designated portage for this one, and I simply pulled out and humped everything the short distance down the road, two trips, maybe a quarter-mile.

I needed water. Not knowing, I guessed the Hudson would be too polluted even with a filter from here down. A rivulet cut under the road above the dam, and I walked up to it, fumbling through the brush. As I pumped, a ruby-throated hummingbird dropped into the little ravine, hovering, its rosy throat distributing overcast light. Capping the bottle, I waded the brush, listening to a chipping passerine. Jerking about a poplar branch, an indigo bunting scolded me, his feathers blue ink. August is late for such behavior, but it may have had a laggard brood. He fluttered from one branch to the next, admonishing. Indigos anchor a famous study. The females choose different mates for different purposes. Gentler sorts build the nest and raise the young, where the rough-and-tumble are tapped for conception. Scientists were quick to translate this to potential human equations. Prior to the trip, I spent most of every day with my daughter, caring for her. The bird escalated his rebuke. And what beguiling vixen, Father Bunting, coaxed you to sit upon those eggs?

Another dam follows in Queensbury, though with a cut portage to river-right. Above the structure, in a dead tree, an immature eagle perched, a kayak remuda below gawking upward, cameras snapping. I didn't blame them. Eagles are pigeons in Alaska. They fight seagulls for cannery scraps and haunt the dump in hard winters, lapping mayonnaise jars. Still, you forget what majesty they project, and I took a moment with the kayakers, grateful for the birds' return here.

This portage is roughly the length of Corinth's, but the ground too rough to do much dragging. Twenty years ago I would've carried that boat with a whistle on my lips. Now, deer flies buzzing, I simply sweated, my back creaking like a schooner mast. More dams lay ahead, I knew, but a stroke of ignorance befriended me that day.

Along with the currentless paddling, the two portages made this the slowest day, maybe ten miles. As such, by the time I cut under I-87—making my way through the many artificial islands where timber sorters built their log docks—the day was ending. I reached a dam, much lower than the others, with dead mills on either side. The portage here is simple, skirting a busy road on river-left. You cross the Feeder Canal, which engineers installed to supply the Champlain Canal with water, keeping summer barter open. It still flows, and the route has been turned into a narrow park, joggers having replaced barge mules. I knew the Champlain Canal would lead me back to the Hudson, I just didn't know how long that would take, so I put back in the river and headed toward Glens Falls, certain I'd have to ditch the canoe under some pier while I slept in a hotel.

You pass through another park here, a municipal one. The roar of Glens Falls has been replaced by industry and traffic, which the park muffles. Picnickers lined the banks, grilling, even swimming. After a mile or so, the hated buoy line signals the dam, and on river-right, a large sign says the portage begins here. If another sign tells where it ends, I never found it.

The dam anchors Glens Falls, where Routes 32 and 9 meet. Beneath the bridge, a laminated placard explains that this site inspired the most famous scene in James Fenimore Cooper's *The Last of the*

Mohicans, where Leatherstocking swears to Cora that she'll not be lost. Alongside an elderly couple, I peered upstream, unable to find the cave amid the concrete. The dam allows the river through, but at nothing like its original force. Few dispute that America's frontier myth began here, with Archetypal Man at its center. Like all myths, it started with actions among living people, in this case Iroquois, Algonquin, and Europeans mingling in wilderness, but was truly hatched in the imagination.

Leatherstocking, or Natty Bumppo, was Cooper's merger of wild and civilized, where Natty's inviolable woodsy ethics steer him through a wash of changing values jumbling traditional racial and gender identities. Capitalism and American expansion, too, played key roles. People strive for individuality, yet the crush of nationalism and free markets work to homogenize us, confining us to civilization and the unmanly lairs of home and office. In an essay terrifically titled "The Last Real Man in America: From Natty Bumppo to Batman," David Leverenz points to Leatherstocking as the first Last Man in America, commencing two centuries' worth of national male fret: "Cooper taunts civilized readers with a vague sense of the shamefulness inherent in the white march westward—not, paradoxically, with the guilt of exercising oppressive power, but with the shame of accommodating to a large-scale nation-state . . . [a]s domestic intimacy and career advancement supersede traditional manliness."

As with the lost kings of the Snickers campaign, even Natty Bumppo wandered through a feminizing world, unsure of what "man" meant. Such paranoia has and continues to be ridiculed, maybe rightfully so, but we shouldn't go too far. As Henry Kissinger said, "Just because you're paranoid, doesn't mean nobody's after you."

Today, the Last Real Man in America lives in Alaska, the Final Frontier. As always, He's more myth than matter. Shows such as *The Deadliest Catch* and *Harder in Alaska* dramatize what can be torturous labor, but the Alaskan bush remains one of the safest places to work and live. Gasoline and satellite phones get you out of most scrapes, and while Indians can still upend a Saturday night, they're now as addicted to dish TV and tater tots as the rest of us. Still, it's a fairly coarse place to live, manly endeavors aplenty, and I was fresh from it. Yet I was a stay-at-home dad now, living in New York, unable to find family-supporting work in the direst capitalist slip in generations. As such, I turned away from Natty's cave, asphalt below, neon in the air, haplessly searching out a portage.

Walking in the nearest dive, I was greeted by several affable lush-es, seated here-and-there along the Western-motif bar, buffalo horns and wagon wheels, arrowheads and headdresses. I said hello, then asked if anyone knew where the portage trail ended. The bartender, blonde, thick-set, looked like she could drop five kids before breakfast and split a pound of bacon with you besides. Why this country wor-ships the emaciated I'll never know.

Before my question was out I knew no one knew what portage meant, let alone where one might be. They were friendly though, proud of their town, and even if they didn't know the answer, they had a cousin that did, if only they could remember that number. I parried the hospitality, somehow avoiding having to do a shot, then did what I should've done from the start—walked out and paddled back up to the Feeder Canal, daylight be damned.

I'm conservative at heart. If I know I have three hours, I count on two. I had no idea how long this canal was, nor what it looked like where it ended, but I hoped to be safely bedded down in two hours. On the way back through the park, I hugged river-left. Trees drooped over the high bank, and frustrated with my decision not to take the canal in the first place, I worked as close to the bank as I could, push-ing off bottom where I couldn't use a stump. A mink loped beneath the undercut bank, right at me, small, probably young-of-the-year. The dark body disappeared a few times where mats of root and dirt overlaid the bank, then popped out again, swimming where a rock or log forced it in. I held a willow branch, locking the boat in place. No matter what you're doing, there's always time for mink.

The dam was in sight, and rather than paddle to it, I took out at the first half-clearing, cutting through the woods, where the feeder parallels the river a while. I pushed off, using the cement wall for leverage. People walked and biked along the cinder trail above. Vines strangle many of the trees here, and what the forest lacks for breadth it makes up in density, providing some understanding of what it took to dig this ditch, built in the 1820s to supply the Champlain Canal its summer flow. Mules, men, and oxen dug this thing, and what a job they did. Narrow and smooth, it flows at a fair clip toward I didn't know where, though if it kept me from portaging through Glens Falls, that was enough.

A mink wasn't the only wildlife. Green-winged teal are a dainty, fine-tasting duck. Coasting by a lumber yard—a mill, maybe, the boards looked rough—five teal paddled from the swampy left bank. I associate teal with marshlands, not narrow-ribbon parks adjoining sawmills. They swam for a while, then hopped off the water, heading toward the river.

Not much later, I came on the last gasp of Hudson paper making, a stout operation straddling the canal. An overpass joins rattling tin structures on both sides. This is the last of Hudson behemoth Finch, Pruyn, and Company. Several workers were on break, casting suspicious eyes my way. Canoes are associated with environmentalists, and environmentalists with lost jobs. I nodded, receiving only leery etiquette in return. This place stank. Sulphur and fire, chemicals of every kind. I stood. To the left, raw logs heaped a workyard, mountains of them, a yellow machine pushing them around, soaked sawdust everywhere. I'd spent the last few days floating through where that wood came from, and though my instinct is to admonish such practices, I need that paper. Besides, much forest lies intact, and as I paddled away from the stink, I had a flicker of hope that birds and books can coexist.

The portaging wasn't done. The day was almost over, so when I heard rushing water, I cursed the bad timing. Canal locks are built to pass boats, but the feeder has been defunct for decades. It still has a series of broken locks, though, that are unboatable. The first couple were easy, simple slide-arounds on the grassy trailside, but then I came to a road, tying the canoe to have a look, taking note of the sign that says no camping.

The park widens here, losing its pencil shape to woods and open fields. It additionally has "The Combines," five locks in a row along a steep pitch. They're busted now, leaving a series of waterfalls. I carried the bags downhill, maybe a mile. Running back, I crossed the road, picked up the boat, and waited for traffic to clear. Headlights were on, and the last car to pass was a cop. I thought sure he'd stop, but watched until his tail lights disappeared, then set the canoe up for a drag. There's mown grass here, mostly downhill. I ran, the bow occasionally clipping my heels. By the time I reached the bags, twilight was done. Beavers have plugged the canal where the land flattens, and the concrete walls are gone, replaced by cattails. Putting in below the beavers, I paddled by headlamp. A muskrat swam ahead, then plunged, and in a stretch where vines drape young trees, I came upon a robin roost, hundreds of birds startling from the limbs. Whooshing overhead, nearly crashing into one another, the commotion didn't stop for fifty yards. An egret, glowing white, hissed soon after, reluctantly lifting into black. All this wildlife, with a spuming paper plant not far away. Borders exist, but it's increasingly difficult to finger them.

The dark was too much. The park had to be home. Stashing the canoe in cattails, I found a clearing off the trail and made camp just before the rain. That cop hadn't left me. Do we ever tire of pursuing and being pursued? Every American heart—even a cop's—houses a dapper gangster, tommy gun at the ready, shouting out a shattered window, "You'll never take me alive!" We're as much outlaw as in, and where those borders are it's never been easy to say.

The Gravity of Greeks

I was in the boat before light and the Champlain Canal before I knew it. Needing a bath, I dipped in the brown water, plugging all facial orifae and hoping for the best. Yick.

Cows greeted me at the Champlain juncture. New York is close to Vermont here and looks like it, with Holsteins sprinkled in green fields, red barn on the rise. The Champlain runs wider than the feeder. I turned right—south—and headed for the Hudson, the scent of cow dung hanging in lacy mist.

A sharp-shinned hawk dropped off a limb, heading toward the farm. Sharp-shinneds are bird killers, following migrants south to north, north to south. The heat belied the season. August was getting on, and in the brush and in the trees, movement tickled the birds.

Float the Hudson anywhere from Henderson to the Battery— even a few miles—and you can't help but think about labor, bloodshed either. Mines at Tahawus, pulp in Corinth, every manner of factory all the way down, battlefields throughout, the x and y of Fort Knox. In two hundred years, the United States went from colonial wilderness to dominant world power, crammed with everything from space shuttles to high-end architecture to nuclear weapons to flim-flam strip malls, our satellites pocking the sky. The meeting of capital and labor largely made this happen, but only after the cannon fire cleared. It's a delicate confluence, blood, sweat, and money, and the New York canal system is a promising place to brood it.

DeWitt Clinton. Here's your man. He did what George Washington couldn't. Any bozo can run an army, but punching a waterway through the Appalachians, joining West to East, fighting odious bankers, waterfalls, mosquitoes, and endless forests takes pluck, pluck and throngs of guys willing to hoist picks and beat mules until the thing is done.

Washington saw it needed doing too. We laud his military feats, but ignore his intelligence. Knowing that trade cinches people together, he predicted that failure to affect fluent commerce through the Appalachians would eventually see westward settlers fracture off, forming a new nation. The Mississippi, he knew, connected the burgeoning West with Europe, leaving them no ties with America but nostalgia and some distant cousins. His prescience is astonishing. In 1775, before the Revolution, he wrote the governor of Virginia: "The western settlers . . . stand, as it were, upon a pivot. The touch of a feather would turn them away," grasping what escapes so many statesmen: People love their country, but they love stuff even more. Cut trade routes, and off they go.

After independence, Washington commissioned an effort to canalize the Potomac River, and while it improved navigation, it failed to get through the mountains. Rocks, trees, and elevation make difficult digging, as does lack of engineers, which in Founding-Father America was the condition. Clinton fought through all this, through obstinate legislatures, an incredulous nation, and another war with England. By 1825—eight years from the first spadeful dug by his own hand—his ditch was dug. When the first boats hauled material from the Great Lakes to the Hudson, people turned, instantly recognizing it for the history-altering achievement it was.

While I only glimpsed the Erie later that day, the Champlain— even the feeder—served the purpose. Empire was the game in the New World, and though we pretend it isn't today, it remains so. America has played its hand well, and the Erie Canal falls just shy of the Revolution in getting it started, where the fractious symmetry of worker and worked-for, money and muscle, did what very few thought could be done.

The Champlain is one of the Erie's "lateral canals," spurs connecting the Hudson with further territory. Shortly after Clinton "married" the waters of Lake Erie and New York Harbor, the Champlain stitched the Hudson with the northern waterways, siphoning trade from Canada. The Cayuga-Seneca linked the Hudson with the Finger Lakes, while the Oswego connected Lake Ontario. Clinton had incarnated what visionaries had seen as far back as Cadwallader Colden in 1724. Having conducted a survey of the Mohawk Valley, Colden recorded that region's political, topographical, and commercial conditions, but came away seeing grander things. "How is it possible that the traders of New York should neglect so considerable and beneficial trade for so long a time?" he asked, referring to the Mohawk's feasibility as a canal route. Clinton, having surveyed the route himself, in what Peter L. Bernstein interpreted in his *Wedding of the Waters* as an "adventuresome jaunt by a bunch of men liberated from the constraints of office work for . . . the great outdoors"—or the Last Real Men in America—saw Colden's same vision, and burned up much of his twenty-three years as New York's mayor and nine as its governor in scaling the popular and political mountains between America and that 363-mile ditch. He made it, securing barter with westward expansion and insuring that New York City became what he said it would, "the granary of the world, the emporium of commerce, the seat of manufactures, [and] the focus of great moneyed nations." Clinton, though, didn't do it alone. The greater ugliness preceded him.

Paddling the Champlain Canal, you pass through America's womb. We make great fuss now over whether we're an empire, but this is only talk. America has always been an empire. We started as the outermost branch of one, and simply kept going. Indians were to conquer first, then back across the seas. Yet without doings in the Champlain and Mohawk valleys, we likely would have remained a confederate starveling, if not a colonial one.

With America an English-speaking nation, and Indians so long a static symbol of white duplicity, it's nearly forgotten that for roughly half the period since Henry Hudson's voyage—nearly two hundred years—Iroquois battled Algonquin battled English battled Dutch battled French for control of the Hudson, Champlain, and Mohawk valleys, and that highly unpredictable outcome played out right here.

Nowadays, Fort Edward is a burned-up mill town, once home to a pig iron furnace fed by Fort Ann mines by way of the Champlain Canal. Its origin, though, was as a Seven Years War British fort. If I'd have turned north, toward Lake Champlain, I would've neared Lake George, glacially severed from the Hudson long ago. Here ugly battles took place, culminating in a bitter event at Fort William Henry. This turned moral momentum Britain's way and did much to ossify colonial hatred of Natives, registering consequences through Wounded Knee two-thousand miles and many generations later.

History, though, has problems. "History is bunk," Henry Ford said, implying that it's open to interpretation and therefore biased, or untrue. Jill Lepore's *The Name of War* explores this, delving King Philip's War, Fort William Henry's harbinger by a hundred years. The war itself is of secondary concern, Lepore's tool to explore how history's framework is fought over as much as the events themselves, which are nothing but raw resources for posterity to shape.

The war pitted colonial New Englanders against several Algonquin tribes, and might be the most foul conflict on American record. Both sides gutted, beheaded, tortured, and otherwise mutilated one another (white on Indian, Indian on white, Indian on Indian). Women and children were dismembered and houses burnt. Lepore's title comes from contemporary William Hubbard, who wondered if the struggle even deserved "the name of war" (though he himself was shilling for the colonists, implying that Indian behavior didn't hold up to honorable warfare). The Indians lost, stifling their voice in the scrum that followed. With a shrunken frontier filled with unhappy heathens, the colonists wrote prolifically, calling any Indian victory a "massacre" while downplaying English bloodlust. Native outrages were "savage," "barbarous," "inhuman." A century and a half later, though, with the Eastern Indians either moved West or turned to demoralized ghosts, Lepore notes the colonist shift to revision: "John Adams wrote from Massachusetts, 'We scarcely see an Indian in a year. I remember the Time when Indian Murders, Scalpings, Depredations and conflagrations were as frequent on the Eastern and Northern Frontier of Massachusetts as they are now in Indiana, and spread as much terror.' Adams, clearly, had little nostalgia for New England's Indians . . . but by the 1820s and 1830s many . . . writers expressed only sorrow at their disappearance." Native resurgence—ever since busy to fashion a more secure identity—dove-tailed this white nostalgia, fertilizing white America's noble savage that persists today. Fact, of course, has blended with fiction in this centuries-old scramble, losing precision if not the name of war.

The British held Fort William Henry, losing it to the French and Algonquins in 1757 after a grinding siege. Assured of generous terms by French general de Montcalm, British colonel George Munro surrendered, thinking the French would march them to Ticonderoga for peaceable cashiering. Such was French intention, but the Indians' claim to promised war trophies—scalps—went unfulfilled, and when the British marched out along with officers' wives and children, those scalps were had. The French tried to stop it, the British inflated the carnage, but it's generally agreed that heaps of wounded soldiers, women, and children were among the many killed. Reports of a Native dashing a baby's skull against a tree are many, but none confirmed. No matter. Once colonists heard this, Indian policy was set, though today, in combining all the literature, accounts of what truly happened at William Henry are a muddle. History can, in fact, be bunk, for how often do we make it what we need it to be? Cultures, however, are built on stories, motivated by them too, and if myths are the only bricks we have, history is their only clay.

Knowing I was near Fort William Henry, my white guilt welled up, a perennial nemesis. What happened? I couldn't say, but my bias swung toward massacre. Walk a mile in my moccasins, goes the Native proverb, and so I do. *Je sens mon coeur, et je connais les hommes.* When the guilt becomes too much, I need balance, and rely on this formula to partially achieve it.

They had their reasons, I know, but Indians did, in fact, slaughter people all the time. In one incident, Schenectady, New York, in 1690, was burned to the ground, with residents of all sixty homes murdered or imprisoned. What had the whites done? Something, no doubt. From a canoe, three centuries distant, it was easy to look back on such an occurrence and surmise the many Native motives, but what does that mean when I go back, kin to the slaughtered, come over that rise, the scalp-shorn, cut-up corpses smoldering in ember? *Je sens mon coeur.* What history might be in the classroom I'm not sure, bunk maybe, but while it happens it's more emotion than reason, and emotion can only be touched with emotion. "Not everything's in your books, Stephen," *Master and Commander*'s Lucky Jack says to Dr. Maturin, and so it isn't. Though then makes now what it is, now is never then, nor will it ever be but by feeling.

Emotion is no small portion of labor either. Set yourself up before ten yards of New York forest, ax and shovel in hand, and see what helps you more in clearing it—thought or rage. I've never seen the Mohawk Valley, other than glancing up its mouth where the Erie Canal merges with the Hudson. I am, however, deeply intimate with northern hardwood, and the rocky, root-webbed soils that nurture it. Today, we have backhoes and front-end loaders for such stuff. We also have unions, though, and wonder if such a thing as the Erie would be possible today.

There are people who run the world and people who keep it running. Alaska's fish and game department has a traveling handyman, bopping from outpost to outpost, fixing pipes, repairing roofs, tinkering all that needs tinkering. This guy was great. He came to Yakutat every October, capable of anything a hammer, saw, or welding torch required, decked in a one-piece union suit and spouting gorgeous piths like "All's a lock does is keep honest people honest."

One year we needed a new pump house, a simple day's work of tacking studs into four walls then a roof, slapping tin to the sides. A sunny day, too, rare for Yakutat, and I hammered where he told me, soaking up his babble. The four walls erected, we stepped on buckets to nail the roof tight. "You know," Jim said through a mouth full of nails, "for all our computer what-not, we really haven't figured out anything the Greeks didn't figure five thousand years ago."

He was talking geometry, of course, but his observation has range. If the Greeks didn't get it all right, their philosophy certainly posed the right questions, pulling us back again and again. Thrust all you want, you'll never get out of that atmosphere.

One Greek, I forget which, said, "Every society must be half-slave and half-free." Aristotle maybe. With a democracy far beyond what any Greek envisioned, we recoil at such maxims today, but rather than retreat, we might take a closer look.

What this most likely meant was that in order for a civilization to serve humanity best, it needs philosophers to philosophize and carpenters to carpenter. Poets can't versify if they're banging nails, and nail-bangers must bang nails, not dream themselves into metaphor. The Greeks made this easy, as did the Romans, Egyptians, Chinese, and lest we forget, the Americans. They had slaves. Real ones. Beat down, unpaid, miserable, and wretched. Humans are crafty though. Where one historical trend brings you down, another lifts you up. America banned slavery in rivers of blood, and ever since, the requirements of full, free citizenship have grown leaner. If white men of property were its original members, now all our democracy demands is the age of eighteen. Yet labor questions remain, and the Greek magnet draws us back.

Clinton finally won his funding, and his state approval too. After twenty years of legislative patty-cake, the New York representatives relented, scrambling seven million dollars in state bonds and giving Clinton the go-ahead. Now to dig the thing.

Prior to accelerating the fast-growing American tradition of "Hard Job? Put an Immigrant on It," Clinton did something wise. He made construction local. Rather than contract the whole thing to a single bidder, ensuring provincial snubbing by importing labor and engineering talent, Clinton contracted short sections to local communities, leveraging human pride. Each group dug from one natural waterway to the next, a string of mini-canals. The project took eight years, however, and eventually immigrants—mostly Irish—were employed, flooding Upstate New York. For twelve bucks a month, this blend of foreign and native-born labor toiled away. Trees were whacked down, stumps hauled, mud moved with picks and shovels, a pinch of blasting powder where needed. Through mosquitoes and deluge, heat and disease, they hacked from sunup to sundown, praying God they didn't get hurt.

The divisions between labor and capital are well known. Money hates muscle, muscle hates money. Philosophically, human beings are rarely equatorial, rather thriving at the poles. Somewhere in the mix of worker dignity and industrial efficiency lies *isle paradisio*, we just can't seem to locate it. Today, people are shocked to learn that 363 miles of man-dug ditch were constructed across New York in eight years, most of it within budget. Men were tougher back then, but that doesn't explain it. Without organized labor, without ten thousand nano-laws restricting what workers can and can't do, without weekends and holidays and eight-hour shifts and overtime and health benefits and everything else, management was simply able to get more out of people than they otherwise could. Don't like it? Tough. Sean and Pat here will do it. Hurt? Good. Leave. Dead? Even better.

And yet. In a hundred years—from 1820 to 1920—American money and muscle went at it hard. It was bad before and has been rough since, but these decades saw live blood. (The worst of it, of course, is related but a different subject. Southern blacks were still slaves for much of this time). Indians were killed, moved, and sequestered, with all that land opened to industry and resource extraction. Fortunes were made, but on the backs of rapidly depreciating labor conditions.

Workers organized, were repelled, struck back, gained ground. By the early twentieth century, this near-warfare became tangled in a national identity crisis, the precursor to Commies and Capitalists. People died. In 1914, in Ludlow, Colorado, twenty people perished in coal violence, including children, while in the early twenties, assorted West Virginian gunfights left dozens dead in Mingo, Logan, and McDowell counties, again over coal unions. These were the worst, but violence was everywhere. Through doggedness, the unions eventually won, doing much to create a taut middle class. Even where unions didn't form, their ethos did. Factory owners often treated workers—and the town—to dignities any nineteenth-century tycoon would have deemed feeble. Now, however, unions have largely become what people feared they would—many-tentacled monsters strangling production, threatening the work itself. Over the seas such jobs go, and along the Hudson you see the evidence, among the first regions the phenomenon took place.

With the Erie Canal, America exploded. People poured West, and their farm output matched that of their resources—coal and lumber—providing Eastern industry all it needed. Along the Hudson, factories popped up everywhere. Early to this outbreak were Troy and Cohoes. Troy is on the Hudson, Cohoes the Mohawk. Four miles separate them. The rivers powered many industries, but iron and textiles—particularly collar making—were dominant. Detachable white collars were a new fashion, giving an economic class its name. This was the first half of the nineteenth century, real Charles Dickens stuff. Manufacture abruptly leapt from small houses of twenty employees or less—with the owner often on the line—to high-powered, specialized operations employing hundreds of workers, the owners often far away.

As with canal work, factory days were long, conditions grim, pay grimmer. Worse, it was all inside—fumes, heat, butchering machinery. Job security existed as long as you were on post performing at an exaggerated clip with no mistakes. Women in the collar industry soaked to the elbows in bleach twelve hours a day, often more, overtime not yet a theory. Vapors, along with direct absorption, must have cut countless lives short. The Sabbath was honored, but six-day weeks were mandatory. Men in ironworks lived similar lives, puddling molten ore. Foundries were shut down in summer heat, but only because human beings simply can't exist in such conditions, let alone work, something even the floor bosses noticed. These stories are old but unweary.

Dickens dug through the English grime to find human spirit, and American workers found their own. Troy and Cohoes particularly standout. Bucking existing mores, men supported women here in their common plight, while immigrant diversity differentiated each town from the more uniform New England mills, allowing greater empathy. Kate Mullany organized the first women's union in 1864, improving conditions while reciprocating male foundry efforts, which formed their own tight-knit outfits.

As with unions to follow, these initial organizations sought only dignified lives—reasonable hours, livable wages. Even so, such modest gains had a price. Jobs fled. Not overseas, but to the South and Midwest, heretofore nonunion. The South took the linen mills, the Midwest the foundry jobs. Pittsburgh. Youngstown. Cincinnati. Unions eventually won there too, but in August of 2009, as I paddled along, not much remained of them.

It can't all be blamed on unions, or even half of it. For one, less than twenty percent of the private workforce is currently unionized. That more than seven million manufacturing jobs have left the country in the last few decades contributes to that number, but nonetheless, we're not uniformly union. Secondly, human nature played its own hand. At their outset, institutions are lofty, born to great principle in opposition to oppression. Kate Mullany in 1864 or miners in 1930s West Virginia risked all to benefit all (one of the wittier bumper stickers I've seen says, "The Labor Movement: The People Who Brought You the Weekend"). Right through to the post–World War II era, unions allowed people to work with dignity, and the nation thrived. By increments, however, unions themselves became the oppressor. Everyone knows that the United Auto Workers force Detroit to pay more for health benefits than car materials. Once again, we hopped right over pragmatism for the opposite extreme. Teachers' unions provide one example. They're necessary. Without them, any helicopter parent who wanted to fire you just because their idiot kid got a D could do so. As it stands, however, anything short of YouTube bestiality keeps you your job.

This had relevance. Deep in a recession, out of work, I was paddling for dollars, or at least the hope of them, mother and child at home. My bias was showing, but it wasn't unwarranted. More than twenty jobs I know I could do turned me down with a word. Union. While in Alaska, I was in a union for ten years, though never thought about it. They clipped some bucks from each paycheck, but otherwise had no requirements that mattered, and the benefits allowed all that we take for granted today, union or no—overtime, health insurance, holidays, vacation, the works. Across the seas, people grind out our goods in Dickensian horrors, Troy's and Cohoes' too, with capital having gone where the unions aren't, as they did to Pittsburgh and Charlotte long ago. Where are the Greeks? Whips and shackles aside, we wonder if there's no other way than half-slave, half-free.

Working down the canal, I came to the first of several locks, simple things first designed by Leonardo da Vinci. Unlike the feeders, these are fully operational. You paddle through a gate, wait, then paddle out the other side, the lock having adjusted you to elevation. Iron doors hold water out or in as needed.

At the first I learned three things. Waiting for a gate to open, I was surprised to see a fish swirl, no minnow either. Canal water is oozy brown, but there it was, a modest leviathan. The lockman, too, wore a Red Sox cap. I asked. Just as I'd feared. They'd dropped five of six to the Yanks. "Screw it," he said. "It's over anyway. I stopped paying attention two weeks ago." Then how'd you know they dropped five of six? I wondered. He also said I was the first of two canoes that day, sometimes half of what they see in a year. A woman had radioed the night before, saying she'd be through that afternoon, paddling from Burlington to Manhattan. We never met, but leapfrogged one another over the next couple days. Meantime, I paddled from lock to lock, making time, passing boats on their way to Vermont. With the last lock cleared, I rejoined the river where the Hudson receives most of its filthy reputation.

The Shadow

Anyone who hasn't seen Monty Python's *The Life of Brian* is living paycheck-to-paycheck intellectually. Human folly, futility, foibles, fecklessness—all of it, right here, stripped clean for our little minds to mull. Tyrants, mobs, radicals, religiosos, conservatives, and revolutionaries alike take their licks, prophets too, and we come away as we should from artistic enterprise—we've looked in the mirror, and the mirror said, "You're ugly." Mark Twain, the Master of American Rivers, would've memorized each frame, happy at last after a life of dejection. In it, the Boys give us the aqueduct scene, which neutralizes poo-poohers of THE STATE more effectively than any form of torture could.

For the unlettered, *Brian* is set in Jerusalem, 1 AD. A Jewish hooker births a son in the manger adjoining Jesus'. Throughout, he's mistaken for the Messiah. In the aqueduct scene, the Boys pick apart hapless liberal oppositions everywhere. Twenty commandoes huddle in sedition, plotting the capture of Pilate's wife. Reg, the leader, gives a talk:

> *Reg*: They've bled us white, the bastards. They've taken everything we had, and not just from us, from our fathers, and from our fathers' fathers . . . [a]nd what have they ever given us in return?!
>
> *Xerxes*: The aqueduct?
>
> *Reg*: What?

Xerxes: The aqueduct.

Reg: Oh. Yeah, yeah. They did give us that. Uh, that's true. Yeah.

Commando #3: And the sanitation.

Loretta: Oh, yeah, the sanitation, Reg. Remember what the city used to be like.

Reg: Yeah. All right. I'll grant you the aqueduct and the sanitation are two things that the Romans have done.

Matthias: And the roads.

Reg: Well, yeah. Obviously the roads. I mean, the roads go without saying, don't they? But apart from the sanitation, the aqueduct, and the roads—

Commando: Irrigation.

Xerxes: Medicine.

Commando #2: Education.

Reg: Yeah, yeah. All right. Fair enough.

Commando #1: And the wine.

Francis: Yeah. Yeah, that's something we'd really miss, Reg, if the Romans left.

Commando: Public baths.

Loretta: And it's safe to walk in the streets at night now, Reg.

Francis: Yeah, they certainly know how to keep order. Let's face it. They're the only ones who could in a place like this.

Reg: All right, but apart from the sanitation, the medicine, education, wine, public order, irrigation, roads, a fresh water system, and public health, what have the Romans ever done for us?

Xerxes: Brought peace?

Reg: Oh, peace! Shut up!

I don't know if the cast knew of Hudson Falls, New York, or even of General Electric (GE), but as the Hudson River's many ecological woes are considered, "The Aqueduct" needs consideration.

Out of the canal, all I saw were snorts. As a toddler, my parents read me the book *Are You My Mother?* in which a creature mistakes many things for its mom, including an excavator whose only utterance is "Snort!" Here they were, battalions of them, yellow and shoveled, floating on anchored barges—the heavily litigated, much ballyhooed Hudson River vacuums. Not long into the General Electric cleanup, however—decades in the making—the operation halted, as early efforts had suspended too many polychlorinated biphenyls, or PCBs.

The last lock-master told me to hustle when I hit the river, as a large vessel was bound for the canal. I had time, but a research boat cut a wake my way. I aimed for the other side, then disembarked. This was Roger's Island, named for Captain Robert Rogers, who trained irregular forces here during the French and Indian War, then went and did vile things to Indians. Rogers is said to be the only man George Washington feared, and even today, this place is considered the inspiration for the United States Special Forces.

I dug out a couple energy bars then sipped some water, needing to conserve. From here down it was store-bought only. A white-throated sparrow chipped in the willow scrub. At my feet, pearly mussel shells—pried by raccoons, herons, and mink, maybe an otter—washed with the pea gravel in the boat wakes. Across the water, an osprey took in the river—barges, snorts, powerboats, and with luck, a fish. Such life was promising, but little more, for not far above Roger's Island begins the Hudson's bleakest chapter.

PCBs started as so many human innovations—well and well regarded. A synthetic oil made of chlorinated biphenyl rings, it insulates electricity without altering the current or itself heating up. This was great news, for electric fires were common. GE built plants a mile apart in Hudson Falls and Fort Edward during World War II, providing bomber parts. When the war ended, they converted to manufacturing transformers, capacitors, and other electrical parts, including PCBs.

Ironically, it was a dam removal that did the damage. Currently, environmentalists are gangbusters to remove every dam they see, with me mostly behind them, as dams impede bio-traffic, affecting what species can live there. The Edwards Dam on Maine's Kennebec River was recently removed to good effect, allowing troubled species like Atlantic salmon and alewives back to old spawning grounds. That dam, though, didn't have over a million pounds of PCBs behind it.

Hudson dams have come and gone for three centuries, and when the Niagara Mohawk Power Company petitioned to remove one more in 1973, no one cared. Out it came, and down the already foul flow went decades of semi-legally dumped carcinogens—fish killers, human killers, everything killers. The river hasn't recovered, and few think the dormant snorts that I drifted through would have much effect beyond the usual political badminton.

PCBs are heavier than water, catching where other stuff stops— log jams, eddies, dams. Largely insoluble, they're sucked up the food ladder and poison water as far out as several hundred human lifetimes. None of this was known at the time they were concocted, but by the 1930s their toxicity was undisputed. Still they were made, and when Hudson Falls and Fort Edward became the largest transformer and capacitor site in the nation, PCBs spewed out of them in gross tonnage, often straight into the river, sometimes into ramshackle containment attempts beneath the factories, creating the reservoirs that make the dredging project mostly a farce.

The New York Department of Environmental Conservation (DEC) is charged with keeping the land clean, water too, but laws are only as good as they're enforced. The DEC, though, has a rough row. New York City is America's economic engine. America is wild for profit. Environmental regulations cut profits, which raise costs, which rankles consumers, which cuts profits further. According to many, then, the DEC's primary job is not to shrink the bottom line, and as such, laxity was their key strategy when it came to curtailing GE's Hudson River runoff.

Admit nothing, deny everything, make counteraccusations—a ploy of politicians and corporate flak shields alike. GE, in spite of every fact and law against it, still maintains everything they did was legal, and because of long-standing DEC complicity, they have wiggle room. The federal Rivers and Harbors Act, along with the Refuse Act—both passed in 1899—clearly prohibit the type of discharge that occurred for decades at Hudson Falls and Fort Edward, but with laughable government oversight the laws meant little. After the Clean Water and Water Pollution Control acts of the early seventies, GE had to at least pretend, applying for dumping exemptions that they exceeded with blind-eye DEC sanctions. It wasn't until the Niagara Mohawk dam came out that people noticed how sick the river had become (eating a single eel around Stillwater was said to supply half a lifetime's PCB quota), and as David Gargill wrote in *Harper's*, by the early eighties the DEC finally "warmed to the idea of doing its job."

I first ran into GE PCBs long before. They're probably still with me. Northwestern Connecticut is one of the prettiest places you'll find, the Housatonic River its chief boast. Cutting through the southern Berkshires, it stitches deep woods to farmland then back again—magnificent to the eyes, nose, ears, and fingers. Just don't eat anything.

At sixteen, some high school pals and I made the hour's drive to Cornwall. Trout were our aim, but booze and Led Zeppelin too, along with whatever teenage mayhem we could wreak, driving while heavily intoxicated high among it.

Cornwall is a peach—dusky, broken-boarded covered bridge spanning the Housatonic, New England hardwood glutting either bank, steep, rocky ridges crowding it all. We crossed the bridge then fell out of the car like circus clowns. Trout were had, and by afternoon a bonfire lit up a high-water silt bar. With much beer drank and fish consumed, we couldn't be beat. As usual at sixteen, though, we had no idea. Looking up, there were two signs. One said no fires. Good. Another law broken, laurels all around. The other said don't eat the fish, they're choked with PCBs. Oof. Today, then, if I were to pick apart my liver, I'd find chemicals from the GE capacitor plant in Pittsfield, Massachusetts, where the leakage is horrendous.

Tim Gray, the Housatonic River Initiative (HRI) director, told me Pittsfield is a petri dish to see how many PCBs humans can absorb before damage is done. "The town is marinated in them," he said before describing a spill within fifty yards of a school. GE employees called such patches an "ax-yard," where pallets of waste oils were taken and emptied with an ax. "The EPA was too gutless to make them clean it properly," Gray added, explaining how PCB sites were "capped" with blacktop, all with the EPA's blessing. After the feds were court-forced to study the problem, they summed their findings this way: "We think your children are safe." GE, then, was let off for the price of a little pavement and some legal fees, but the problem remains. "Plumes" exist all around the old site, where wayward PCBs burrowed into bedrock and surrounding soils, the same problem that undermines the dredging below Fort Edward.

The company did attempt to contain the toxins, but failed. PCBs slipped into the fractured schists and shales beneath Ford Edward, where they will seep into the river for generations. Dredging will stir what's actually on the bottom, sending much of it downstream, but the problem—perhaps unfixable—lies in the bedrock. What began as environmentalist glory, then, has ended in melancholic gloom.

Maybe it can be fixed. Maybe not. I don't know. The EPA, GE, and many other people much smarter than me don't know, so why guess, and when you can't guess, blame. GE is an easy target, as is the government. The company ran a horridly sloppy operation, sneaky too, from polluting through litigation. The DEC and EPA largely let them do it, and even when the EPA forced a cleanup, their own court-ordered research undercuts the method. Dredging won't make the river any cleaner than waiting it out, and without addressing the bedrock plumes pooled beneath Hudson Falls and Fort Edward, PCBs will ooze into the river for unknown lengths of time. All the stereotypes of corporate turpitude sleeping with government impotence are here, juicy bull's-eyes for anyone who cares to shoot.

Still, something's missing. Rome brought misery to Jerusalem, but it also brought the aqueduct, sanitation, the roads, irrigation, education, medicine, order, and public health, even wine. Being largely an environmentalist myself, I often grumble about Corporate America and all the horrors it's enacted. Details are many, facts too, but the general, well-justified essence is "They're screwing us." As companies grow larger, they've stripped much out of community life as they trot around the globe looking for lower and lower labor costs to match slacker and slacker environmental regulations. Advertising misleads ("Beyond Petroleum," for one), pollution continues, and the faceless nature of leviathan business practice gives every impression of an unslayable dragon. They've bled us white, the bastards, and not just us, but our fathers, and what have they ever given us in return?

Enter the aqueduct, enter General Electric. When we ignore GE's considerable offenses, they do indeed bring good things to life. Toasters, refrigerators, stoves, ovens, heaters, air conditioners, electricity—every modern gizmo that takes so much of the "Oh, my aching back" out of life comes from GE and outfits like it, and they've been successful largely because they're cheap. Enter the consumer. Enter us. Enter me.

Drifting through the moribund dredges, nodding to bearded men and ponytailed women taking water samples, I paddled over the goop that would taint me and my daughter and her grandchildren and all the ones after that. The sun slipped through the clouds, and in the inky depths I looked for but couldn't see the invisible venom. This was a good place, then, to study America's most dour savior.

The Puritans put a stamp on the national consciousness that hasn't rubbed. Their direct descendant, John Edwards, spread his Calvinist gaiety throughout the eighteenth-century Connecticut River Valley, and it's still with us today. His most famous image has every sinner dangling like a spider over fire, saved only by a whimsical God. While this gloom hasn't done much for our sex lives, it at least lent a hand in ending slavery, not completely annihilating Natives, and eventually allowing all other groups—including women—full citizenship. It makes us feel ugly, and only by feeling ugly can we gussy ourselves up and do it right. Twice I've seen peregrine falcons swoop over an otherwise frolicking teal flock, every bird freezing beneath the shadow. Such is Edwards' effect upon us when we reach too far. There's a predator out there, and it's us.

The genius of the Calvinist stamp is to combine introspection with the certainty that somehow it's all your fault. Much of me, for instance, hates GE. Much of me hates the favored station American profit enjoys to the diminishment of other pursuits. I look outward, and snipe fat, well-deserving targets like DuPont, GE, and the U.S. Government. The Hudson didn't have to be this way. Neither did the Housatonic, or all the other industrial stink pits across the country. Industry dumped it in, though, and the government mostly watched. Cost-cutting, however, was their chief impetus, the shadow hovering above.

I use refrigerators. Ovens are dear friends. When I walk in a dark room I want to flick a switch. I wash clothes in spin cycle then toss them in a dryer, and when I seek out these rote amenities I do so with one adjective in mind—cheap. I want the aqueduct and my low price too, and for this it may not be all my fault, but there's a spot there that won't rub. Were I willing to pay more, it may be that GE would do more to keep rivers clean. Until people—me—stop wanting so much for so little, corners will be cut and government agencies made blind in what remains of American industry. For the balance, we've made filthy rivers the rest of the world's problem. Across the channel from Juneau, Alaska, on the west side of Admiralty Island, there's a mine. The Green's Creek hauls out silver, zinc, and other ores, boring into mountainsides. With strict environmental regulations, however, and high labor costs, the dirtiest part of metal making is sent overseas, where half-slaves slop around in chemicals and high heat, dumping all waste into nearby ecologies. They send the finished product back here. I called to find out where this happened. Admit nothing, deny everything, make counteraccusations was the answer, but it won't stop me from using metals, not if they're cheap enough. Industry captains are mostly abhorrent creatures, the government often the Keystone Cops, but I'm in on it as well. I've cut usage, turn off lights when necessary, and have learned to live without when I can, but there're many hurdles I'm sure I'll never clear. D. H. Lawrence said that any-one can draft a novel, but to write one, edit, re-edit, then a hundred times and again, that's the trick—"the grip and slog of it." We want a cleaner world, but with all the booty we've had before, relying on the Romans to supply it. It's a simple thing to dream up a world where rivers are clean and skies pure, but how many are willing to stagger through the grip and slog of it, and how far?

Still, Still Water

This second part of the canoeist's river, the lock-dam-industrial zone, is a grip and slog in itself. Not difficult water, it plods, the current nearly imperceptible. Anything, though, to avoid loaded-down portages, deer fly Rollerball as you go. For that reason alone locks are pure joy, and if a genie granted me one trip in a time machine, I'd fly straight back to Brave Leonardo and hug that man firm.

Still, the middle of most things presents the test, and the middle of the Hudson is no different. I missed my family for one. For the first time in forty-one years that meant something other than the nuclear unit of my childhood. Nine months of pregnancy and five of infant life hadn't quite brought me through the transition. Were there really two people waiting down there? A family? My family? Or was this just an East Coast jaunt, followed by a plane back to Alaska?

Not so. Shannon might have sprouted a tooth. Maybe she was crawling. I didn't know, but didn't want to miss it, and this broad, lazy water wasn't getting me back any faster. Karen, of course, was another matter. We weren't yet married, and already it seemed like everything between "I do" and "Until death do us part" was the middle, the two of you exchanging body blows like Frazier-Ali, the grip and slog indeed. Endurance, though, has rewards. "We've done this," you'll say at the end, and it will mean something.

Lock Number 5. Schuylerville. The sun had won the day, drawing the evening's rain back to nose level. Weighted air. Out on the water there's nowhere to hide. The tops of my feet will likely be brown for the rest of my life, and I doubt the white of my bottom and healed burn of my lumbar will ever merge to one color. I broiled, then, and after the many months of urban indoordom, nothing could have felt better.

I ate in Schuylerville. Below Lock 5 the town is a mile walk, maybe less. On the way in, grasshoppers lifted from the frost-heaved sidewalks, fluttering into milkweed. Cars passed, and I could feel passengers staring at my filthy pants and the alien glow of my forehead.

In the diner I quaffed three iced teas before the tuna sandwich came, then two after that. How many Schuylerville's in America? Ten thousand? Fifty? Post office and a general store, a few odd businesses, two-lane cutting through, the people sweet but guarded. This one's named for Philip Schuyler, of landed Dutch stock who made general during the Revolution. Not far downriver, in 1777, he missed glory by a few weeks.

From about this point to Manhattan, the Hudson is a who-did-what-where of the American Revolution. Britain never controlled it entirely. Had they done that, history would be different, and so would we. Benedict Arnold. Each year, from 1775 to 1777, he did what few could have done—kept Britain from coming out of Canada to win the Hudson and therefore the war. New Englanders, they knew, were the troublemakers, and severing them would see the South sue for peace. In 1775, Arnold led roughly eight hundred men through Maine in October. His force was repelled trying to take Canada, but the effort showed the sort of heart the Brits didn't think the rebels had, and throughout the war they stationed troops badly needed further south in Canada. The next year, the Brits came down Lake Champlain with a navy. Arnold built a navy on the lake's shores, then engaged. Again, he didn't win, but crippled the English enough that they retired. The following summer, they sent their best man.

Johnny Burgoyne was a gentleman and entertainer. He was also cocky. He took Fort Ticonderoga in July, whereupon General Horatio Gates had General Schuyler removed. Gates took all the credit for the Battle of Saratoga on the Hudson's banks a few weeks later, despite his every effort to lose it. Arnold and a Polish engineer, Thaddeus Kosciusko, were the Continentals best assets. Kosciusko designed fortifications at Bemis Heights which turned Burgoyne back, while Arnold, after being ordered to stand down by Gates, rode a horse into battle just as things were turning against the colonists. The Americans followed. Arnold nearly had a leg shot off and was pinned under his horse, but the momentum changed, and Burgoyne was through. The victory convinced France enough of American success that they lent Ben Franklin badly needed money and troop support, which eventually won the war.

Saratoga is a national historic site today, where a statue of Arnold's leg stands. He went on to become synonymous with treason, and was no less reckless in treachery. Fighting for the British, he raided coastal Virginia, asking a captive American what the Continentals would do if they caught him. "They will cut off (your wounded) leg and bury it with the honors of war, and hang the rest of your body on a gibbet." Even the people who hated him most, then, and should have, knew what they owed him.

Back at Lock 5, I pushed off, eventually cutting the day short. Pleasure boats passed up and down the widening river, and the factories ceded to corn and hay. A windless day, boat wakes supplied the rocking, stirring up each shore as well. Miles passed, scattered houses too, increasingly large. Near Stillwater, a woman haled from river-right.

"There's a storm coming. Nasty one. You should find a site if you're camping."

Her hair was whipped in the sort of Appalachian Beehive that only says "trust me."

"Thank you, Miss. I appreciate it."

"You can camp down at Cucamonga, on the right. You can't miss the sandy beach."

"I'll look for it. Thanks again."

The Hudson is famous for summer lightning. Two hours of daylight remained, but a broad river is no place to be amid scattershot lightning bolts. Besides, when you have a chance to camp at a place called Cucamonga, you take it.

It turns out she was wrong. Cucamonga was on the right—a bit of white sand before forest—but the rain never showed. Such storms dance about, though, and I'm sure it squalled somewhere. With the tent pitched and tarps strung, I had more daylight than I was used to. I swam. The Hudson is black and still here, and the breezeless day made it more so. Hold your breath and dive deep. No sound, little sight, all peace. My kingdom for a set of gills.

On shore, I took out *Augie March*, reading on the beach. A song sparrow chested atop a sumac, trebling happy notes. *Melospiza melodia*. Schools of fry dimpled the river just off the sand. I could identify such sized fish in Alaska, but not these. Shad? Stripers? You have to spend time on a river, put your hands on things. I extended a leg, and the fish made for the depths.

A motor boat full of kids whipped a tuber upriver. In their early twenties, there were a half dozen of them. The kid tumbled off the tube, and the boat put-putted to pick him up. All in, they cut the motor and kicked up their legs, tattoos aplenty, drinking beer and enjoying the day. Two women were on board, pairing their laughter with the sparrow.

These people reminded me of what I often forget, what most of the country often forgets. Two wars were being fought, far away and for what purpose beyond nihilism few could any longer articulate. A painted turtle swam upriver, stroking a couple feet from my toes. Yellow streaked its face and the gray shell skimmed just beneath the water. It froze. I again moved a foot, and like the fry, it vanished in black. At twilight I called Karen. Tomorrow she'd know if she and Shannon could come up, somewhere below Albany. I said I hoped she could.

The next day was much the same. From the map I thought I could make Albany, digging hard, relishing the continued calm. Mechanicville is just below Lock 3, where I tied up next to a semi-yacht heading to Montreal. Two parents ate with their daughter on the stern deck. They spoke French, but the woman asked where I was going in English. I said not as far as you. She smiled. Montreal is something of a teenage Shangri-la for American boys. Strip joints— "peeler" bars to Canadians—are rife, you can drink at eighteen, and French accents are French accents.

Mechanicville is tough to see, a *memento mori*. I'm sure there's more to it than what I saw, but its likeness is splattered all over New England, where most old mill towns aren't more than what they seem. Boarded-up factories pox Mechanicville, and the people seem as despondent, like some bony hand reached in and took out the important parts of them. Many towns here are the same. Waterford. Watervliet. Troy. In Waterford, I drifted past the Erie Canal. The history outdoes the image, brown water seeping into brown water, banked by unloved dwellings, cracked pavement, and concrete flood walls. Troy is gruffer. The last lock is here, run by the Feds, the estuary behind it, but my enthusiasm was dampened by the anaerobic hush whispered from tenantless structures. What happened? We had a new continent, green and alive, with the energy to transform it, but cut ourselves deep in the process and have yet to heal.

From the river at least, Troy is red brick and white brick, brown brick and gray, most of it crumbling, save the odd machine shop limping along. Busted windows pock these old sweatshops, where labor unions once thrived at a time when they needed to thrive. They're gone now—the factories, the unions, the work. American history is repetition. Renewal, decay, renewal, decay. From the 1840s to about the 1970s, industry surged on American rivers. Where one died, another cropped up, shape-shifted by trend and innovation. Immigrants poured in, moved, moved again, chasing work, but there was land to put them on, and little global competition to hook those jobs away. Time, though, has passed. Paddle through Troy, New York; Bridgeport, Connecticut; Manchester, New Hampshire; or Youngstown, Ohio. Gary, Indiana; Pawtucket, Rhode Island; Bradford, Pennsylvania; or Fall River, Massachusetts. Look. Listen. Pigeons and stupor. Silence. Vacancy. You'll find these, but not renewal, nor many of the components that comprise it.

Inside Troy's federal lock, I sniffed for salt but didn't catch it. I'd spent the last ten years in estuarine systems. Penned up for the moment in the last lock, I could feel that old titillation as tides sift through eel grass, and what that means to fish life, our life.

I should've remembered about the salt. Another boater, a Rhode Islander, reminded me. I held my canoe against one concrete monolith while he chatted from the stern of his sailboat along the other, the water draining beneath us. He was curious of the canoe, a bit skeptical of my chances.

"As soon as you're out of here you'll be in tide water, though the salt won't pick up for a hundred miles."

I'd forgotten that. As the ocean pushes into rivers, the salt water acts like a dam, pushing the fresh back up the gradient. That the Hudson is an old fjord leaves it with scant incline, and on high tides the fresh water tumbles back a hundred and fifty miles. Paddling against tides isn't difficult, you simply go slower. Usually enough eddies and still water exist along the edges to make a guerilla game of it, and tides, of course, turn. Not wanting to sound smug, I didn't say this. Besides, I'd never been on a river this wide, or in a tidal zone this long.

"Well, if I make it, I make it," I said. "If not, I'll cut it short."

I asked where he was heading.

"We were up in the Lakes. We'll head out through Hell's Gate to Long Island Sound, then tuck up into Narragansett Bay and home to Tiverton."

The Hudson and the big bays, Narragansett and Chesapeake, might be our last hope. What lives were once lived here? Clams, oysters, mussels. Blue crab and stone. Lobsters. Sturgeon. Halibut and flounder. Cod. Muskrats, mink, and otter. Beavers, and O Christ the ducks and geese, blotting out whole coves. Anadromous fish up the rivers—alewives and shad, striped bass and herring, along with the eels, the catadromes. Deer, even elk. Life out in the reeds, waiting, watching, learning, gathering food, then back home for the slow cook. Family. Music. We've gained much in poisoning and paving these places, but lost much too, and a look now at the dilapidated postpartum of the cities we've chosen makes you want to revisit that crossroads. These aren't things you say to a stranger in a lock, but you think them.

"Happy trip to you," I said.

"And you," he nodded. "Good luck."

The bottom gate opened. He went through, and I followed him out of the Hudson's last impediment into shifting waters.

PART III

&

O HUDSON

Red/Blue

I made Albany, a great relief. Tents are fine places, but I needed a shower. That's one advantage of ageing—you're no longer afraid to say, "Alright. Enough." Besides, between Troy and Albany I never felt at ease. The tide was indeed coming in, providing a long look at the camping options. Either train tracks or buildings run tight to each bank, and these towns have a rough go of it even in high times. On the cusp of Depression, then, what demons prowled the strip of trees between city and river I didn't want to learn.

Interstate 90 was the marker. Many highways converge in Albany, and I-90 spans the Hudson. The river has a few slight turns between here and Manhattan, but not many, due to the fact that mile-thick ice doesn't bend much. I cleared one crook and saw that bridge for miles. Sticking to the edge, I worked the tide's eddies, using the erosion boulders—"rip-rap" in Hudson terminology—to push off where I could, ducking limbs as they came. After the frenzy of the Hudson Gorge, the water here isn't in a hurry. They've dropped painted sticks in this stretch, finding them at the mouth 126 days later. The crossing cars seemed like they'd never get bigger, but soon enough I was under them.

In 2002, Albany put in a river park, bucking a longtime tradition of turning its back on the river. When Dwight Eisenhower sanctioned the interstate system in the fifties, the Hudson was unwanted. Accordingly, when I-787 was built in the 1960s, connecting the New York State Thruway to downtown Albany and points northward, they ran it tight to the river. Now that the Hudson flows a little cleaner, and fish swim rather than float, the town has scrambled to reconnect to its riverfront. Despite the static drone of the several connecting highways, they've done an admirable job. People walked and jogged along a cinder path, scullers stroked upstream and down, and parents chased toddlers about the thin strip of mown grass while fathers and sons tossed bass plugs to inedible fish. The rest was a corridor of trees, with the evening birdlife settling down.

Directly under I-90, I used the bank's slight pitch to shield myself from passersby. A snarled catalpa tree—a jewel of eastern hardwoods, common on riversides—wilted its heart-shaped leaves over the bank. This was August, early nutting season, and the tree's phallic pods dangled in breezeless air. I slid the boat across stone, turning it over at the catalpa's base a couple feet above the wrack line, a weave of leaf and grass with remarkably little trash. Joggers crunched cinder twenty yards away. Staying low, I tied off the bow and stern lines. Taking my phone, wallet, and toothbrush, I slipped out of the weeds and became just another ambler, heading toward New York State's own wrack, the capital city.

Albany looks like an old boxer, one with a long, undistinguished career, maybe 45-42-1. Bulbous nose, cauliflower ears, swollen eyes. The punchy, normally genial demeanor has a flair for the old violence, though through healed bones and bloated knuckles the stiff right is gone. On the drive up to Henderson Lake the week before, my brother-in-law's minivan popped a flat coming off I-90. All the tires were bald, so he decided to have them replaced right there, giving us four hours to kill.

Capital towns seem to share the same afflictions—row houses that look as if they were never new, rundown business sectors with patches of people in their prime wafting about poorly kept streets. Pawn shops, dime stores, and government are the chief industries, and while history may be here, both it and the future seem buried in the present malaise.

The sun was down, the park grew dim, and I had no idea where I was going. I picked out a gentle peak of dwarf high-rises. An elevated catwalk takes you beneath the highways, over a mishmash of commuter lots and pallid business fronts. Well past work hours, few people passed me, but those were donned in business formal. Sales staff. Data entry. Marketing team. Amanuenses. IT support. Oversight Chairwoman, Region IX. No smiles, no felicitous symptom of any kind, just ashen solemnity in uncomfortable attire. What did Thoreau say, nearly two hundred years ago in a far-wilder nation than we'll ever know? "Most of our citizens lead lives of quiet desperation." Maybe, but under a roaring highway you have to apply Ed Abbey's amendment, Thoreau's half-daft desert descendant. Most of us now lead lives of unquiet desperation, minimized by dreary jobs and blistering paces away from family, friends, and natural process. Abbey said as much in 1980, reflecting on a trip down Wesley Powell's Green River long before cell phones and IPods and the World Wide Web. "We are belabored by the insistence on the part of our politicians, businessmen and military leaders, and the claque of scriveners who serve them, that 'growth' and 'power' are intrinsic goods, of which we can never have enough." What would he say now? Either way, his words would be denounced and worshipped at once. My prophet is your crank.

Off the catwalk, I blundered into a Hampton Inn. Finding my room, I took a shower. Pumice would've been preferable to soap, but my odor was neutral enough now to venture an evening out.

Albany at night, 9:30 p.m., scarcely a restaurant serving. I found a little place, though, tables outside, and had a delicate cut of flounder. People smiled. People laughed. People talked. People enjoyed the night. They looked happy. Albany might even be a pleasant place to live. I wouldn't know. You have to spend time in a city. Work there. Put your hands on things. That's the trouble with cranks. They see much, maybe deep, but they don't see all. Abbey knew this: "Yes, there are many who seem to be happy in their lives and work," he wrote. "But strange lives, queer work."

Back at the room, I flicked on the One-Eyed Monster. Television. Sweet Surrender. First things first. The Sox still slipped, the Yanks still rolled. God hates me. Next up. The world. For this, I begrudgingly went to cable news. Henry James may have called Tolstoy a "windy, baggy monster," but James never had cable TV. Today's carcass was healthcare, the summer's feast. After eight years of one president, the nation had a new one, ushered in with great fanfare. Now he seemed as befuddled by America's political bowels as the forty-three people before him.

I scarcely paid attention to politics prior to September 11th, then took a hydrophobic interest in them, straining family bonds and friendships. Watching the waning days of George Bush's presidency, though, and the onset of Barack Obama's, I realized it's simple to run the country as long as you're not running the country. Three hundred million genius savants, one in charge. The older I get, then, the more

I hold to Charles Dickens at the head of *A Tale of Two Cities*: "There were a king with a large jaw and a queen with a plain face, on the throne of England; there were a king with a large jaw and a queen with a fair face, on the throne of France. In both countries it was clearer than crystal to the lords of the State preserves of loaves and fishes, that things in general were settled forever."

It's silly to say that all politicians are the same. It's silly to say that your vote doesn't matter. Democracy stinks. The only thing worse is everything else. Fine, but Dickens' words aren't throwaways. They're sharp. Wrapped in everyday life, it's difficult not to see politicians as a template. The tax code might edge a percentage point this way or that, we're always tromping in some foreign land warring or threatening war, and particularly since 9/11 there's constant jabber of Our Forefathers and patriotism and all that, but none of this seems to effect life's mechanics—jobs, family, the scoop-flip-catch-jump-twirl-fire-pick beauty of a 6-4-3 double play, the relief of dinner cooking all day and the friends coming to gather, or when your kid looks up at you like you're the only thing that can help her out, because you are. God, of course, is its own mystery, and what country are any of these for large jaws and plain faces? Johann Goethe, rapt in Europe's governmental identity crisis at the time colonial America faced its, said he was royalist, that not having to worry about who was serving or why freed him to ponder things worth pondering—god, love, life, evil. I can't go that far, but he wasn't fishing. Obama, on the other hand, was an interest, a thinker, someone who seemed to understand life's complexities, or at least that life was complex. He'd unleashed something though, a furor, or rather it had been unleashed on him.

Red, Blue. As with any generalization, filing swaths of geography into political ideologies has a nit of truth, like saying anyone who looks like they haven't had a job in seventeen years is a Democrat, while anyone who looks like they haven't had an orgasm in seventeen is Republican. A few yucks, perhaps, but hardly precise.

The Red Tide that had Obama stacking sandbags all summer wasn't new. Though it had its own nuances of race, religion, and political ideology, it was founded by a rural/urban divide that has prominent roots in Albany, New York. This president was simply the latest working to bridge it.

Nothing says "city" like Manhattan, and despite strong performances across the West and South, nothing says "goober' like Upstate New

York, or "Upstate." Oliver Stone's *Platoon* follows a group of GIs though Vietnam. Bunny is their resident evil, named for the Bugs Bunny tattoo on his forearm. Wiry, nasty, two years of high school, tough as nails, he rapes, murders, and courageously soldiers his way through the film, fond of neither his Asian hosts nor his black messmates.

"I'll bet that guy was from Alabama," I said to my father.

"Nope. Upstate."

A couple years later I read the book. Upstate it was.

This would be no surprise to Manhattanites, who since the country's birth have derided Upstaters as toothless inbreeds gathered in Albany every year to thwart urban agendas. "Apple-knockers" and "hayseeds" they were called in DeWitt Clinton's time, and are still. For their part, the hayseeds thought as little of the city, a popinjay-sewer good for little beyond taxes and degeneracy. America, though, is messy. Things are never as simple as Camp A and Camp B. As time went on, much of the friction lay not with the popinjays but with city dwellers as equally rough-hewn as the mountain people with whom they quarreled. These were the Irish, this was Tammany Hall.

All this, of course, precedes America by millennia. Though it predated Christianity, the word "pagan" came to mean a "rustic," or rural dweller. Christ first took in Roman cities, and the converted derided the conservative farm-types who feared the new religion threatened their way of life. That model probably started the first time more than ten people lived in the same place, and it's never changed—quicksilver mores in the cities, calcified ones in the country, each working to shape the other.

Tammany Hall started just after the American Revolution, and, looking back, it seems little different than Fred Flintstone's Grand Pooh-Bah Society. Named for the Lenape chief Tammenund, the founders gathered in a Manhattan bar they called the wigwam, dubbing themselves "sachems." This group sided with Thomas Jefferson's American vision, preferring his somewhat Romantic ideal of the individual to Alexander Hamilton's *Pax Corporata*. Tammany, then, sided with the mechanics and laborers that industry regarded as beasts. As it grew, its relationship to immigrants was natural, and when the Irish Potato Famine hit in 1845, Tammany came to represent poor tidings to the countryside's Protestant throngs—Ireland, the papacy, corruption, change.

Under the influence of "bosses," most notably William Tweed, Tammany Hall did much to aid immigrants in exchange for political

favor, namely, a "vote early and often" stratagem. This birthed ethnic political machines, still holding on today in places like Chicago
and Rhode Island. Famous for corrupting city politics, it's forgotten
that apparati like Tammany helped create America's own pagan/urban
divide. In nineteenth-century New York, for instance, fears that urban
Catholic influence would palsy the nation's Protestant country back-
bone ran deep, while in twenty-first-century America, Barack Obama
represents a future of mixed race, progressive thought that mostly
white, government-fearing citizens despise. The script, then, never
changes, just the players, but at the moment this hotel bed felt too
good to be bothered with such things. Just the same, the discord
was flaring to worrisome temperatures. Not tonight though. I called
Karen. She'd meet me in the town of Hudson in two days, a distance
I thought I could make. I'd have to.

Imaginarium

I was in luck, thrice over. Having checked out at dawn, I still wasn't sure if Albany's castaways had found my boat, and re-crossing the catwalk, passing more office-bound dread, I turned over the prospect of theft, even ignoring the band of robins marshaling the park's dewy grass, hopping and halting, tamping the ground for worms. My worry, though, wasn't warranted. The canoe was there, bags too, and unbundling the map, it looked about twenty-five miles to Hudson, a day and a half to get there. Easy money. The tide, moreover, was high-slack, when the swell stills for an hour before turning. I'd begin paddling pond water, then, before six hours of riding the drain plug.

Albany is still an active port, receiving ocean vessels a hundred-some odd miles inland. This seems to be the area's station. Chased from the Ohio's banks by drought and famine, the Mohawk filed down the river that would later bear their name, settling along the Hudson/Mohawk confluence, terrorizing the native Algonquin for trade supremacy. Later, though Henry Hudson grounded out not far from here, his Oriental dreams led to Dutch claims, who named the first settlement Beverwyck, or Beavertown, for the countless pelts pouring from every watershed. They later named it Fort Orange, for their King William of, and later still, during the tussle of empire when the Brits took New Amsterdam, the place became Albany, honoring a lord of that country. Now, timber piers and steel frontage line the west bank, mooring hulking rust buckets while squeaking cranes lurch cargo to and fro. Wanting nothing of this, I made for the east side, Rensselaer, and stayed there, anticipating the trip's first big wake as a red barge pushed upriver.

Skirting an old refinery—Chemicals? Oil?—I paddled by wooden pilings, most badly eaten by tide flow. Algae-stricken rope lashed tires to pier posts, and fresh signs warned off river travelers. These I heeded, thinking them from Homeland Security. The last thing I needed was some psychotic frogman pumped with rhino hormones popping out of the depths, Glock in hand, begging me to make his day. Scrap metal heaped both banks here, heavy equipment pushing it around. The tanker's waves had crossed, nuzzling me from trough to crest, crest to trough, the waters otherwise still.

Passing the last wormy timber, I gauged river-left and the skeins of flat-leafed greenery ribbing it, called "river lettuce." Willows blocked the escalating sun, and beneath them, thirty yards from piles of bent copper and twisted pipe—front-end loaders plowing old factory guts askew—a muskrat emerged from the plants, its head cutting a V-wake downstream. Behind it, on the bank, a Louisiana waterthrush skitched among the rip-rap, pausing intermittently, probing algae for nematodes. The Hudson here once ran the color of paper-dying operations upstream, which along with the sewage, dioxins, cadmium, PCBs, and other of prosperity's outwash, nearly killed the river, but the ecosystem is changing. Two eagles—mature, white-capped, one side of the river apiece—studied the flow. I looked for 'rat sign, then closed my eyes. At high slack, the world feels like it would toss you one way or the next.

"It's a lack of imagination," said John Elder, buttressing Bill McKibben's thought. I met these two the winter following the float, at Vermont's Middlebury College, an unnerving encounter. McKibben is fairly famous, a global warming activist who wrote the first accessible accounts of what perils might lie ahead, in books such as *The End of Nature*. Having lived for years in the Adirondacks, he's a former staff writer for *The New Yorker* and regularly appears in big lumber like *Orion* and *Harper's*. He'd been to Copenhagen the week before, heading his advocacy group 350.org, advising world leaders on carbon emissions. I get nervous talking to myself.

Elder is one of those bastards that makes you wish you were someone else, namely him. Possessed of that ease leading you to believe this guy has never been nervous in his life, you wonder if he's even been ticked. What kind of a man doesn't hate anyone? Raised near San Francisco Bay, he might be the only reverse émigré I've ever met, having come West to East, loving the place too much to leave. Brought up Baptist, he holds to Christianity, but studies Buddhism and generally feeds on an omnivorous American theology. (Be it god, government, or rock-n-roll, America's true genius is for synthesis.) He's an English prof, a poetry man, and therefore my kind of guy. With his sons, he runs a sugaring operation near the college, having spent his adult life putting both mind and hands on God's hieroglyph, the natural world. The three of us sat in Salma's diner, fresh snow outside, and I'd asked McKibben if he thought the Hudson could support its past industrial might while maintaining its ecological recovery.

"It's a dead question," he said. "The industry's not coming back. Those jobs are overseas, and the technology is changing too much anyway."

I looked at Elder. He has opinions, but doesn't feel this is his field, so holds them until prompted. His eyeballs are a professor's, swollen, wrecked on the printed page, but not his hands. These looked used up by boiler wood and ax handles.

"I think," he said, "it's a lack of imagination. People look at those old buildings and just see the past, the industry. There's another future there, as important now as industry was then. We need that vision, but with an end relevant to the moment."

I liked this. Together, these two make up the best of human thought. Lean and lithe, McKibben is mostly science, nosegays of facts for every occasion, the type that drives me nuts. I'm a Humanities guy. I hate facts. Without them, however, imagination has no seed, and without imagination human beings aren't human beings, nor do we look past the surface, where more facts lie, and therefore more imaginative gristle. The Endless Onion. In their own way, this pair reminded me of a trapper and a game biologist—one all metaphor, the other all math. Combine the two and you move toward understanding.

Below Albany the river changes. For the first time since Corinth, it loses the industrial dominance of its past, becoming pastoral if not outright wild like its headwaters. You can build a dam where the water flows one way, but not otherwise. Besides, from here down, the Hudson doesn't have the juice to run much of a mill. This, then, is the estuary, 150 miles of it, with everything imagination can provide.

There's a painting in the Hudson canon quite adored. I love it too, both for its promise and irony. Many books use it to show the Hudson's past bounty as a fishery, and it graces the Hyde Park whistle stop, or at least the façade of a small tourist hut nearby. In it, three men wrestle an enormous sturgeon from a net, the fish thrashing enough to heave their skiff aloft. The crew wear placid, lemonade-on-a-summer's-day smiles, as if this fish were in a bowl, there to ease their worried minds, real Currier & Ives stuff, but enough to go on.

The promise, of course, looks back, taking from the past much of what the future might hold. Having seen—and in some ways lived—an estuarine economy for ten years, imagination wasn't the sole agent as I drifted toward Hudson, picturing what might lay ahead for this magnificent belt of habitat. Salmon—chinook, sockeye, coho, pink, and chum—is the river-word in Yakutat, with Dungeness crab, halibut, and cod in the bay, but this was a different river, with words of its own. The grammar, though, is the same.

Spirit and Flesh. It's to these gods we make our offerings, in constant desire of fellowship, and food is our chief conductor. John Elder doesn't know the Hudson, and for all I know he's never seen a salmon. Vermont, though, is covered in sugar maples, and throughout the year he puts much sweat into mending lines, sawing wood, and maintaining equipment, all in preparation for that tight March window. God—at least as we sense it—dwells in these movements. "The woods are where I converse," he said, describing among other things the labor he puts into syrup, what most people during most of human history have put into food-creation. There's education here, as it's not all serenity, but an acquired knowledge that rage and calm often segue while wresting our meals from nature, which makes the irony of the sturgeon print.

I worked for two guys in Yakutat. The first, Al, hired me, a grumbly Hoosier down from Fairbanks where he'd worked for Sport Fish, the division managing people who fish for fun. After a couple seasons, Al left, replaced by a guy who'd worked Commercial Fish for thirty years. This is the world's decent fiber, Gordie, full of good cheer and stories to tell. He was there when the heavies hired Al, whom they hadn't met. Al had only one knock against him, a Sport Fish man, a guy who frolicked with anglers making dainty presentations to Arctic grayling and other interior guppies. When Gordie mentioned this to the bigwig, a veteran of having crab captains and salmon trollers scream at him for forty years, the guy said, "Crap. You mean he's never seen a fish killed in anger?"

Fury, then, is every bit the essential ingredient as composure when procuring food. Given enough time, rubbing against one another like cricket legs, the two produce reverence along with the suste-nance—food for the spirit, food for the flesh. Music. Anyone, though, who hasn't seen commercial fishermen at their trade, or slaughtered an animal, or furrowed a row of beans during black fly season, or done or witnessed any of the thousand things that go into food-making, would look at the Hudson crew gazing fondly on their dear netted fish and be moved to belief, rather than fall down laughing. This dissonance, unfortunately, is a prevalent affliction in American life, one which could be happily rectified with a little vision.

The Hudson would be a fine place to start, though not yet. In much greater health than it has been in a hundred years, the river still needs deep convalescence. I visited Frances Dunwell a month after the float, the author of *The Hudson: America's River*, probably the valley's most comprehensive register. Writing, though, is her night job. She, too, is one of the beautiful people, giving her professional time to fisheries management. The Hudson River Estuary Program is a large branch of the New York Department of Environmental Con-servation (DEC), based in New Paltz. Dunwell combines her commu-nication skills and biological knowledge with a lifetime of recovering the Hudson's natural splendor—and concomitant food bonanza—for future generations. Now in the top brass of the Estuary Program, she can look back with pride on decades of town council pugilism and national news frenzies, trading dukes with industry honchos such as those at GE or Chevrolet, for though still ill, the river is a marvel once again.

Grown up near Poughkeepsie in the fifties and sixties, Dun-well, like most river-dwellers, avoided the Hudson. Once, before a family took her on a boat, she had to get shots in case she fell off. Now, with the industries mostly gone and the sewage largely treated, Dunwell beamed a bit when I mentioned how clean the river was, but deflected the accolade. "We tapped into a national consciousness back then," she said, referring to the otherwise bizarre congeries of fishermen, developers, artists, politicians, and most every other diver-gent block of humanity that helped clean up. It worked, or rather is working, but questions remain, and I asked Dunwell the same one I later asked Bill McKibben: Did she think the Hudson could continue recovering were the industries—or jobs—to return? I felt awful. As the words reached her, one by one, thirty years of anguish flushed her cheeks, and I knew she'd been asked the same question in town meetings up and down this valley, from Albany to the Lower East Side, on camera and off. Her eyes shut, and she took a long breath.

"Yes," she said, lifting her lids, not letting out much air. Dunwell looks a bit like a hippie couching a dedicated samurai—studied, disciplined, kind, and, if need be, lethal. This combination has served the Hudson well, making trips like mine both possible and pleasant, and I had no interest in pressing for details. Assuredly, they're sticky. Besides, we seemed in line. As she writes in *The Hudson: America's River*, the watershed "has something most do not: a following, a diverse and growing cadre of people who will fight for it and argue about it . . . men and women who listen to the river and imagine new things, contributing to our nation's heritage and our sense of who we are." In her own imaginings, then, I guessed Dunwell doesn't see industry either. I don't know what she does see, but beneath the August sun, lush green to the sides and big water underfoot, I know what I saw.

To kill one fish is simple. You pop a gill and take it home, dinner served. There's a spiritual dilemma in taking a life, but it's fleeting when that flesh flakes off the bone. Fifty fish, or a hundred, or a thousand, is something different. What in the singular had been a rite of both stomach and soul has become a living, a job, mechanical, yet one still laden with death and all the sweat, fatigue, frustration, and metaphysical abuse that entails. This is contact, the place where hand meets source—the origin of our food, and therefore our selves. It's abhorrent to many, but it's how we're nourished, making it—to the Godly and no—holy. The starkest division in our labors isn't blue-collar/white-collar, then, but those who touch food at its source and those who don't. The same might be said of our shelter, clothing, and heating needs. A butcher is one thing, a steer gutter another. Bread makers do one job, but people who tear up earth, water it, then thresh what they grow know the world differently. A lumberjack is a source worker, roughnecks and cotton harvesters too, while carpenters, loomers, and fuel transporters are not. The world has changed. We work as hard as ever, but nearly all of us far from what can rightfully be termed living—the destruction and decomposition of one being to sustain another. Life is physically easier under this divorce, far less bloody and conflicted, but that gore and that conflict make up much of our worth—our connections to each other, the earth, and speculations on what might have brought us here. This is how we converse, and a slice of redemption can be had along our rivers, where ocean-lived fish return to spawn.

Schodack Island, just below the Berkshire Spur of the New York Thruway, is a place to ponder. Part of Governor George Pataki's Hudson River Greenway, it's been turned into a public access. Islands distinguish this stretch from Castleton to Hudson, and thin Schodack Creek isolates the thousand-plus-acre park from the east bank.

It wasn't noon, the sun already smothering the atmosphere. Salt doesn't make it this high, but tidal flotsam enriches the air just the same. Even beneath the humming spur I didn't know I was near a park. A mile down, though, drifting along a stone jetty, the signs were apparent. Old men held fishing rods beneath recently planted trees, their lines tightening with the tide. Above, on a cleared knoll, parents and kids romped about a jungle gym, while uniformed employees spread mulch around the base of a wired sapling. Needing a leg stretch, maybe a little water, I tucked into the jetty's slight harbor and tied off, walking up the causeway.

They thought this place out. Trails crisscross the island's deep forest. Catalpa trees are prominent, cottonwoods too, vinery dripping toward the dense understory. A sign tells you that fishers live here, and cerulean warblers—cerulean warblers!—are a feature of spring. I'd never heard of these, feeling cheated. Returned from the Andes, they nest atop the deciduous canopy, where bright blue males croon in lusty competition. I walked the trails, happy for the shade, knowing that in August the songs would be gone. Somewhere in the leafy crown, though, young-of-the-year ceruleans plucked inchworms off catalpa leaves, and if that knowledge won't bring you contentment, your day is lost.

At trail's end I came to Schodack Creek, a tidal ribbon just wide enough to make this an island. Southeast Alaska came flooding back. Juvenile salmon rear in such places, the calm, woody-banked creeks bird-footing every watershed. Here, on Schodack, branches hung low to the water, now rapidly depleting as the ocean tugged it away. Such growth gives shade while providing young fish predator cover. I'd worked several smolt projects, catching finger-length salmon by the thousands, tagging them for future population estimates. No salmon reared in these muddy waters, but fish were down there. You could feel them. I walked out on the kayak launch. Downstream, a kingfisher hunched on a maple limb, scowling a tide swirl, while close by, beneath an undercut bank, a mink had worked the previous night. Its tracks were there. These creatures fed on fish life, and walking back to the mainstem, I crawled inside my memories to join them.

A cork bobs. If you're lucky, another, then one more. You stretched the net at low slack, anchoring it in the river, then to a parallel point onshore. The corks keeps it afloat, the lead line brings it down, finds bottom. Patience. Anadromous fish—those living in the ocean but river-born and reared—are most active on a rising tide. Sockeye and chinook are the prize in Alaska, the first of a dense, burnt-orange flesh, the second but muscle and oil. Commercial fishermen do it for money, while others make a day of it, called "subsistence," hauling in what they need for the year. Even a day, though, is enough to feel the anger, paired with the joy writhing within it.

No-see-ums never help. Sockeye and chinook are taken early summer, when estuaries teem with the hellish mites. No larger than a deer fly's nose, these creatures consist of a giant tooth, congregating by dozens on every uncovered inch of flesh, digging in. You swat. As the fish slime builds, you stick with death and mashed bugs, hatred. These are the sweaty months, and your own goo ferments with the rest. A fish or two might hit, struggling in the net. The idea, though, is to bleed them quickly, not let the blood coagulate. You lift the net over skiff gunnels, pulling yourself through the incoming tide. The monofilament diamonds make a deep bag, where you dig through the cocoons that twisting fish have made. Fingers feel for lenience, stretch webbing, work kypes and gill plates. The salmon freed, into the boat they go, knife up the anus onshore, gills and guts to the river, milt or eggs saved if you want them, the body packed in ice. Five, ten, sometimes thirty hit at once, an upriver push, goaded by sex and death. Goaded by sex, food, and death yourself, you scramble to keep up. Fins and teeth poke as you go, while sweat, bugs, blood, and glop make a canvas of you. The knife works through fish while screeching gulls hover for guts, fighting flounder and eagles, and the absurdity of it all—pinned down by gobbling insects—has you laughing, only because to do otherwise means madness. Creation made this cauldron of murder that you now touch. The gasping fish you find are head-thumped harder and harder with the gaff, and with the net finally in the tote, coolers of fish and bagged roe on the beach, the seething subsides. Food has been won for the year. The hands that took it—yours—will take it through the canning and freezing, pickling and smoking. This is life at the root. If it doesn't put you in touch with God, it puts you in touch with the terror and inquiry that attend it, elation too, and in this whorl you'll feel closer to yourself and everything around you than you ever have. Those faces like your own—two eyes, two nostrils, the mouth and teeth, all with the shared aim of reproduction and dread of death. Your life is their life—fear and joy, fury and fret, tranquility and jubilation, urgency and repose. Flesh. Spirit. The quest. It ends and starts here, in the pursuit, capture, and consumption of food. Life.

Schodack has other signs posted on the jetty, telling anglers to release any sturgeon they catch. What marvelous monsters, these fish, prowling oceans and estuaries since the Mesozoic. Bottom dwellers, they've no face for kissing, with shrunken eyes unaccustomed to light, the mashed, platypus mouth fringed with silt-whisking barbs, feeling for food. Rather than scales, sturgeon have scutes, plates that slipped through evolution to keep protecting these fish from disease. The Hudson has two species, the short-nosed and Atlantic. Short-nosed grow to four feet and rarely leave the estuary. The Atlantic, an anadromous fish, has grown to fourteen feet and many hundred pounds, but is now in deep trouble, though this hasn't always been so.

Atlantics have traditionally been the most important to people. What we know best as caviar comes from these fish, but it was their flesh that made the most critical food. Once known as "Albany Beef," it was sold door-to-door to late nineteenth-century immigrants hungry for Old Country preferences. Natives, of course, knew sturgeon patterns first, gorging themselves, as Jan Weber writes in "A Short History of Sturgeon on the Hudson," "until their flesh reeked of it." This was according to early Dutch settlers, who, not fond of the meat themselves, nevertheless "staved off starvation and survived on sturgeon they could kill . . . with frying pans," exemplifying the anger, and telling of sturgeon runs once plugging the Hudson.

Yakutat had similar seasons, with coho and pink salmon thick enough to pave the stream bottom. Walking the banks, fish crammed in pool after pool, stirs you in deep strokes, hunger and the thrill of surplus chief among them. Any river with an estuary used to be the same. Standing on the jetty, I looked out on the Hudson. Earlier travelers, anchored on sloops, remarked of sturgeon breeching throughout the night, clapping the surface with their feet-long bodies walled by oily flesh. Imagine. Where to anchor? There, atop that eddy. The corks gradually nudged by the ocean, I'd wait—club in hand—for the first to bob, no smile on my face as I rapped the skulls of distant kin, days of filleting, canning, drying, and smoking ahead, sweltered in summer heat and clouded mosquitoes, to be followed by the communal deference for satiation, surfeit.

Two hundred and six fish species live in the Hudson, including a few Midwesterners—like the buffalo fish—that have slipped through the Erie Canal. In late September, I met Bob Adams of the DEC at Croton Point, twenty-five miles from Manhattan, near where I'd camped just six weeks before. He and three others seined here often, primarily to estimate juvenile out-migrations of shad and herring. This was my former occupation. You never feel more unemployed than watching peers do your old job. Croton Point, another park, juts into the Hudson from the east. Six-thousand-year-old oyster middens show long human use. As the crew set their fine-meshed beach seine on the north crook, a husband and wife team held it to shore while Bob reversed the skiff, making a half-moon from depth to beach while an agile woman fed net off the bow. Eight o'clock. Our breath plumed, and the wader-clad crew soon had a full net. Nice set. Now let's see one of you petunias hump this thing five miles through bear country, rifle in hand, then scoop up two-hundred sockeye on your own. Envy only sharpens a tooth though. I stood on the bank, pencil in hand, taking notes.

The lead and corks formed a purse, holding the captives in water while Bob and his bunch tallied numbers. A half dozen adult carp were released, gold-plated archaics introduced from Europe, with the remaining catch no longer than a finger per fish. Bob and two others processed samples, while the fourth recorded data. Some fish were tossed in a bucket for later sampling. To me it looked like a considerable set, five hundred or more squiggling figures in woven kelp. Not so, Bob said, separating plant from fish, calling out "shad" or "blueback" as he spoke, pulling an occasional striped bass from the mix, "These numbers are way down. It started a few years ago with the shad and it's getting worse, herring too. We'll probably shut down for shad this year. A few guys still fish herring in the creeks for striper bait, but corking the rivers the way they do, I don't how long it will last."

I'd caught a few corkers in Alaska. Nets can legally block no more than two-thirds of a river, but corking, stretching mesh bank to bank, allows only the smallest fish through. Do that long enough and the crash will come. I asked about the shad decline. As is often the case with science types, no one gave a specific answer. Science demands clarity, and trying to pin a fish down who lives most of its life in the ocean doesn't promote that coveted aim. Only catches are known, trends, and even those aren't exact. Dredging for shipping lanes was mentioned, as was pollution, but shad don't eat in-river, leaving them mostly toxin-free. Let fisheries people talk, though, and eventually they drop the empirical pussyfooting and tell you what they know, data or not. The crew's collective conclusion, voiced by the bearded Adams, was off-the-books clear.

"By-catch," he said, dropping a wriggling herring in the bucket. "Too many are caught in the ocean." The crew members nodded, hushed, as if passing secrets through prison walls. I understood the reticence, but they pushed an open door. I'd been on the regulatory end for ten years, knowing the topic to be flammable. Nearly everyone is implicated, and livelihoods are at risk. Fishermen, driven by the people they feed, have depleted most fisheries worldwide, the Hudson included.

During World War II, upward of thirty million Hudson shad returned, a spike in an otherwise decades-long decline. Shad spawn between Kingston and Albany, and fishermen spread out from the Tappan Zee to Hudson to pick them off. The eighties saw another spike, but stocks are back in freefall. The first overharvests occurred in the nineteenth century, when sturgeon took their own pummeling. After Pearl Harbor, the nation reaped its protein where it could, understandably, and shad were scooped up without restraint. Only a few gill-netters remain, though Dunwell and others told me of the coming closure. She crimped a bit, saddened, as did Adams. "They're old families, fishing a long time," he said. "But there's no future if we don't protect what we've got."

Unfortunately, the Hudson's shadmen aren't the only harvesters. The fish—a large herring—make their way up and down the Atlantic coast, becoming "by-catch" in any net or trawl that nabs them. It's a pressing problem in Alaska, where pollock trawlers filch dwindling chinook stocks. To catch fish in the numbers that an increasingly Omega-3 fatty acid–crazed world demands necessitates inexact methods. Nets and trawls kill fish indiscriminately, making vulnerable species like shad susceptible to sudden slaughter. Shad netters, too, aren't immune to by-catch, killing striped bass, short-nosed sturgeon, and anything else the meshes choke.

Atlantic sturgeon biologists weren't as hesitant. Less than a thousand are now thought to spawn in the Hudson, and the fishery was closed in 1996. Amanda Higgs, a biologist with the Hudson River Estuary Program, has placed sonic tags in sturgeon for several years, finding them far wider traveled than previously thought, traveling anywhere from the Carolinas to the Bay of Fundy before tracking back. I asked what caused the decline.

"Fishing," she said by phone.

"That's it?"

"Yes. The short-nosed were never in real trouble, but the Atlantic's had commercial value, suffering losses they couldn't withstand. They can live for sixty years, and females might not reach sexual maturity until twenty. That kind of recruitment only takes so much."

Mark Bain, a biologist with Cornell, concurred. I asked him if short-noseds were less threatened due to their estuarine permanence, eliminating the threat of high-seas by-catch.

"No," he said. "The river fishery did the Atlantics in. Commercial pressures kept them open until 1996, whereas the short-nosed—which weren't as bad off to begin with—were a charter member of the Endangered Species Act in 1972. Atlantics were already badly depleted, but weren't shutdown for another twenty-four years."

Along with shad and Atlantic sturgeon, blueback herring are in trouble too, as are the river's catadromous fish, the American eel. Catadromes are reverse anadromous fish, living in freshwater while spawning at sea. The ropey adults throng from the river mouths each year to the Sargasso, where they mate and die. Eel larvae spend a year drifting ocean currents, turning to the inches-long, clear-bodied glass eel. These turn brown, a bit larger, easing into the elver phase. Yellow eels, adults, find the estuaries, where males stay while females head upriver, ripening up to thirty years. In cold winters they'll burrow in mud, absorbing ambient substances like PCBs. Eels also live in European rivers, sharing the Sargasso nursery. Both populations are in peril, though it's difficult to say why. Overfishing, naturally, hasn't helped. Adult fisheries are now reduced to eat-them-if-you-dare recreational takes, but glass eels, a delicacy, are still snatched in great numbers. Eels are being considered for the endangered list, a status that shocked me. Fishing Connecticut as a kid, eels were thick. Particularly at night, we'd pull them lashing onto banks, hooked on any piece of dead flesh we threw.

Karin Limburg, a fisheries professor with Syracuse University, seemed frustrated by the continued harvests. Speaking of the forty-year sturgeon moratorium, she told me this was important. "Management takes into account much more of the salient features of fish life history and ecology than it did in the past. That's a good thing. What countervails is greed and impatience to wait for stocks to rebuild." Switching to eels, she mentioned that they were once abundant enough on Lake Ondandaga for a pot-setter or spearmen to take a thousand in a night. "Talk about greed," she said, adding that blueback herring—a sardine-like fish spawning in Hudson tributaries—are at historic lows, while the DEC has to "position" itself to bring forth a closure. This struggle is ancient, as visceral as it is intellectual. The need to preserve, the need to consume, paralleling Jones Ordway's seeing dollar bills alone in Adirondack timber, dismissing the long arm of regulation. "From what I can tell," Limburg said, "if you remove the influence of people, give an ecosystem time to recover, then yes, things will come back."

I have no interest in removing the influence of people, as I doubt Limburg does, only in finding a balance after we've given our estuaries the requisite time. How long that would be I don't know, but if generations have to leave hands off, then let us have hands off.

The water stayed mild, the day long. Greenery—forest and field, pasture and overgrowth—lined each bank. Miles passed. The river widened, widened again, while the estuary turned, the water creeping up by inhale and exhale before the steady reverse toward Troy.

Close to Hudson, on the east bank, they built the railroad out in the river, or at least patched it along the tide flats, asphyxiating land beyond the tracks from ocean play. No matter. Plenty remains to imagine, and enough signposts exist here of the old fat-of-the-land economies to make reverie simple.

Sticking to river-left, I passed cove after cove, islands here and there. Dormant duck blinds rested above the thatched river plants, the tide swelling beneath them. Each fall, waterfowl pour out of Canada, down arterial drainages like the Hudson, rafting in larger and larger numbers. Decoys would soon decorate the water ahead of these platforms, where hunters crouch. Mallards and teal, widgeon and wood ducks, Canada geese—rich meat, fat and red. In addition, I twice passed identical structures to Yakutat's fish camps—slap-together, chip-board hovels, tin roof on top. These were on islands. I doubted they had anything to do with subsistence fishing, but given enough time, allowing stocks to recover, they certainly could.

Bill McKibben was right, John Elder too. The industry is shot—if not the production, then the jobs. While it's true that offshore labor conditions have bled out most of America's manufacturing class, technology is precluding its return. I asked Daniel Walkowitz, a professor at New York University, what this means. He said though conditions in developing countries resemble those of nineteenth-century American factories, others are better harbingers. "Japan and Germany have modernized, using robotics, which eliminate most of the jobs, a result which contemporary Hudson Valley citizens whose grandparents may have worked in the mills know only too well." Even were the factories to return, then, they'd be largely run by cyborgs, and wouldn't need waterpower to operate, leaving the river unmolested

Daylight remained, but Hudson was in sight. I pulled past a cove, admiring the thick plaits of river lettuce stitched throughout. The tide increased, saturating the mudflats, and I watched a cottontail nibble junkus, large eyes cocked for danger. Slipping into an eddy, I studied the muskrat cuttings swirling about. No trouble taking animals here. All's you'd need is a canoe and a few days.

Across the river, the Catskills adorn the distant southern view. The day's only clouds laced the purple peaks, while the sun touched up each in auburn. I looked left. A mature eagle, riveted to a cottonwood, scanned the cove. It would take what the tide offered, I imagined, but had visions of its own, awaiting the old mythology's upriver teem.

I pulled ashore, dragging the canoe through the second growth out of tide range. A woodcock jumped, stuttering off in its wing-whistle way. Riparian ground is soft, rich, bulged with worms, the woodcock's primary diet. I pitched the tent in rotting leaves, then sat on a piece of slag to watch the tide. The sun was about done, suspended over cross-river mountains and farms.

What do we see? Generations have passed. Shannon is gone, her children too, and theirs, and theirs again. All were patient. All left the estuaries alone, but that time is gone. No factories blemish these banks, only communities, tight-knit to the river. Spring. Nets stretch for roiling shad, while anger rolls with the joy as corks bob and smokehouses cure. God hunkers in the interstices, sensed, unreachable.

Mothers line tributaries with their broods, celebrating herring, casting nets in gloried love and primitive horror, while all await the big fish, the sturgeon, and the year-round feasts they'll provide. Eels, too, split and flayed, drape willow racks, drying in the sun. These aren't for commerce, at least widespread. Lessons were learned, and in this aspect we live more as the Iroquois did, looking seven generations hence. This is what we see, this is how we speak, at night, by lamplight, wet to the waist, gig in hand, waiting for what Ted Hughes called the eel, "the moon's pilgrim, the night mind of water." We dream, a dream with encouragement. Beavers were extinct here, fishers too. Wait. Be patient. This isn't for you, but creatures and people to come. The river.

Such fond visions to have in a twilit niche, but we need more. People don't live by eels alone. We need fruit and bread, vegetables and livestock. Fortunately, Hudson is the seat of Columbia County, where you don't need much imagination for these. I slept, and woke the next morning for the short paddle to town.

Into the Wild Frontier

Blessed are the sauce-buckets, for they plunge us through their wine-dark seas to critical depths, where life springs. Here they chant their verse, interpreting, grafting beauty to the terror we behold. I don't know what makes many of our greatest poets such spectacular drunks, but it's so, and none more than Dylan Thomas, whom Karen likes. Thomas was Welsh, she all Irish pride, detesting even the thought of English muffins. When forced to concede that the Brits have produced some gems, she honors Wales. Shakespeare was a Welshman, the Beatles too, but with Thomas she voids the pretense.

He died on the Hudson's forgotten loop, that passing round Manhattan. Like so many cities, most residents scarcely know they're near a river. Pie-eyed, he collapsed in the White Horse Tavern, aged thirty-nine. Nearly from the start, he besotted himself, but out of that drench came some of English's prettiest riffs, trenchant too. This opens "Fern Hill":

> Now as I was young and easy under the apple boughs
> About the lilting house and happy as the grass was green,
> The night above the dingle starry,
> Time let me hail and climb
> Golden in the heydays of his eyes,
> And honored among wagons I was prince of the apple towns
> And once below a time I lordly had the trees and leaves
> Trail with daisies and barley
> Down the rivers of the windfall light
>
> . . . And the Sabbath rang slowly
> In the pebbles of the holy streams.

Phew. Much more of that and you'll think you've scampered up Jacob's Ladder and claimed the prize. Natural and revealed religion split from the same cell here, darkness damascenes the light, while carcinogenic time cracks lush innocence, but none of that matters as the pretty pastoral pours down, flowed and eddied like river cadence. The rhythm is the beauty, and would feather your spine even if you didn't speak English. Thomas talks of Wales, rural Swansea, but walking the orchards of Columbia County, bathed in the golden heyday and windfall light, you'll swear he was still here, has always been here, by the pebbles of the holy streams, prince of these apple towns.

Quite fitting that Karen and I would meet in Hudson. Just prior to her pregnancy, she'd had enough, fleeing the city for a smaller life. She rented an apartment on Warren Street, plump in the middle of Hudson's five-block Renaissance. Flying back from Alaska, I moved here, flailing for work in a rural economy during the onset of global paralysis. About the time I realized I'd be jobless for the rest of my life, she realized that a two-hour Amtrak commute while pregnant wouldn't cut it, and back to Queens we went. Nonetheless, we knew Hudson a bit, and were happy to meet there.

I'd called the night before, the cell conversation befouling dreams of pickled eel and sturgeon festivals. Still, absence does a union wonders, and hearing her voice with Shannon gurgling below dissipated every thought. I'd see them soon. Tomorrow. We tremble at blindness, shrink from deafness, but what of touch? Strange what gentle powers lay in a hand, there upon a knee, or the impress of skin to lip. I asked about the plan.

"I'll be there at four. My dad will meet you at Baba Louie's at two. My parents are coming."

"Great," I said. "What?"

I was kidding, at least a little. Time alone with love and child, or in-laws in the rumble? No matter. You marry the family, we know, not the person, and luck again has been my genie. I'd have some time as well. I could see Hudson from camp, and two o'clock meant God knows what. It might be politically subversive, I'm not sure, but the Irish take to Greenwich Mean Time like cats take to water. As with Californians, "meet you at seven" means "we'll traipse in at eight with you on your fifth drink, blotto." Adjusted for wind and County

Kerry, then, "2:00 p.m." is 3:17. I'd be in town by 9:00 a.m., giving me five-plus hours.

Hudson is beat up, but with new life, or at least the hope of it, and has a spiritual twin in Haines, Alaska. I worked Haines for two springs. Once the Tlingit had been carted up the Chilkat River to Klukwan, whites scratched Haines out of the river's mouth. No Harvard grads here, just fishermen, loggers, trappers, and miners spitting and swearing their way through ocean and forest, making a living, building a town. Nature beaten back, others came. The Chilkat is rafter friendly, and hikeable mountains line its valley. Haines is comparatively cold, too, making good skiing, and soon people trickled in who recreated in the wilds rather than went at that them with a grudge.

Overlap was abundant, lifestyles accommodated, but when *Outside* magazine wrote the town up as one of America's best, things changed. Here came the activists, as enraged as their chainsawing binaries but endowed with crib money. These were the trustafarians— well-meaning, often well-doing hipsters plugged with family loot. They often hate their parents for how that money came about, but rather than forsake it, they turn their rage against the confounded pioneers, elbowing into town boards and thwarting everything rednecks do. Logging was pared back, along with mining, while cruise ships, which bring money to local businesses but are floating sewers, were nearly tarred and feathered. Accommodation has imploded. Goobers and trusties shop at different markets, go to different diners, and town votes are right down the middle. Oddly, nearly everyone smokes dope. My second spring there I worked a smolt project. A new guy, a biologist, was learning the ropes, wife and son in town. He said the day after they moved in, dignitaries from both camps came courting, pies and brownies in hand, prying as to how the two might vote. Ugly stuff, but hardly unique.

I don't know Hudson as well as Haines, but that same rift seems to be here, its unease torquing the atmosphere. Warren Street slopes up from the railroad abutting the river, where in another age whaling vessels docked. By the tracks live the old guard, children and grandchildren of industry, which here mostly meant cement. Blacks mix with whites, stitching together what work they can, floundering as people do two generations gone from fixed identity.

Like many upstate towns, slate is everywhere, reflecting both local geology and past industries. Slate roofs, slate sidewalks, slate for breakfast. Slate, slate, slate. Residencies and offices display regional architecture—big-box, flat-roofed structures with finely framed windows and well-crafted cornices. Warren Street is the future, from about Sixth to First, where for two decades outsiders have sought simpler lives. They've opened art galleries, wine bars, and a specialty meat shop; bed and breakfasts, antique stores, and a clutch of fine-fared restaurants. We lived across from the Spotty Dog, one of our kind's better inventions. It's a creakily floored bookstore serving booze. You can have your Hemingway and Pinot Grigio too. Great stuff.

As in Haines, though, new money has freshened up old problems. "Gentrify" is the fashionable term, where new energies are thrust upon remnant greatness—or at least steady paychecks—by well-funded zeal. The last stroke was when the St. Lawrence Cement Plant was publicly rejected during the permit process. In truth, the St. Lawrence would have closed a plant further down river, the net job loss/creation cancelling each other out. "One job would have been created," Harvey Flad, a professor at Poughkeepsie's Vassar College told me. "Still, there's an underground sense that blue-collar is the authentic Hudson and that most of the St. Lawrence opponents were new to Columbia County. There's certainly tension over it."

Gentrify, though, shouldn't be the dirty word it's become. Old economies die. If they're not revitalized, populations suffer degeneratively, from depression to atrophy to ruin. Though renewal has been America's persistent salvation, we now seem slow to embrace it, being miserly of the mid-twentieth-century boom. Those ways, though, have decayed—the gargantuan farms and factories with their outrageous output and crippling social costs. Besides, the United States had no competition then. The world spent thirty years in World War II's ashes while America nursed it with wheat and durable goods. Now, technology is ousting muscle, the world is back on its feet, and carbon fuels are both finite and filthy. Change comes, and equal verve is the only way to befriend it. If Hudson's trendy merchants represent a move from the old industry, then that's one thing. Other change, however, is afoot, grander in scope, progressively regressive, and it's happening up and down the Hudson Valley, with food again at its heart.

Manhattan is many things. The city that never sleeps. The world's financial engine. Broadway. Madison Avenue. Central Park. Eight million women, all telling perfect two-hundred-dollar-an-hour strangers how horrible it is to have a father. None of this, though, matters, or with luck will matter less and less, for New York is quietly rediscovering the agriculture that makes it great. From the west's rolling hills to Finger Lake orchards to the Hudson's fecund till, this place grows stuff, and grows it well, and after decades of shunting it, people downriver are again paying attention.

Once upon a time, dairy was the WORD in Northeastern farming, and it remains so in Washington, D.C., where dastardly lobbyists vie for its life support, colluding with price-controlling mega-wholesalers. Currently, milk isn't dead here, but it needs to change, not rely on subsidies, a lost cause scuttled long ago by monster herds elsewhere. The Northeast's forested, dismally wintered hills afford few cows per farm, where more temperate, pasture-friendly places like California and Florida kick out the milk demanded by three hundred million people. Yet here's the pivot. To survive human commerce, you melt down the sword meant to kill you and hammer out something new. Three hundred million don't need to be served. In every watershed rather, in every furrow of every field nationwide, markets exist right down the road, something to which Hudson Valley farmers are gainfully adapting.

With the heat of the day already tearing moisture from the river, I pulled into Hudson's modest marina, tying up amid the pleasure craft and walking into the empty restaurant. The harbor master charged sixteen bucks, a dollar per foot per day, even for a canoe. I asked him how far to Manhattan. Ninety-eight miles. My God, I thought. Two-thirds down, just ten days in, but it ain't over till it's over. We begrudge Great Yogi his pinstripes, but laud his aphorisms.

Bidding the harbor master good-day, I walked past the train tracks, ambling up semi-familiar streets. I'd left eleven months before, at the recession's first bite. Expecting closed shops and boarded-up windows, I was delighted to see the galleries still open, restaurants too, polished as ever. The early hour didn't see much foot traffic, but the West Indian deli reeked of rice and jerk chicken, and further up Warren, bagel-munchers gaggled Nolita's patio—reading papers, sipping coffee, preparing for the day. This wasn't my aim though. I had hours to kill, and open space to revisit.

Jogging was my salvation in Hudson. Only so many résumés can be set free in cyberspace, never to return, before an existential gloom sets in. I'd don the running shoes in early evening and set out, east some days, west others, north or south when it suited. Up north they say Anchorage is five minutes from Alaska, and the same can be said of Hudson, New York. Jog outside the city, just a few strides, and you're in Columbia County at last—not wild like the mountains above it, or anything you'd find out West, but more rural, which is to say cultivated, farm country blended into recovering forests and undulant hills.

Like most of the Northeast, this whole area had once been cleared for firewood, pastureland, and hayfields. Those days gone, many clearings have returned to woodland, while smaller scale farms have back-filled the rest. These are a fresh breed, though, joining hippie idealism to sound business practice, with a few derring-do wrinkles. If you don't sense much future within the Hudson River's industrial towns, you get a good whiff of one out here.

One of my favorite runs took a right at Columbia Memorial off toward the Taconic Parkway. Route 9. Immediately outside of town, pit-patting along the cinder shoulder, you pass the Old Way—cement chutes, concrete plants, rows of big rigs, all derelict. Technologically speaking, humanity crawled for a great while—a hundred thousand years or more—not gaining ground beyond fire and the wheel. Suddenly, we leapt, harnessing our brains, brawn, and industry to put us up with Icarus, thinking we'd finally outpaced the Gods. All through the twentieth century, our buildings grew higher, our energy more powerful, our lives easier and easier. Nature, it seemed, had lost, but this wasn't so. Any doubts of earth's plodding superiority over our achievements will dissolve with a glance off this gentle New York road, where not long ago factories pumped out the quick-lime that founded our greatest architecture. Inanition passed to abandonment, and now to rot. In front of one old plant, fifty or more concrete transports lay whole where they died, like frozen megafauna, while atop the many-storied silos an entire ecosystem has sprouted, head-high trees and all, creating bird habitat where smoke once plumed. One by one, year after year, the bricks below crumble and break as windows succumb to sunlight and vandals. Ginger Strand, a Brooklyn-based writer who studies America's ruins, told me they have much to say, "that the world can change," she said. "Just because we have an economy based on burning fossil fuels, say, doesn't mean we can't have another kind in the future. Civilization and its infrastructure are always subject to being rethought. What does that tell us? That we can make it better."

I didn't know it the year before while jogging by, and I didn't know it now, but inside one of these old husks, if you cared to look, you'd find the New Way churning apace.

Todd Erling is my age, with a daughter of his own. He's the executive director of the Hudson Valley AgriBusiness Development Corporation (HVADC), a misnomer. The Hudson Valley is nothing like the agri-business of our collective mind, the country-sized corn, wheat, and soy seas, themselves buoyed by seas of tax money. Similarly, the HVADC is not the faceless giant squid of corporate America—huge, ungainly, monstrous, indifferent. It's a handful of employees, working in the shadow of the forested concrete silos, with Erling as its high-energy, high-hope face. I met him there in September, not long after the float.

Regarding agriculture, here are the extremes:

Hippie: Hey man, you've got to subvert the corporations, grow it all organic, sell only local. We can feed everyone that way, and better, too.

Corporations: You're an idiot.

I'm more hippie, wishing that way was the only way, but I have doubts. Erling here was a great comfort, wanting only what works best. That's normally corporate mantra, but Erling is of my generation, with influences far beyond the top-hatted, diamond-soled barons of yore. What works best is now multifaceted, not merely dollars at the end of a day. Social fabric is weighed along with bankrolls, as is the environ-ment we bequeath. This isn't Aquarian gold alone, but business. If you waste the earth with the Old Way, Erling knows, there's no future, and besides, the behemoth model with its scatterbrained distribution and wasteful farming techniques is simply bad business. This is America, by God, where there's always a better way, and these hippies may be onto something. Let's make it work.

Erling isn't a hippie. Clean cut, well spoken, sharply dressed, he seemed like an MBA candidate, but with an adaptive mind that bunch usually lacks. Sitting in his office, I asked if he thought organic agriculture was the answer, if it could feed nine billion people by midcentury, as are predicted will exist. Reluctantly, I'm not convinced it can, and doubt I disguised this sad suspicion.

"It would be terrific if it could," he said, "but it's highly debatable."

Rats. I knew it. We're doomed. Before I jumped off a bridge, however, he went on. "Right now I don't think organic crops produce enough. If we think about it, we all want that, but it's not there, and may never be. Things are changing, though, in all facets. Farmers used to spray trees in clouds—crop-dusters and industrial sprayers. The stuff wafted everywhere. That's changing, or has changed. Like drip irrigation, the chemicals are better directed, and there's far less pesticide use per acre now that it is. Integrated Pest Management (IPM) is building too."

That sounded like a dating strategy. I asked about it. It turns out this blends organic methods with other means, though broadcast spraying is only used in desperation. Rather than habitually dusting fields, preventative measures are taken, such as crop rotation and selecting pest-resistant stock. This costs next to nothing and can be quite effective, not to mention toxin free. Should pests appear, as eventually they will, they're identified by species, followed by determining if their numbers present a threat. If they do, everything from unleashing aphid-devouring ladybugs to pinpointing deterrents is used, toxic or non-toxic. If all else fails, out come the nukes, the stuff that kills me, you, and everything else, bugs included, misting all in its path. According to the Environmental Protection Agency (EPA), this method is seldom employed, and IPM is currently having standards set that will eventually see foods labeled as "IPM-approved," much as the "organic" tag is used now.

This sounded like progress. Erling continued. He's a native of the region, telling me that fruit-growers here doused orchards the way rain falls, covering everything. "That's simply how it was done," he said. Now, he and his wife tend a small orchard of their own, using IPM techniques undreamt of thirty years ago, but much less costly and equally effective, without the grim environmental results, including the pulmonary horrors associated with old sprayers. Once, I heard Michael Pollan—the pithy, increasingly famous food theorist—on the radio. Speaking of public demand for perfect, blemish-free potatoes, he said that after spraying the fungicide that makes this non-necessity possible, farmers—dressed in moon-suits at the time—don't go into the fields for five days. If crop-growers need respirators, he said, we should take note.

"Realism is the aim," said Erling. "Patience and pragmatism. The idea is to use what works, keep farmers at a comfortable living, always evolving. This is as true for growing techniques as it is for business practices and marketing strategies. In time, behaviors become reflexive. Organic and IPM were fringe methods forty years ago, but now they're exploding, becoming integrated into the culture. That's largely because they're cost effective—at least IPM—and friendly to the environment, which people are recognizing more and more as good business. The same is true of 'local.' That was fringe, too, but it's become the Hudson Valley brand name's greatest asset, and it won't fade for economic reasons. People are seeing this. Whether organic can be the sole provider I don't know, but it's certainly an important component, and selling locally, where people know where their food comes from and support those growers, that's probably more important. I think New York can grow all its own food."

This might be so. I don't know, but walking my old jogging route, skirting the road crew sweeping tar resin from patch jobs, I headed for the fruit stand, dreaming of tomatoes and other joys. I love these roads. Field to forest, forest to field, they're as beveled as the land, providing rich views of rich country, foliage shading the shoulders, the Hudson in the pollen-heavy air. You walk them, seeing nothing but farms and what farms promise. It's all here, small-scale, focused, industrious, diverse, and it's not just Columbia County, but Ulster, Dutchess, and Green, right down to New York City's bedroom, Westchester. Goat cheese. Sheep cheese. Cow cheese. Laying hens and chicken yards. Beer-makers, fifty-head beeferies, vintners, vegetables, rows and fields of them, all kinds, neatly tended, immensely productive, and then there's the fruit, endless bushels of it, any apple you want, peaches and pears, linear columns of trees, fed by the broken light punching through the shroud, clouds hung-up between the Catskills and Tacon-ics, the Hudson splitting the ranges.

All through Route 9, through nearly every road in Columbia County, runaway pear and apple trees fleck the countryside—dropped in deer pellets, borne by birds. The orchards from which they come appear over hillcrests like Creation itself. Such a weighted word, orchard, Saxon and ancient, fused and wise. *Wortgeard*—plant garden, with *geard* from Proto-Indo-European *gher*, "to grasp, enclose." This is old stuff, where we took hold of nature, enclosed it, husbanding its properties, becoming a new species. Both earthbound and celestial, sto-ried and practical, they're portals, these fruit yards, conduits between what we were before the farm and what we've been after. No mistake, then, that Eve accepts knowledge in an orchard, passing us from a creature among fellows to a creature apart. Find a quiet one, apples and peaches, a few pears, maybe a plum grove. Sneak down off the road. There, by the pebbly brook, down amid the unmown stretch, the grass. Lie down. Bees buzzing, sun shining, water crossing stone, all day. Listen to the fruit grow. We've defined each other, these trees and ourselves, and you sense a similar awareness in that swelling pulp. This union is where something began.

My dreams were answered. The fruit stand was open. Four peaches and a fat tomato, change in the jar. I walked a little further up Route 9, where it breaks east, and found a patch of hickory shade, eating that tomato like an apple, seeds and juice running through my stubble. The peaches were next. Four up, four down, sweet as can be. I stood. Buckets of Irish time left to burn, I resumed walking.

I could've trekked for days, weeks. Some of these farms were familiar. Rather than stands, many have full-blown stores now, advantaging both the trend and wisdom of selling locally. No middlemen, no distribution, no retail costs—more profit. In the short two months I was here, unable to shake the hands-on thrill of food procurement enjoyed in Alaska, these places were nearly home, Hudson's farmer's market, too. People are looser here than at superstores, more animated. This stuff is right off a tree or out of the ground, earth upon it. Cheese is in the open air, the rank-dank vapor of exquisite taste hovering about. In the orchard stores you smell cider, knowing the mash is fast by, and if you're not the one growing and making this stuff, you don't feel entirely severed from it. These markets have sprouted everywhere. In *Deep Economy*, an un-psychotic manifesto arguing for small, local-market farms, Bill McKibben writes that in 1970 America had 340 farmer's markets. By 2004, there were 3,700. That number grows, and here's where Erling's rounder business approach shines. Not only does selling regionally eliminate distribution links and raise profits, but people are happier, communities stronger, and, because it's good business, the world is cleaner.

The year before, I'd visited other Columbia County farms with jobs in mind. The Old Chatham Sheepherding Company, in Chatham, is the nation's largest producer of sheep milk products. Chatham is terrific, smaller than Hudson, without the rancor of industrial obsolescence pricking its underbelly. Well off the river, it has some fame for its Shaker museum, but is otherwise just a quaint one-street town burgeoning with unquaint, youthful energy. Karen and I enjoyed the Blue Plate, a nice corner restaurant, while everywhere, on the menus and in the air, you sense the surrounding farms, a solar contentment all its own.

The Old Chatham Sheepherding Company is about what you'd picture—long, clean barn nestled in a vale, hills all around, tufted pastures partitioned by motley deciduous strips. The farm manager was Beth, compact and fit, ruddy with sun and earth-splattered work. Farmhands were in the barn, milking sheep. As gentle as their animals, the workers coaxed ewes in and out of stalls, draining their milk and herding them out. Most of the rams were slaughtered nearby, sent to Greek markets in Boston and New York. Who wouldn't want this job? Beth eventually offered, but at ten bucks an hour it was no go. Life takes its turns. Without a pregnant girlfriend, free as the forty years before, I'd have taken that work without thought, probably still be there, in the fields, keeping vigil, mucking stalls, minding coyotes, putting my hands on food before it was food. Much later, in Queens, I came across their yogurt, tinged with maple, right next to the Dannon. I dared, and wasn't disappointed. They've found a niche, the sheep people, and it keeps them thriving, their community too. We pray this is the New Hope—small farms, multiplying by day, old industry hands filling the slots, pushing products downriver.

Reservations, though, persist. Attitude is more a deterrent than soil limitations, but I may be wrong. As Erling pointed out, give patience and pragmatism time, and behaviors become reflexive. Still, people like their yummies on both sides of the food spectrum, much of which can't be produced in every region. No limes, for instance, or kiwis, will ever come out of New York, Twinkies or Cocoa Puffs either. Volume, too, is a concern. What we now call industrial farms started roughly around World War II, with "get big or get out" sloganeering sponsored by government and industry captains alike. This has been no mean strategy. Modern agriculture—characterized by petro-fertilizers, petro-insecticides, petro-fuel, and rampant consolidation—has performed "two feats that all of human history has spent trying to achieve," Bill McKibben counters himself in *Deep Economy*—"[produced] a lot of food and produced it cheaply." This couldn't be more true. As farms become bigger and farmers fewer, soil more bombarded with fertilizers and irrigation, yield records break every year, and prices, as demanded by mammoth, high-volume, low-margin wholesalers, keep dropping. That soils and water tables are cracking beneath this system's strain, or that the millions forced off small farms for a life of assembly-line claustrophobia have become social tinder is irrelevant when you're living cheaply yourself, standing in the well-lit, county-sized aisles of bright-shiny food.

I asked McKibben about this, relaying an anecdote. Gordie, my Yakutat boss, had several biologist chums in Juneau when the Soviet Empire caved in. In character, America bubbled over to show their former enemies the Proper Way. Capitalists, free-market-eers, and consultants of every kind poured into Russia, bent on turning the alcoholic, infrastructureless, endemically corrupt nation into Wall Street and Las Vegas by this time next month. Our government got its licks in, too, setting up communication between "sister" cities. Vladivostok is on the Pacific Rim, Juneau as well. One of Gordie's friends corresponded with a biologist, eventually inviting her over. They picked her up, then drove to Fred Meyer—a Walmart-like place—to pick up groceries. The woman walked in, stood before the rows of fruits, vegetables, cheeses, butter, milk, juices, cereals, breads, pastries, lamb chops, pork chops, sirloin, hamburger, whole chickens, chicken parts, seafood, canned food, boxed food, jarred food, every food, and collapsed, weeping on her knees. Gordie and his buddy were as flummoxed by spontaneous tears as most men, here compounded by a considerable language barrier. "I mean, how do you say, 'Maybe you should call your mother?' in Russian?" She eventually composed herself, then extended an arm. "This," she said. "This is why you won."

McKibben understood the argument—it mirrored his own in *Deep Economy*—but wasn't deterred.

"Well, if you're looking for superior systems to the old Soviet food economy, you won't have to look far. The trouble is, as productive as our modern food system has been, it can't last. Local economies—farms—are the future."

Prior to those two months living in Columbia County, I wouldn't have believed him. I'd want to, but reservoirs of cheap, easily accessed food are tough to work around. As McKibben has explored in depth and Erling knows from experience, though, the Old Way has torn up land and communities in equal shares. At its current pace, farmland worldwide will be owned by a handful of companies, board members being continents away, while those who work it will be little more than sharecroppers. No one will know or care where their food comes from, and with so little connection to sustenance, land abuse will continue until dust and shriveled vines produce problems of a different order. What the answer to this is I'm not qualified to say, only knowing that an answer needs to be found.

Sam Simon, an orthopedist-turned-dairyman in Poughkeepsie, New York, provided me declarative opinions, reflecting Todd Erling's views and affirming my own hunches. I called him. Simon grew up dairying in Middletown, New York. That was the Old Way, producing as much as possible and selling to giant wholesalers at a loss, soaking up government cash for the balance. Retired from his surgeon practice, farm life called Simon back, but he took a different route, starting the Hudson Valley Fresh Co-op in 2005. I trusted this guy immediately. He swears more than I do, which is like saying he's killed more Romans than Hannibal. For Simon, Hudson Valley Fresh—eight farms across Columbia and Dutchess counties—isn't meant to change the world, only provide a handful of local farms new opportunities. Like Erling, he's only interested in plucking strands from various paradigms until he stitches a tapestry that works. I asked whether organic was the answer, and was peppered with a poesy of oaths. Cleaned up, his response was something like this.

"Organic? No, that's bunk. I mean not entirely. Organic started pure. The idea was to have a few cows and a few chickens. You graze the cows in one pasture, then have the chickens come in behind and eat the seeds and maggots out of the manure, fertilizing the pasture with their own nitrogen-rich waste. That way your cows live stress-free in the open, producing better milk, same for your eggs, and you don't need insecticides or fertilizer. The trouble is . . ."

"You can only feed yourself," I said.

"Exactly. You can only feed yourself, maybe a neighbor. Organic now is just a label. Distributors mix up everything in the same vat, making crap. They'll put anything you want on the carton. 'Organic,' 'hormone-free,' anything. It's bunk."

This Dr. Simon was an interesting duck. I would have been too afraid to say it, but his philosophy of dairy, and farming in general—in addition to being on-the-job-informed—is heavily marbled with hippie fiber. He might have laughed if I said this, but he also might have tracked me down and shot me.

Bovine Growth Hormone (BGH) is another of dairy's recently unearthed bugaboos, being accused of everything from male lactation to early menstruation. I've drank enough nondescript milk in my life to fill the Pacific, so can only hope this won't lead to a career in wet-nursing. I asked him about it, after he said he uses certain methods that preclude Hudson Valley Fresh from the organic label, such as commercial fertilizer.

"No. We don't use it. It's not necessary. All BGH does is make cows think they're pregnant, so they keep producing milk. That way you can get five to six hundred straight days out of them. It's hard on them, though, and cuts into quality. Our only chance here is putting the best product on the shelf."

This "hard on the cows" is gaining ground throughout both animal husbandry and the consumers it serves. The notoriety of live-stock treatment on factory farms is now well documented and justly abhorred, being pointed out not only by PETA but conservative activists like George Will. It was all through Simon's voice, too, that he cared deeply about his animals, but for him, economics was the only discussion. Stressed cows, like stressed people, produce lactic acid and other fluids, and when crammed into pens and not allowed to free-graze, they rub against metal gates and each other, producing infections and a high white-blood cell count. All this leads to both bad-tasting milk and a quickly spoiling product. The same is true of pork, chicken, and beef. Happy critters make happy dinner plates, something which Simon's clutch of customers—from Albany to Manhattan, right down the valley—are recognizing. He went on. It turns out that the big southeastern and Californian herds are reared in exactly the conditions that produce poor quality. "Crowded, stressed, and hot," he said, adding that cows don't like heat, at least not all year. "It raises stress levels, promotes infection, and while it produces a lot of milk, none of it is any good."

This wasn't all. Part of Hudson Valley Fresh's mandate is to preserve open space in the valley. Like everyone everywhere, Simon has watched farms disappear throughout his life, making subdivisions of a once rich bungle of cultivated and wild tracts. In the seventies, Dutchess County had 275 dairy farms. In 2010, there were twenty-six, with most sold to developers. "I don't blame them," Simon said. "Make a bunch of money, quit working eighty hours a week at a loss. Problem is, all that open space is gone." That's right out of the hippie handbook, but I didn't dare ask if he lamented the loss of so much pretty bird habitat. Farms mean food, and food means people. Slashing the farm-based infrastructure—which supplies quality products while preserving the open space needed to grow it—"that's no future," Simon finished. Entwining idealism, then, with practicality, he and his collective have opened new opportunities in the vestige of others.

Simon isn't the only one. Local-based farms now blanket the Hudson Valley, some organic, some not, some tapped into a co-op or name brand, others not, an entrepreneurial polyglot trying to figure it out. It's attracting more and more people, young people, and there's every bit the feel of "Wagons Ho!" here. With the American frontiers all sewn up, the adventure and peril gone, things seem to be looking back, to recapture that sense of newness and wonder by returning to the farm. Across the river from Simon, in New Paltz, I visited the Phillies Bridge Farm Project. I'd sent a résumé there, and the manager offered me an internship, not the salaried slot I'd needed. The following September I met her, Jesica Pasqual, in the cleft swale where Phillies Bridge operates, shadowed by Shawangunk Ridge, a Montana-like butte rising from Eastern hardwood. Education is her priority, hosting elementary kids to show them that food is made elsewhere than the grocery store. I asked her how agriculture has changed in the last thirty years. Maybe not thirty herself, she said younger people are going back to it. "Educated people, activist I think, but a new activism, more pragmatic than starry-eyed." She'd come to it recently, and walking by the stacks of cut squash, the harvested plots awaiting spring rotation, and the grazing sheep, all wet with Hudson mist, it wasn't hard to see what brought her here.

If most of these pioneers are rediscovering the simplicities of farm life, mixing new and traditional methods to redefine a region's food base, some are adding the necessary innovation to round it out. When Todd Erling finished talking, he asked if I had a minute. I did. "Great," he said. "Follow me."

We didn't go far. In one of the dilapidated cement plants behind HVDAC's office, the Mediterranean has found Columbia County. Erling liaised between investors and an Israeli aquaculturist, inaugurating zero-discharge fish farming in the Americas. Fish farms are Alaskan pariahs, and I normally recoil at their mention. Alaska had most of the international salmon market locked up until people figured out how to raise fish in pens. Alaska's prices plummeted. Fortunately, salmon farms, while producing cheap flesh, are loathsome in every other way. They swamp the surrounding ecosystem with fish waste, the meat is full of dye and antibiotics, and escapees threaten native species. Alaska worked to point this out, and has had noticeable success.

This farm, though, looked different. If the old plant was nothing else, it was certainly large, big enough to house dozens of plastic tanks roughly the size of backyard pools. Behind them, a tinkertoy apparatus is a marvel of dripping water and bacteria sinks that purifies and recycles the water. The fish I didn't see. In the fingerling stage, they were quarantined until disease-resistant, when they'd be distributed among these larger tanks. Markets awaited in Boston and New York, local enough. The species were Mediterranean bream and sea bass, with the hope of adding two flounder species and a type of tuna. The filtration mimics natural ecosystems, and if it works, if fish really can be farmed cleanly and sold locally, the world will change in terrific ways. Wild stocks will get the reprieve they've long awaited, and landlocked human populations will have jobs and fresh food they otherwise wouldn't. Adjoining technology with small-scale farm models and revitalized notions of local markets, installing it all in the Old Way's rotting core, this Hudson fish project had every desirable element of the old and new, giving it the great promise of human endeavor.

Walking back to town, I returned through the same fruit fields I'd walked before, the apples ripening, ladders poking into peach branches. "Peaches in the summer time," goes "Shady Grove," "Apples in the fall. If I can't have all your love, I won't have none at all." Since Albany, I'd floated by several farms as well. Agriculture is a mix of the same enraged placidity as fishing, the blend squaring up mind and body with questions that matter—God, love, life, and their opposites. Dylan Thomas isn't the only one to plunge these depths. Everyone from Virgil to Robert Frost to Wendell Berry has made a name here, but nothing as complete as John Keats in "To Autumn."

Shannon knows "To Autumn," or at least that's the hope. We want our children to experience the freedom we ourselves desire, and yet it can't be helped—they're not five breaths old and we saturate them with all we love, trying to shape them. I memorized certain poems, racking her in the Baby Bjorn and wandering Queens' congestion, whispering what I hoped to be a lifelong love of words. "To Autumn" is Keats' peace with death, but more—a reconciliation with uncertainty, arbitrated by a faith in hunch and the agricultural arcanum that summons it.

The first stanza is glut, the frame between summer and autumn when everything lazes with plenty. *To bend with apples the mossed cottage-trees / And fill all fruit with ripeness to the core . . . To setting budding more, and still more, later flowers for the bees / Until they think warm days will never cease.* The third stanza, the last, is the boundary of autumn and winter, or death, as swallows flock south, leaving behind the winter red-breast. It's the second stanza, though, the harvest, where Keats brushes against God, coming away affirmed of its existence but unaware of form or intent, only its constant presence in the labor between earth and people.

> Who hath not seen thee oft amid thy store?
> Sometimes whoever seeks abroad may find thee
> Sitting careless on a granary floor,
> Thy hair soft-lifted by the winnowing wind,
> Or on a half-reaped furrow, sound asleep,
> Drowsed with the fume of poppies, while thy
> Hook spares the next swath with all its twined flowers.
> Sometimes like a gleaner thou dost keep steady thy
> Laden head across a brook,
> Or by a cider press, with patient look, thou
> Watchest the last oozings hours by hours.

Not explicitly human, vaguely female, this presence shadows our movements through the paces of harvest. In doing so, it's as subject to the raptures of excess as people, along with the grinding wastage that produces it. Depending how it's tilted, this imagery provides either great horror or great comfort. There's a god, sympathetic, even empathetic, but one that may be as vulnerable as we. It may also be that divinity is simply the vapor engendered by human muscle and intellect as they work the soil.

As with Thomas, Keats didn't write of America. This is England, but once more, walking through the broken landscape around Hudson, the hayfields and cornstalks, the garden plots and pastures, the rows of ripened and ripening fruit, root crops and livestock, you feel your own hunches gather, where natural and supernatural collide, maybe collude, and you search for a rhythm to articulate it. Whatever you exhume, you'll know that if America really is turning back to these old fron-tiers, it will find more than apples and goat cheese in the enterprise.

Just prior to the trip, I'd taken Shannon for a walk, the long rect-angle down Forty-Third to Queens Boulevard, along the East River, then back up Skillman, chanting what poems I could, "To Autumn" among them. It was Saturday. Two blocks from Karen's apartment there's a modest farmer's market, trucks from Jersey, Amish country, and the Finger Lakes, but mostly the Hudson Valley. We stopped. Shannon stared at the people, at the vegetables I handled. That bunch. There. The beets. Dots of mica and powdered siltstone caked the ruby skins, first from the glaciers, then the Adirondacks. Buying them, I wet a finger, then made a spot of mud. Shannon faced away. I daubed her cheek and felt a half-smile, craning my neck to see rich dirt on fresh skin. Mica twitched in the sun, and she felt the same presence I did. I was sure of it.

Conjugal

I made Baba Louie's, 1:55. Karen's dad, I knew, would be the first to show, unharried by his inveterately harried wife and daughter, and as such might be a tad punctual. He was right on time, 2:27. I stood. The river had stripped some pounds from me, and he commented on my color as well. We shook hands and sat.

There's an ease among men without women. A separate language arises, where each word throws a shadow. After forty years on Wall Street and five of retirement, he'd soon be teaching history at Poughkeepsie's Dutchess County Community College. The syllabus was complete, and we went over what might be missing, interspersed with his questions about the river. His bike trip came up, Spain to Ireland, and though we talked of the Old Country's green hills and the Adirondacks' surprising wild, the necessity of breaking free from women for a while was plain to both of us—not leaving, not doing anything but loving partner and family, just the wide-ranging lust for open-aired furlough. Women have it too. Karen's pregnancy—and the suddenness of our engagement—terrified her. She'd spent months at a time abroad, taking leave when she pleased, working orphanages from Vietnam to Argentina to Costa Rica. Men came and went, and though she'd always wanted settlement, it seized her too quickly, and women, of course, have their own language.

There's a rule in Great Quotes: If Mark Twain didn't say it, Oscar Wilde did. England and America, then, are divided by a common speech, and we can say the same of men and women. The abrupt departure of our freedom affected Karen and me in ways we wish it hadn't, but whatever common grammar we had expressed resentment, not empathy. We had the same reservations, but couldn't understand a word the other said, no matter how direct the language. On the other hand, her father could speak of biking through French vineyards, sunset on the make, and I caught every inverse inflection because they were my own. Domestic life has its charms, we agreed, but so does oxygen.

Baba Louie's is the New Hudson. Chic enough, it features heaps of local produce. Signature pizzas are its fame, but the courses are well rounded, and while Karen and I lived there, my nights were sad nights when she was denied her mixed-berry cobbler.

River life changes you. I was now good for one meal a day. Saving myself for dinner, I ordered salad, while Emmett went for the chicken sandwich, local greenery to the side. He spoke of his son and daughter-in-law, both architects, who had bought a run-down farmhouse in nearby Kinderhook. Work had proceeded famously, but then came their own child, a son. I listened to him, the shuttered panes and drained pipes, but only heard the death of his own aspirations as his children came. Such expressions are often thought to be misogynistic, clichés of pythonic feminine coils squeezing spirit from masculine lungs, but they're not, and I never look farther than my own family to prove it.

My pop was the family type, my mother the itinerant. She constantly redefined herself, being a sixties reformist, a writer, a poet, and finally fulfilling a dream by becoming a horsewoman, driving to all points of the compass to watch her daughters ride the shows. She never seemed settled. Months after she died, I asked my dad about it. "The truth is, it's possible she was never happy. Not really." He didn't have to elaborate. She laughed and danced her way through life, but often times it seemed defensive. In word-shadow, then, my pop said that domesticity never suited her, that a spouse and children held her back, but that she'd knuckled down and did what her choices demanded.

Baba Louie's fills up quick, and the chatter-and-clank of late business lunch welled around us. The waitress came, stacking plates. Coffee? Just the check. I looked across at the gray hair and slight stoop of my soon-to-be father-in-law. By my age, Emmett had a son in college, my own parents the same. In every generation before mine, in fact, forty-one-year-olds were either grandparents or soon to become them. Gender isn't the only fault line along a mother tongue.

We walked the few blocks to Ca'Mea, the Bed & Breakfast where Karen had checked us in. It's more Bed & Five Star, being owned by a couple guys from the city, bringing the culinary prowess of Manhattan while keeping the inn small-town friendly. Emmett wasn't staying. One of the owners showed us the rooms, and I followed him downstairs to make dinner reservations. When I opened the door to the street, lo and behold, there they were, Karen and her mother, on time at last. Any doubts that Shannon would remember me vanished. She smiled wide, burrowed into Karen's chest, then as quickly looked up. I snatched her, and at the moment couldn't think of a better life.

We took a walk, Karen and I, carrying our daughter along the streets that might have been home. Above the Amtrak station a park overlooks the Hudson. We jostled Shannon about while she giggled, passing her from one set of arms to the other. Dense brush dresses the steep drop to the river, and a long, thin island partitions east bank from west. Along the island a trio of blue herons sentineled the river lettuce, hawking striper smolt as the sun dropped, while somewhere down the declivity a red-winged blackbird wheezed its call.

When Karen gave birth, the hospital hosted a gratis breast-feeding class. I thought we'd be the oldest there by ten years, but crow's feet and gray hairs abounded. One lady must have been fifty. Such a jolt to family dynamics, and it evolved within thirty years.

Night came. With Emmett gone, I sat in the lavender-heavy ambience of Ca'Mea's back patio, Shannon on my knee, trying to decipher the lee meanings between Karen and her mother. My own parents were in this brood, crammed between the Greatest Generation and Baby Boomers. The Silent Generation. They're the last group, really, who doesn't understand divorce, or the delays in reproducing, or feminism for that matter. Some things are difficult to accept, or even see when you're in the middle of them, but year by year, step by step, American generations become successively selfish, with my own a far needier bunch than my parents'.

Carol talked of a party they'd recently attended, where she'd bumped into one of Karen's classmates. The woman had divorced, telling Carol they just couldn't make it work.

"I don't understand that," Carol said. "What does that mean? You never used to hear that. It didn't matter what problems you had, you stayed with it."

My mother was a great *Golden Girls* watcher. This was back in the three-channel television era, so I often sat with her, pretending not to admire the show's moxie. In one episode, Estelle Getty, the elder, spoke on the same subject, and I played it back in my head as Carol went on: "I mean, hey, we talked, we dealt with it, we got a little on the side, we made do."

Karen returned serve.

"Well, things are different now," she said.

She was right. Between the two of us, friends and family have snapped off marriages at the national rate, leaving the usual residuum of open wounds, lawyers' fees, and diminished childhoods. I bopped Shannon up and down, cooing, making faces, praying Our Heavenly Father that the linguini would show any second. Carol knew that Karen had problems with me, and this talk of the party was her way of saying "don't walk away from this; schlep-with-no-prospects or no-schlep-with-no-prospects, you got yourself knocked up and better stick with it," while Karen, in her generic speak of generational differences, had said that she was independent, that her decisions were her own.

I once installed an Invisible Fence in Ojai, California, where James Dean died, stapling wire to the sun-baked ground. A dozen or so *obreros*, performing grounds tasks, were on break. I speak enough Spanish to know that between chuckles they said I looked and moved like Jeff Spicoli. One even ventured a half-English, "Awright, Dude." Shifting subjects, another said to the *jeffe*, "Ese alambre es para el perro?" I looked up. "Si, mano. Es para el perro," but did no such thing at Ca'Mea, just sitting across from mother and daughter like a man who couldn't understand a word the foreign sophisticates were saying.

As for the generations, it's all true. When my father gets together with peers, you hear a lot about the old days, when people "just shut up and did what they were told." Fair enough. His is the last of them, the forty years and a gold watch generation, the divorce as a last resort squad. They grew up in the Depression's shadow, when Soviet Russia was an easy Devil and America looked upon guilty continents smoldering in a world war's cinders. You marry at twenty-two, have kids, put on your Willie Loman hat and hit the sales trail, retire at sixty-five. What's to think about? My bunch came up in Vietnam's shadow, Watergate, the sixties' assassinations. The country had—and continues to have—an identity crisis, and as such "mine" is the ruling word. It's hurt marriage and it's hurt the country, or at least my father's generation's vision of what the country might be. It's difficult to say where it will lead. It may be for the best. In the Civil War, many recruits didn't know left from right, but knew hay from straw.

Sergeants stuck a piece of hay in one boot and a strand of straw in the other, chanting ditties like "Hayfoot, Strawfoot, belly full of bean soup" to give the country boys a chance. Whenever I hear my elders brag up their adherence to mission, expressing bafflement at today's wayward youth, I mutter "Hayfoot-Strawfoot," denoting people too stupid to do anything but put one foot in front of the other, exactly as they're told.

The night went beautifully, as did the day. Shannon slept between us, flopping and smiling, smiling and flopping, babbling all the while. Karen said she'd never been so vocal. In time, we all fell asleep, waking in that nimbus of family contentment the pine for which ten days did nothing to evaporate. We spent the day ambling Hudson—father, mother, daughter, grandmother—buying Shannon knick-knacks, lunching at a sidewalk café, visiting the harbor. By four o'clock they were gone.

"A taste of honey is worse than none at all," Sweet Smokey sings, and so it is. You get married, you have kids—maybe it isn't incarceration after all, but paddling out of the marina, past the herons returned to fish the island, it didn't matter. There were less than a hundred miles to go, and despite all the uncertainty at their end—the job hunt, Karen, figuring out twelve hours a day with an infant, city life—I wanted those miles gone.

Purging Strangelove

I didn't get far. A few hours into an oncoming tide doesn't promote headway, and after slipping beneath the Rip Van Winkle Bridge, where I'd first looked at the Hudson during a jog and said, "There's something to paddle," the sun sank precipitously.

Hudson's cross-river rival is Catskill. Motor boats and jet skiers boffed about its marina, the boats coursing in and out of the little delta where others were slipped. Après-boaters enjoyed late-day drinks on the club's deck while gulls circled above, hoping for leftover slaw or discarded fries. A decent-sized creek enters here, the Cauterskill, deep, thickly planted water. What sequence? I thought. Herring all spring, muskrats through the fall, shad nets at tide, crab and eel pots besides. Make haste, Great Days, make haste.

Paddling against the current, you can better a mile an hour if the eddies are right. An Albany-bound barge chugged upriver, a white-orange Coastie boat fast behind. Allowing the wakes to pass, I aimed south-southeast for the more camp-friendly river-left. Past a certain point, I intended to stick to the east bank—where I'd pull out—even if it cost a day or two. River travel is quickest from inside bend to inside bend, but about here the Hudson is wide enough to be more ocean than river, subject to crosscurrents and sudden wind storms. In a dead calm, then, a mile by canoe takes time, but that far from shore, white caps lapping the gunnels, tears and a long swim will likely ensue. Yet we take what the river gives us, and despite the tide, with the sun's strength draining away, the still water proved no trouble. Good thing, because what looked like decent camp sites were false palms in a desert.

I had to get right up on them to see. Looking over my shoulder, the Cauterskill was two miles back, the sun nipping the western peaks.

The trains run tight to the east bank here, and what I'd thought were natural jetties jutting from the tracks were indeed that, but too wracked with brush and driftwood to make camp. Besides, from the looks of it, spring tides pushed over these little peninsulas. I beached at a couple, looked them over, but found only birdlife. Only birdlife. Forgotten square yards like these, along with the big preserves, might save us. I asked Rich Anderson, a bird expert working Audubon's Constitution Marsh across from West Point, about such tidbits.

"These 'fringe' wetlands may not be big," he said, "nor their individual bird populations great, but their cumulative acreage and the life it supports is impressive."

Critters, too, then, take what the river gives them, or at least what we give the river. On one jut, bushed out with willow and sumac, a yellow warbler, two yellowthroats, and a hermit thrush shared ten yards by twenty, along with four chickadees, a downy woodpecker, and a recently abandoned cardinal nest. Fine stuff, but a machete and five days couldn't hack out a campsite here, and across the tracks lay private homes, which even *tag-your-it* vets such as me avoid. What to do? I looked across the river. From the marina I couldn't see it, but a wooded cove lay just upstream from a Hudson relic, the active cement plant the St. Lawrence closure had saved. "Well, cowboy," Jon Voight said to his reflection in *Midnight Cowboy*, "you know what you have to do," and so I did. The tide had settled to slack, and by the time I crossed I could scarcely make out the "No Trespassing" signs the plant had posted. In fact, I didn't see them at all, just pulled the boat up in the forest and pitched the tent by headlamp. Damp ground lay yards away, dotted with cedar. Barred owl country. I listened for the *who-cooks-for-you*, but heard only the plant's generator, idling for the next day's work.

Later, with a better map, I'd learn that I camped in the appropriately named Cementon, across the river from Germantown. Downstream from there is Rhinebeck. German Protestants, kicked about Europe by the Reformation's two-hundred-year afterbirth, settled here. Originally, they were England's semi-slaves, who sympathized with their religious difficulties but knew cheap labor and scalp-fodder when they saw it, putting them to work in the early eighteenth century when the understandably irate Iroquois contested the area. These people were from the Palatinate, similar to the Hudson Valley with its forested Rhine, and enough of them hung on to eventually make settlements of their own. Thus are nutshelled the Palatines, one of the hundred thousand splinters making up the American timber.

Do we ever speak of race in America? Truly? Shame if we don't, for this is the place to do it. God might be responsible, evolution maybe, but the question is immaterial. Our species is comprised of different colors, all inter-breedable, producing shades and hues of their own, and over millennia these have coagulated into ethnicities among like cultures—deeply tribal, deeply defensive, deeply paranoid. Continents have given rise to the different races, and what have all these done, but come across the seas to perform a chemistry experiment. We look for origin, want source, and what better place to find the human core than how we cope with difference? America, then, is your corpus, the collision of all difference, and the Hudson a prominent artery within that frame.

We talk of race, of course, *ad nauseum*, but our speech is deflective, displaced, not the introspection it needs to be. Objectivity may be a canard in any field, but it's particularly so in race-speak. You are the race you are, religion too, with the denomination after that, and your grandparents hailed from whatever homeland plain, valley, or hollow that further distinguished them. We may be born free, but in terms of how we see the world this has limits. These limits can be pressed, but again, as with much of history, academia only brings you so far.

Listening to professors, sifting libraries and the Internet, you can find out much about everything, the Hudson Valley included. Race-wise, you'll likely discover things you didn't know, but nothing that shocks, nothing that will change the way you feel, at least directionally. Our deflective brand of articulating race in this country has done many things, some of them well, including preparing us for the worst. This inurnment, though, has both insulated and numbed us, keeping introspection from where it does the most good.

Look in the books. They'll tell you this: America began as a slave nation, including all thirteen colonies during the Revolution. New York had the North's highest proportional slave population and a higher percentage of slave-holding households than some Southern states. Most Northern slaves worked in the home, meaning most

Northern slave-holders owned one or two slaves. Up to forty percent of Manhattan households held a slave. The Hudson Valley, however, differed, being the North's closest model of Southern plantation life. Dutch traders, working for the Dutch West India Company, brought the first Africans in 1626, eleven of them. Dutch émigrés often came for the fur trade, leaving when they'd made their money. Others avoided farm labor for more lucrative trades. Holland, though, wanted to build a colony, which meant it needed on-site food production, and culling slaves bound for Caribbean sugar plantations to serve Hudson Valley patroons proved little trouble. Here the slaves learned the diverse husbandry the Valley boasted, working the grain and fruit crops in sizeable numbers. When the British took New Amsterdam in 1664, the practice continued. By 1756, slaves comprised twenty-five percent of many New York counties. Blacks, naturally, weren't pleased, something whites knew. In 1702, no more than three blacks were allowed to gather, the big Valley farms excepted. In 1712, a Manhattan revolt left five whites dead, fanning panic, resulting in more racial unease.

By the Revolution, the Colonies faced a problem. Clamoring for freedom while holding slaves is an odd strategy, something the British noted vocally. Though Northern slavery continued after independence, a combination of economics, politics, and abolitionist sentiment phased it out. New York was among the last to emancipate, banning the practice on July 4, 1799, with the strange codicil that anyone born prior to that date would remain enslaved until the age of twenty-eight for males, twenty-five for females, making slavery legal in New York until 1827.

Even with slavery banished, it remained complicated. Manhattan brokers took forty cents for every Southern cotton dollar, giving slavery a blushless imprimatur from New York's financial class, so much so that when war broke out Mayor Fernando Wood suggested secession.

There's more, naturally, but that's the gist. Books, however, cause problems. Without them, we're lost, but especially with historical lore, we too often detach ourselves from the subject. Like fiction, history is a way to better understand human nature—and therefore yourself—rather than paleontology, studying other periods with their incomprehensible creatures. These people are you, and must be approached accordingly. In learning of the many American dreads produced between the races, it's simple to distance yourself from the actual subject—how humans react to difference—in order to displace your own unease onto a primitive "other." This is a problem.

Unsure of cement plant security, I was in the boat at first light, pushing into a windless tide. Over the next two days I covered fifty miles, Germantown to Beacon, much of it through Millionaire's Row, the estates of Roosevelts, Vanderbilts, and the like. Most of these can be seen from the river, palatial manors now hosting guided tours rather than debutante balls. On the west bank, perched on a Catskill ridge, there's even a castle, poking its crenellated little towers through the trees.

I know little about architecture, and care even less. Entire libraries have been written on these mansions' designs, but I'll live happily without reading a single paragraph. This isn't to misspeak. I'm greatly pleased that the world has architects, people as fascinated with building design as I am with theological poetry, mink, and the '75 World Series, not to mention table-dancers, but to me it's nothing more than piling squares on top of squares. That these estates still exist, though, providing a rough parity of what the riverfront resembled centuries ago, this was something.

Tom Lewis, an English professor at Skidmore, in Saratoga Springs, wrote a 2005 book concisely titled *The Hudson: A History*. It's a joy. In it, he includes a great deal of Hudson artwork. One painting is by John Heaten, an itinerant working for the Van Bergen family, a prosperous line but hardly of Hudson supernovae like the Livingstons or Van Rensselaers. In 1720, Pere Van Bergen had Heaten paint a mantel piece, an idyll of the farm's everyday. There are horses here, Van Bergens greeting Van Bergens, barns, cows, pastures, and other bucolic whatnot. There are also slaves. The professor returned a phone call.

"That's near Athens, New York, I think. It's just a farm, not one of the great manors. That says a lot. New York doesn't have a terribly honorable relationship with its past."

Who does? Who, for that matter, has a terribly honorable relationship with their present? Lewis' meaning is clear. Many New Yorkers probably don't know slavery existed here, while those who do often think it was confined to the larger estates. "The Dutch thought nothing of selling human flesh," Lewis continued, which applied to the British afterward, though thought was certainly put into it.

In terms of a Hudson farm's treatment of slaves, it was slavery. It stunk. Yet here's proof that at least some New Yorkers were indeed looking inward, trying to find if such a thing as slavery could be justified. It turns out it could.

Lewis talked of Anne Grant's *Memoirs of an American Lady*, a record of pre-Revolution life. Her position was standard. She'd visited the Schuyler estate in Albany, where "even the dark aspect of slavery was softened into a smile." The prevailing valley notion, then, Lewis said, was "that we treat them better than they do in the South." Who knows? Maybe Treblinka was a better gig than Auschwitz, but this isn't the point. Northern slaveholders looked to the South and Caribbean for the same reason many people look to history—to seek solace, finding in the comparison creatures far worse than themselves. Grant and her hosts warmed to thoughts of Hattiesburg and Jamaica, knowing, as the Lady put it, that a New Yorker's relationship between master and slave was "better understood here than in any other place." Ironically, though slaves did receive more *Gee, thanks* liberties in the North—such as the right to occasionally negotiate sale to another master—troublemakers were threatened with elsewhere, or as Lewis put it, "If you give lip, you'll be sent south." Many were, making it a toothy threat.

Today, though slavery and the Holocaust are extremes, people look for such sanctuary all the time. Seek out the greatest trespasses, preferably from a time not your own, and ignore whatever touchy matter swirls in your own soul. Months after I left the river, Joshua Alston, a *Newsweek* columnist, reviewed the growing population of white supremacists in fictional television, an apparent reflection of reality with the inauguration of a black president, American decline, and a lousy economy. Such articles are common, but rather than the usual finger-wagging, Alston breaks away:

> The reason the card-carrying white supremacist lingers in the public imagination is not just because he's scary, but because he fortifies our self-regard in an area where we all occasionally need some convincing. As the puppet of *Avenue Q* sang, "everyone's a little bit racist." On some level we all recognize this, and to acknowledge—or even inflate—white supremacists is to assuage our guilt with

the knowledge that there are people out there far more prejudiced than most of us could ever be.

I saw *Avenue Q*. Along with the Constitution and the infield fly rule, it's America's greatest achievement, a heavily adult *Sesame Street* with actors using hand puppets to sing stinging, raucous songs, with one declaring that while few of us would think to commit hate crimes, we're all a little bit racist, or at least discomfited by variance. Truth, they say, hurts, and to avoid it, we scramble our jets and make for the wild blue, parachuting into history's tender arms, where barbaric minions await our condescension.

So easy to do. Reading a book, walking the street, paddling a river, you simply disappear from the most uncomfortable parts of yourself. As I paddled out of Cementon, I was in full view of Olana, the east-bank studio-home of Frederic Church, Thomas Cole's painting student, who helped imprint the Hudson on the public imagination. This stretch begins the River of Myth. Apart from occasional industrial pockets such as Kingston—endpoint of the now-defunct Delaware and Hudson canal, the D & H, that once fed New York its Pennsylvania anthracite—these miles largely retain the pastoral visions stoking Church and others. (Professor Lewis said they painted a Hudson of the mind. At that time, the Erie Canal was bankrupting valley farms, and iron-mongers and tanneries had stripped most of the trees.) If you don't see many active farms now, great wealth has been drawn here, with mansions and semi-mansions enjoying sloped views to the estuary. Paddling by, if you close your eyes, turn the sod to wheat and the irises to oats, Jaguars and BMWs to oxcarts and hay wagons, twin-250 pleasure boats to oak barges hauling downriver grain, then look again, you'll be drifting through the eighteenth century, and have a series of Van Bergen–like farms to behold.

This is great treatment for whites. There's a bit of self-flagellation to it, using images of slavery, Jim Crow, Indian Wars, and other misfortunes to whip ourselves in reminder, the way certain monk tribes practice self-abuse to recall Original Sin, but turning it over, there's far more sanitarium in it than wailing wall.

I saw them, too, the slaves, scything grain and pruning apples, digging ditches and driving oxen, all beneath the glare of punitive eyes. Through each of these rural townships I could envision purple-black African skin, sweating off humid summers, bitten by cold it had never known, threshing the crops that fed these restless colonies, all on land wrested from Natives. Being white, and what's worse, a WASP, the monster of all whites, I can bathe in these historical salts and hear my dominant voice say, "THEY were worse than YOU." Pity this is so, for two divergent reasons.

Such dodgery, for one, misses the arc. As awful as race relations have been in this country, the graph is remarkable. Geologically, we talk of ten million years as no time at all. What, then, of human time? An average lifespan is seventy-five years. Very good. I paddled in 2009. A black man was in the White House, and African Americans had recently served in the government's top posts. Seventy-five years before, it was 1934. My father's older brother, Owen Osborne Freeman, Jr.—Uncle Chip—was born, and Franklin Roosevelt, of Hudson Dutch stock by way of Hyde Park, struggled with how to mollify the South while stopping lynch mobs. In the end, he failed to support an anti-lynching bill, as Southern votes still went to Democrats for what the Republican Lincoln did sixty-nine years before. Lynchings occurred in the open into the 1950s, when my father was in high school, and up until roughly my own high school days, blacks didn't have many opportunities beyond sports and entertainment—Hispanics, Indians (east and west), or Asians either. In two lifetimes, then, worlds have been made, against the odds of human history.

Much of this, of course, is on the books, legislative progress that has little to do with how people feel. There's truth to this, but it's a cynic's getaway. As Todd Erling said of farm practices, after a while behaviors become reflexive, a transferable maxim. Days after Barack Obama won office, Karen and I visited my sister in Connecticut. She has three kids, at the time nineteen, fourteen, and twelve. I drove the two youngest to their respective activities, asking if their teachers had talked about the election.

"Kind of," my niece said. "I mean sort of. Not really. I don't know."

My nephew, fourteen, was in the timeless boy-man process of not speaking to anyone over fifteen.

"Uh, yeah. I guess."

The Children are the Future? I thought. Toot your horn, Gabriel, but I wouldn't be denied.

"I'm not sure if you guys know what a big deal it is that a black guy was elected, but however people feel about his politics, it's huge."

Looks say more than words. I could tell they had a vague notion, but simply because of their generation it wasn't a shock, no more than a black guy winning the Heisman was a shock to my own childhood, though it may have sent at least one grandfather to an early Reward.

That spring, in April, Karen and I took Shannon south. Karen has friends in D.C., and coming off the winter she needed warmth. We circled the Chesapeake. St. Michael's, in Talbot County, Maryland, lies on the water, a place that had me drifting from Karen's words toward endless back marshes. My God, I thought, a muskrat house, rivers of cattails all about, and here I am talking Roth IRAs. We reach for Jeremiah Johnson and end up as Babbitt, the nation's tragic graph.

Carrying Shannon along Main Street, milky-orange sky to the west, we looked for a place to eat. At a nondescript intersection, two boys, maybe ten, road bikes up and down a rise, one white, the other mixed-race. They moved and talked like people who had come up together. Above them, nearly lost in an unpruned tree, a rusting metal sign tells you Harriet Tubman and Frederick Douglass came from these swamps. A hundred and seventy-some years before, these two separately escaped slavery, fleeing Maryland for better deeds up North. Both knew the Hudson. Douglass found harbor in Manhattan's Underground Railroad, while Tubman, based in the Finger Lakes, helped break a fugitive out of jail in heavily abolitionist Troy, scaring off the slave-catcher. That's not three lifetimes ago, and here, beneath their marker, two kids with trace inklings of the racial hatreds that sent slaves north killed a friendly spring evening together—anecdotal to be sure, but pertinent. Things are changing, which unveils the other blind spot in historical convalescence.

The more obvious component of this patch is refutation. By picturing slaves toiling Hudson manors, by looking upon their masters and saying, "Weren't they awful," I fail to look inward, acknowledging my own bigotries. If I do, I make the comparison—as Anne Grant did—and say, "Well, okay," if anything feeling better. This is the not-so-strange case of Dr. Strangelove.

Dr. Strangelove, we know, is among the greats, a film gaily exposing the lunacies of absolute power. Peter Sellers steals the show, playing an ineffectual American president, the incorruptible Lionel Mandrake, and Dr. Strangelove, the beyond-kook who seduces everyone with glories of nuclear winter. This may have been the first film to satirize Nazis comically.

Strangelove is a German scientist turned American, lurking in a Pentagon war room as the U.S. and Russia head for nuclear combat. Crippled from the waist down, he has a half-mechanical right arm he can't control. When excited, the arm shoots a Nazi salute. At the end, realizing his machinations have turned the American president, he miraculously stands, firing a salute and shouting, "Ya vol, mein Fuhrer!" Earlier, George C. Scott's Bucky Turgidson learns of Strangelove's original name, Merkwurdegliebe, and shrugs his shoulders. "Oh well," he says to a colleague. "A kraut by any other name, eh Stainsy?" Well put. All of us have that inner Strangelove, our reliquary of tribal pride. Denying it, we seek trouble. Embracing it, we might find ease, but it's by searching out the Doctor's motive—our motive—that we seek to understand this remnant imp living within us, and that motive, of course, is annihilation.

Ken Burns is to documentary-making what Van Gogh is to painting. He changed things. His *Civil War* is hypnotic, a trance of America's most fertile epoch, along with its most lethal. Things died here, things were born, while others caught the cold that would kill them.

Late in the series, in the aftermath of Grant's one-hundred-thousand-casualty Wilderness campaign, Burns personalizes the carnage, showing us period photos, gorgeous things of cracked-glass black-and-white. One by one they appear, soldiers in dress, Garrison Keilor's honeyed-homey voice narrating. Bearded and proud, most are from the 77th New York, drawn from Saratoga. Keilor relays each name and rank, and then the fate. "Killed at Cedar Creek." "Killed at Wilderness." "Eye shot out at Spotsylvania." "Union officers, all killed in battle." It's brutal, it's beautiful, and prior to fatherhood may have been the one thing that quashed my normal dread of sentimentality. The Civil War does that to WASPs, one of the few recollections that can. Richard Brookheiser, of *The National Review*, wrote *The Way of the WASP*, claiming that when WASPs vanish, America will remain a WASP nation, given the group's foundational work. In it he acknowledges WASP romance with the Civil War.

"Well," he began when I called him. "Such a complicated question."

I dug the receiver in, awaiting the outpour, but he drew back.

"Of course, I can't recall what I might have been thinking in 1990, but I'd say it was the death toll. Everyone thought it would be an afternoon affair."

Rats. That's true, but all war casualties evoke lamentation. The romance runs deeper.

Reasons vary, but the prettiest ones are thrust out to conceal more unseemly matter, though this doesn't disqualify them. The Portuguese may have started African slavery, other European states may have partaken in it, African kings may have profited from their catching and selling of rivals, Brazil may have been the last nation to ban it, and the Middle East may have the bleakest role with millions of East Africans vanished in Arab sands, but in America, WASPs own slavery. Catholics by and large hadn't shown, and were scowled upon when they did, and Jews were equally marginalized. America has always been a muddle, then, but from colonial times through about the 1960s, the mainframe was WASP—flesh, philosophy, creed.

I worked a field camp one spring on Alaska's Unuk River, in Misty Fjords National Monument. Among the crew of four were a Tsimshian Indian and an Italian American. The five-week project went well. By the last night all the gear was stowed. All we had to do was break out the booze. The Native, Roger, started in on the Italian for white transgressions, beginning with Indians but ending with slaves. It never got out of hand, but the Italian, using the same defense I would have, cast disapproving eyes my way.

"Well, actually, Roger, my people weren't here then," he said.

The darkest devil in me wanted to say, "Well, gee, thanks for showing up when all the work was done," but the darkest devil in me stayed dumb. I shrugged my shoulders.

"Guilty as charged, Rodge," I said, and the night proceeded without incident.

Roger, of course, was right, the Italian guy too mostly. Grimly enough, however, the dumb portion of me had its own point. WASPs were the dominant American class for generations. Slavery and Indian policies are our beastliest endeavors, but emancipation and the fact that Natives weren't wiped out completely—eventually being built into a superior myth, an extreme rarity for conquerors—must be put on the same display. This brings up annihilation, the real reason the Civil War squeezes such emotion from WASPs. Black freedom is the emollient. Emancipation doesn't redeem slavery, but it certainly eases my kind's conflict with it, providing the distraction. My darkest devil that night was simply Dr. Strangelove, throwing out a desperate salute to stave off the inevitable, something fomented by the American Civil War.

The heat of these days didn't quit with dusk. Paddling by what I took to be the Vanderbilt Estate, sweating as I did at noon, I camped in the open woods below. Shortly before, I'd pulled into Rhinecliff, the river-side whistle-stop serving Rhinebeck, one of the valley's most pleasant towns—shady, prosperous, entrepreneurial in small, productive ways. With Manhattan on my mind, Rhinebeck was too far to walk, and the Rhinecliff Hotel is all Rhinecliff has to offer, but what an offer. A colossal yellow-boarded building with white trim, its restaurant is too posh to seat a single customer eleven days on a river, but the maître d', an Aussie, obliged, and I sat among the *bon vivants*, sheepishly eating a Caesar salad with pickled sardines and downing a dozen iced teas. I apologized to the waitress, who couldn't stop smiling, loading me down with raw sugar. A group of kayakers had blown by me a mile back, and here they were, two tables over. The guide, a youthful Long Island Baby Boomer, said hello.

"I passed another canoe with yesterday's group," she said. "She'd come down from Champlain. Said she was going to spend a couple days in Rhinebeck."

I paid the bill and walked back to the dock, hoping to get two or three hours further. Lady Champlain had obviously passed me in Hudson. That was the last I heard of her, though I'm sure she made it. The good weather never faded.

The woods I'd chosen were a state park. Since the mountains, it was the quietest place I slept. No trains, no trucks, just the occasional barge. A veery put me to sleep, and a snorting white-tail woke me, one of four by the sound of bounding hooves outside the tent. This was before sunup. I'd camped on a ridge above the shale beach where I'd stashed the canoe. With all gear in the bags, I swiped a foot back and forth through the pressed leaves my body had left. Anyone pass-ing would only think a wild turkey had been here, clawing acorns.

A forested knob lay mid-river off the shale. Fine place for a runaway slave, I thought, and didn't doubt many had used it. By nine, I passed Hyde Park, hoping for a bit of breakfast, but found only the sturgeon painting at the train stop, aptly including a black crewman. Franklin Roosevelt was reared here, making later decisions not on slaves but nooses. Poughkeepsie, I guessed, would be the first place with accessible eateries, and by the time I paddled beneath an old railroad bridge, pulling out under the active auto crossing below, I was ready to eat the gunnels.

Poughkeepsie is like many towns upriver, having flourished and rotted at the whim of American industry, but it's been gutted twice. When all the Hudson sweat trades were gone—paper, textiles, lumber, quarries, iron—the postwar twentieth century produced something else, technology. International Business Machines (IBM) set up on the river, producing mainframe computers that revolutionized human life. For both white-collar and blue, IBM Poughkeepsie filled voids. Engineers, programmers, and the people who soldered it all together lived here, branching into the suburbs. Kingston, too, employed five thousand IBMers, but these vanished nearly overnight. Throughout the mid-nineties, Poughkeepsie got it as well, and while it wasn't cleaned out, the wreckage is tangible. Wander these streets any day of the week, and you'll live Kris Kristofferson's toasted chronicle of small-city America:

> On the Sunday morning sidewalks
> Wishing Lord that I was stoned
> 'Cause there's something in a Sunday
> That makes a body feel alone
>
> And there's nothing short of dying
> Half as lonesome as the sound
> Of the sleeping city sidewalk
> Sunday morning coming down

How much of America has become this, with the great vision beaten out by life itself? Harvey Flad, the Vassar professor, wrote *Main Street to Main Frames*, which details IBM's Poughkeepsie relationship. I asked him if the lay-offs created a permanent anxiety.

"Absolutely," he said. "No doubt about it." IBM had once been regarded as a lineage, as had much of corporate America. "That's who people were, that's who their family was, but the concept of downsizing left everyone feeling anonymous, a real psychological blow. The corporate culture had created a welfare-style capitalism, and it devastated people." This could be said up and down the Hudson, from white-collar Poughkeepsie to blue-collar Corinth, and it's infected America as well. Trust used to run business. Now mistrust does.

As it happened, I was in Poughkeepsie on a Sunday, sauntering into the train stop's substantial food ring a little before noon, the first customer at an Irish pub. I'd been here twice while living in Hudson, once for a tool-making interview, the other for a concrete-pouring job. The concreters offered, but the meager wage couldn't pull us from our Queens trajectory. That these firms still made things should have been encouraging, but the hollow tenor of employees I met said what you sense on every block—it's here now, but tomorrow will snatch it away, leaving fifty cents on the dollar when it does. That was the previous summer, in the same heat and humidity, though this had little to do with the town's fatigue. The Northeast has kept it up for so long it was bound to happen—the place is exhausted.

Something else has changed. Having disappeared in Alaska for ten years, I noticed things on my return that I'd never thought of before. It's expected in Queens, but shows in Poughkeepsie as well, along with more towns every year: Quite soon—maybe fifty years—America will no longer be considered a white nation.

The simple counter to this is partially right—America has never been white, rather always a mix. True, but as the world's greatest unwitting philosopher, *Raising Arizona's* H-I McDonough, said, "There's what's right and there's what's right." While all races and ethnicities contributed mightily to America's build-up, the majority were whites, and for more of our history than not, white meant WASP. Seated outside the Irish pub, inhaling fish and chips while looking out on Poughkeepsie's in-an-out train traffic, this is far from what I saw. Had I not seen it in dozens of other places, I may not have noticed, but the Hispanic, East Indian, black, and Asian faces shuffling about were only half of it. The races are bleeding into one another, something that has always occurred but is accelerating. (Were a WASP of yore to confront me today, he'd grimace. My dad is pure, but my mother was half Welsh, half German, mud people, and while no one blinks at a WASP/Irish couple today, a hundred and fifty years ago you'd have done better to puke on the Pope than mention it.) Black and white couples certainly raise present-day hackles from either race, but it's lessening, and most people under thirty think it's fine. If all rivers flow to the sea, it's true of human color as well.

Ninety-seven percent of me thinks this is fantastic. People make great hay of the Founders' original intent, but whatever they meant by this article or that is irrelevant, for despite slavery, despite the exclusion of women, despite Indian genocides and removals, despite oppressions, inequities, and outrages of every kind, those men really did see a shining city, where everyone mingled on par. It hasn't happened yet, but it's happening, and it couldn't have happened anywhere else. My bunch solely possesses most of this country's grossest crimes, but owns a healthy portion of rectifying them, and if we haven't reached the Promised Land, we sense that it's there, filling my ninety-seven percent with joy. It's the other three percent—my Dr. Strangelove—that scares the hell out of me.

Moving from Alaska to New York City in late 2008 was a queer arrangement. Not long before Karen and I moved to Queens, Sarah Palin, then Alaska's governor, became John McCain's running mate. Yikes. The country hasn't seen the like, and race is the reason. Palin ignited a flagging campaign, summoning an ancient seethe that has nothing to do with taxes, health care, or small government, but the far deeper fear of annihilation. Whites—WASPs and otherwise—can see it, and in seeing it, feel it in primitive places. The country—long considered THEIR country—is slipping toward the color confluence embodied in faces like half-white, half-black Barack Obama, whom Palin opposed. Whether she knew it or not, the governor subsumed this energy, largely from non–New York America, leaving that city stunned.

By force of physics alone, New York City is reasonably tolerant. Bigotry abounds, but as every racial/religious/ethnic permutation exists there, people have mostly accepted an endlessly morphing demographic. As such, why anyone would flock to an unknown, half-measure governor who moonlights as a lingual terrorist was outside the ken of even conservative New Yorkers. Everyone I met who found out I'd lived in Alaska wanted to know what she was like, probing me as if I'd dated her. Not among those who follow what the governor is up to, I knew little beyond that I'd technically worked for her, only knowing that New York can be as provincial as the rubes they universally chide, having little interest beyond the Hudson's west bank.

For WASPs, this matter of white deliquescence is softer stuff, digested long ago. WASP, however, must be defined along a finer gradient. White Anglo-Saxon Protestant is the broad term, but as with any ethnicity, further distinctions break it down. Ever in search of THE WAY, Protestants have spawned quite a broodstock. From Martin Luther to Joseph Smith to Billy Graham, if you believe in Christ and aren't Catholic, you're a Prod, but let's not be hasty. As derided most aggressively by H. L. Mencken, WASP generally means English-derived Episcopalians tied to the Northeast, nowadays roughly down to my father and a homosexual deacon in New Hampshire. Nevertheless, the tent must not be broadened. By our model, Baptists are a rung beneath bonobos, and Methodists, as eloquently narrated by Robert Redford in *A River Runs Through It*, are "Baptists that can read." As for the rest, well, in Judge Smails' memorable words, the world needs ditchdiggers.

Idiosyncrasies, of course, define ethnicity far more than religion or skin tone. For WASPs, our lack of color gives us color. Most of my college chums were Irish and Italian, punching bags for lovers of ethnic provocation. After one particular stream of jabs profiling the slobbering family life of my mates, they failed once again to return fire. "You can't make fun of WASPs," I said. "We're too boring," and I was right. The mere thought of social interaction finds us retreating deep within ourselves, engaging in internal warfare over the meanings of God, Jackie Robinson, or *The Trojan Women*, anything to avoid emotive interplay with a fellow human being. Samuel Ward, after reading Emily Dickinson, translated WASPy reticence for her longtime fairy godfather, Thomas Higginson. "She is the quintessence of that element we all have who are of Puritan descent," he said. "We came to this country to think our own thoughts with nobody to hinder. We conversed with our own souls till we lost the art of communicating with other people."

Having married into an Irish Catholic family, my sense of the chasm between us has heightened, as has Karen's. For most people, the personal comfort zone is four feet. For WASPs, it's twenty-seven yards, while for the Irish it's three centimeters. It's not the long ceremony, then, nor the drinking, that has me dreading my first family wedding, but the hugging. Most WASPs would rather spend a month in a dentist chair than have even the Lord's arms put around them, let alone hives of glad-happy Irish. Ironically, WASPs have no fear of sex, while for all the fodder Catholic repression has provided top-notch comedians, it's been underplayed. Mention coitus, and every papist in the room ducks. I've told Karen that if she ever upsets me at a family reunion, I'll simply call everyone to attention, stand on a table and say "vagina," watching 3,879 people vaporize in Sister Mary Margaret's mnemonic brimstone.

For my part, my family is a cartoon of WASPiness. Drawn from Mainline Philly, my father's side is filthy in banking and finance—"The WASP Mafia" he calls them. Nature is our chief escape. In hunting and fishing, WASPs find all the rugged demands of outdoor living, but are exclusively pulled to upland game birds like ruffed grouse and dry-fly fishing for trout, the most snobbish of their fields. My grandfather taught my father dry-flying and wing-shooting, and my dad taught me. Trapping is for lesser primates, but as mentioned, we're not pure. Even those who don't hunt or fish adore the memorabilia. My Uncle Chip has three kids. Karen and I went to visit them in Princeton, New Jersey. Living in a restored farmhouse, my cousin's walls are covered with bird-dog prints and fox-hunting horns. The conversation was strained and impersonal, just the way we like it. On the train home, Karen said, "My God, I sat there the whole time saying, "Jesus, these people are WASPy." Damn right, sister, and if you don't like it you can cart yourself back to Old Kildare.

Such tribal categorizing constitutes large chunks of not only bloodlines but culture, and our greatest minds haven't shrunk from it. Robert Frost raked it over in several poems, depicting the terror aroused by the threat of ethnic collapse. "The Ax Helve" is the finest, where a French Canadian logger asserts himself into his Yankee neighbor's mind. It's a friendly encounter, but the mutual paranoia of cultural annihilation holds it on a string.

It's said that human nature is a reflection of Mother Nature. If that's true, then orogeny is your allegory for cultural collision. Any mountain chain will do. Land rises and falls, with each event leaving traces of itself as others ascend. Take the Adirondacks. Their peaks consist of Precambrian rock, resisting two billion years of erosion. Human history, too, is strewn with like dynamics. One of my favorite paintings shows a Viking warrior knee-deep in a river, dropping pagan idols under the eye of converting priests. As Thor floats away, this newest lamb grieves for the old ways, yet the Norse/Germanic cultures clung where they could. Tuesday, Wednesday, Thursday, and Friday are eponyms of the lost gods, Christmas trees descend from winter solstice rites, and the Easter Bunny with its eggs were symbols of the spring equinox. The Vikings, of course, are far from all.

Most mountains are built by convergent tectonics. When two plates hit, one slides beneath the other, heating as it nears the earth's core, where it either shoots lava across the dominant plate or metamorphoses rock within standing beds. This is as attractive a metaphor for how Native Americans survived Europeans as there is, and such dynamics predate the species. Athens is gone, Rome too, but what thousands of lesser-knowns have vanished, leaking what magma they could to the surface? Alexis de Tocqueville, in *Democracy in America*, describes the "Mound People" in the Mississippi Valley. Their only remains are a series of earthen mounds, the purpose unknown to "the Indians of our time." "How strange does it appear," de Tocqueville continues, "that nations have existed, and afterwards . . . the remembrance of their very names is effaced . . . though perhaps there is not one which has not left behind it some tomb in memory of its passage!" Races, cultures, and ethnicities, then, have subsumed one another since *Australopithecus*, with the mute residue—Stonehenge, Easter Island—affirming what every human fears most, that our suspicions are not unfounded, that annihilation happens, which is why the Civil War elicits from WASPs such mawkish pining.

For Southerners, it's simple. They were subsumed themselves during the war, relinquishing a cherished culture to a hated other. On the other hand, many Northerners feel that emancipation atones for slavery, the nation's seminal infirmity. Underpinning all this, however, is a recognition, usually tacit, that the war signaled the first cracks in WASP dominion. Its demise would take another century, but the self-appointed WASP aristocracy crested with the Civil War.

Partly this is breeding, partly principle. Appomattox ended slavery. While this didn't free blacks in the way the Fourteenth Amendment expressed, it vaulted the Great Promise forward. Non-WASP whites fared better. The war legitimized their citizenship. America's chief antebellum immigrants were German and Irish, roughly handled by the WASP majority. War changes that. German and Irish units fought on par with Yankee regiments, elevating their status in the eyes of "Natavists." A single anecdote relays at least one Irishman's gunpowder assimilation, a microcosm of the larger spectacle. During one fight, confederates surrounded a Northern standard-bearer, an Irishman.

"Give me that flag, Yankee," one shouted.

"You can have it," the man said. "Because you called me 'Yankee' you can have it."

The next great waves came soon after and didn't stop—Italians, Poles, Jews, Europe in general. These had to prove themselves in the World Wars, and did, but for WASPs, it started with that Irishman's recognition that what separated his kind from our kind was no longer easily discerned.

Nowadays, of course, most parts of most WASPs think this is good, a leading vector in the country's upward racial tilt. Pricked on one side by everyone we've suppressed—blacks, Natives, white Catholics, Hispanics, Jews, everybody—and on the other by our own conscience, WASPs by the 1960s finally kicked open the door, allowing the country's principled equality to fully fruit, something recently acknowledged by several non-WASPs. Joseph Epstein, from "In a Snob-Free Zone," writes, "[M]any children of established WASP families . . . were feeling guilty of their inherited wealth, and looking for ways to redistribute it in the larger society. The WASP old guard put up the white flag without a shot being fired, [and] suddenly bars began to drop." Slightly disgusted by the surrender of such advantage, Epstein thinks WASPs "a little despised for having done so." Fareed Zakaria, on the other hand, laments not the manner of WASP capitulation but the standards it killed. "[I]n the end," he says in *The Future of Liberty*, "WASPs opened the doors to their club . . . partly because they were pushed, but also because they knew it was the right thing to do. Confronted with a choice between their privilege and their values, they chose the latter."

From here, he says, the story is mixed:

It is easy to mock the Anglo-American elite with their striking air of high-minded paternalism, born of a cultural sense of superiority. But it also embodied certain values—fair play, decency, liberty, and a Protestant sense of mission—that helped set standards for society. Of course these codes were artificial and . . . often abused. . . . But so what? . . . Standards represent a society's highest aspirations, not its complex realities. When powerful people acknowledge that there are certain standards for behavior, they limit their own power . . . [signaling] to society, "*This is what we strive for.*"

He ends with a back-door encomium, noting that today, with the fall of WASP self-imposition, we've come to "expect very little of those in . . . power and they rarely disappoint us."

Personally, parts of me find validation here. The nation started with a vision, and though bigotry, fear, and exclusion retarded it, it's now been largely realized, with the erosion of WASP hypocrisy providing the critical mass. This may sound self-gratifying, but history doesn't provide many parallels. "White people have made tremendous progress since the 1960s," Shelby Steele, a black Stanford scholar, said in an interview, "and have never given themselves credit." The trouble is, my dirtier three percent hears these comments and flings out that involuntary arm. This buried tyrant is in most of us. Fortunately, if he's indelible, he's appeasable. All he needs is a little air. As a Brit would say, take him for walkies, where he can pee on trees and roll in grass. Cooping it up, denying it exists, allows it to fester, making a dangerous brew, the likes of which "the real America" to whom Sarah Palin alludes has freely imbibed.

Pushing off from the rip-rap where I'd stashed the canoe, I'd hoped to make I-84 by dusk—Newburgh/Beacon—but wasn't hopeful. The tide shifted, though, and the sun beat any wind into hiding. Sweating joyfully, I stroked away, with barges and pleasure boats futzing toward their own purposes. Gulls spiraled above, while along the banks grasshopper nations lulled their summer hum.

I thought the Ashokan Reservoir might be near, the place inspiring Jay Ungar's stirring fiddle work from Burns' *Civil War*. It wasn't, being near Kingston, but no matter. I remembered a story where someone swam the Ashokan, near a guy playing guitar. She left, only to realize that it had been Bob Dylan. Two miles wide of river makes a forgiving amphitheater, and "Tangled Up in Blue" burst out of me, the sun tickling the river like mosquito legs. "We drove that car as far as we could," it goes, "and abandoned it out West," the line we've been singing since Plymouth Rock. Ain't Bobby so cool.

Below Poughkeepsie, the banks become less farm friendly, more rugged, though none of it had left me—the upriver slave dreams, Poughkeepsie's kaleidoscopic skin parade, nor, for that matter, the sense I'd had in Albany that American racial tensions were re-flaring. For this I needed the Book of Mel, Mel Brooks, and the fat-happy blowhard of *Blazing Saddles*, the perfect foil to a WASP Dr. Strangelove.

Deadeye social commentary separates the likes of *Caddyshack* and *Blazing Saddles* from lesser romps. We laugh and remember because our ugliest parts are tickled. When the black caddy overhears Judge Smails tell one about the priest, the rabbi, and the colored boy, then grinds down the judge's favorite shoes, the image lasts because it mirrors what we know. If non-WASPs, then, want to know how WASPs really feel about The Great Other's encroachment upon our little cotillion, *Blazing Saddles* is the place to go.

David Huddleston plays Olson Johnson, one of many dolts black Sherriff Bart must save. With Rockridge under threat, all meet upon a hill—the inbred WASPs with the black, Chinese, and Irish rail workers. In exchange for their service, the workers demand land. Huddleston—huge, red-faced, unconsciously candid—says, "Alright. We'll give some land to the niggers and the chinks, but we don't want the Irish," and from here Brooks is too good. Several leprechauns, mumbling Gaelic, walk off, with the bucktoothed Chinese and minstrel-tinted blacks in full support. Recognizing his gaffe more as undue inequity than bad politics, Huddleston's great, flesh-bagged face softens to a Santa Claus smile. "Aw, prairie crud," he says, "everybody," the sentiment that started with the Civil War and consummated with Civil Rights.

Having surrendered the notion that I'll ever escape prejudice entirely, I've reorganized, pleased that America's promised egalitarianism will likely take hold. I can only do so, however, by airing out my vestige tribalism with the ample humor ethnic difference allows. Such a strategy keeps me on the upward arc without denying that while racial reconstitution is an overall good, it will be different, and that my spackled reservations signal little more than my humanity.

As I paddled, we had a black president, who refreshingly expresses that race is not simple, but a labyrinth of past, present, and future, a dozen minotaurs for every pot of gold. If my three-percent Strangelove fears the annihilation of WASP culture, I understand that's part of the complexity. Fatherhood compounded it. Shannon's generation will no longer be a white majority, with WASPs ever smaller as "white" segments into Italian, Irish, and so on. Hispanics make bigger gains every year, Africans and Eastern Europeans too, and I'd deny trace unease over this only through dishonesty. America has always had corruption and violence, but it's homegrown, adjusted to in the same way people live with birth defects. Absorptions have been made, the Mafia being the biggest, but Mexicans will import their own brand of corruption and pronounced castes, while Africans have fled grizzly war zones with all that entails. Eastern Bloc Euros are a separate concern. A cousin of mine is on a SWAT team in Denver. I asked him who scared them most. He didn't think. "Russians. Their nasty isn't our nasty."

My guilt over slavery and other abominations remains strong, but mitigates with age. As a kid, I was certain prejudice was unique to my kind. Three cheers for naiveté, for if one thing links all humans, it's the need for group identity. Mexicans have had it rough here, but other Latin migrants say the American border is a cinch if you make it through Mexico. Blacks have a skin-tone hierarchy among themselves, the Japanese are famous for self-supremacy, and we can't toss up the Khmer Rouge, Rwanda, or El Tiempo de Los Zopilotes to the White Devil alone. A great many Native American tribal names, too, translate as "The First People," "The Real People," or "The True Human Beings," and while the Trail of Tears is as low as WASPs sank, the pre-Columbian Cherokee weren't known for cultural accommodation. Lingual studies trace them west, where they cut a swath east. The Lenni Lenape lived in the Hudson/Delaware region, and after subduing them, the Cherokee dubbed them "women," stripping them of their rights. In Alaska, you can call most non-Eskimo Natives anything you want—Native, Indian, Native American—but don't call them "Eskimo," or "dirty *dutna*" in regional lingo. Jews aren't exempt either. Far from it. My pop retired to Arizona, where he regularly golfs. In both looks and humor, his best friend is Don Rickles Jewish. My dad is a screaming liberal, Alan a staunch conservative. They putz around the links, then, having fun with that, but mostly wallow in their shared love of ethnic humor. One day, Alan explained the Jewish totem.

"German Jews are at the top. Russians at the bottom. Everyone else jockeys for the middle."

My pop teed his drive, contemplating.

"Jesus," he said. "You mean even among Jews krauts are the Master Race? That's sick."

Poor Alan. He never looked at it that way.

"I guess it is a little sick," he said, then teed up his own drive.

America has had great racial difficulty largely because of WASPs, but given that all the world's "True People" meet here hasn't made it easier. Nothing, though, is stable. As generations plod forth and we're further alloyed by the Great Homogenizer—human sex appeal—racial and ethnic dilution both relieve and exacerbate tensions. If all rivers go to the sea, most fight it—slowing, ox-bowing, anything to abate the equalizing salts. As humanity blends, resistance will rise, and this, more than anything political, has driven the white upwelling triggered by Barack Obama. Whether this is wicked or evil or reactionary I can't say, only that it's as natural as flowing water.

There is an advanced model. Twenty-five miles from Manhattan, splitting turf between the Jersey side's Hudson and Ramapo watersheds, the Ramapough Mountain People have maintained backwoods traditions and lifestyles normally matched to Kentucky. Racially, they're tough to finger. Calling themselves the Ramapough Mountain Indians, they've been designated as such, but many feel this was done to deny their black heritage. Most bear Dutch surnames bequeathed by the Hudson's first whites, slave owners. Ben McGrath covered the Ramapough in a *New Yorker* article months after I floated. Toxic dumps from an old auto painting factory and colonial iron mine have kept outsiders at bay, but the land is healing. In a disputed 2006 incident, a park ranger shot and killed a Ramapough man, bringing attention.

Derisively, they're known as "Jackson Whites," a name as murky as their ethnic makeup. Runaway slaves were known as "jacks," and one theory has "Jackson Whites" as a perversion of "Jacks and Whites," for it's thought that latter-day hippies had mingled with the runaways and Tuscarora Indians, whom themselves had fled the British. Another offering puts the term with the British General Jackson, who imported prostitutes while provosting Revolution Manhattan. Some ships carried British whites, others West Indian blacks. The blacks were lost at sea, while the whites ran West when the Brits abandoned New York. Here, "Jackson's Whites" ran into the spawn of slaves, Indians, and Dutch renegades, along with AWOL German mercenaries. A final theory sources Andrew Jackson. Old Hickory was famous for many things, the absorption of lower-class whites into democracy among them. Citing vote-mongering, critics said this included anyone, the bronzish Ramapough too, who became locally known as "[Andrew] Jackson's Whites."

Whatever the etymology, whatever the DNA quilt, the Ramapough are a remarkable conflation of America's racial distress, as well as a vestige of the hard-hitting country life that many feel forged the nation's character. That they've lasted this long is astonishing, but generations of cultural isolation and recent infringements have loosed the bolts. As early as 1938, George Weller wrote in *The New Yorker* that "oblivion is gathering around the Jackson Whites," and by 2010, as interviewed by McGrath, Ramapough paterfamilias Roger De Groat anointed himself "The Last of the Mohicans." McGrath's article is titled "Strangers on the Mountain," leaving undecided who the strangers are, but to anyone reading, the slippage of one culture beneath another is razor on bone.

I hadn't heard of the Ramapough when I moved to Queens, but knew the lifestyle. Hunting, fishing, trapping. Growing a garden. Work with dirt, work with blood. It's myth mostly, but many see this as White Life. To those asking, I tried to explain this as Sarah Palin's appeal—the white, church-going sex bomb who dropped like a meteor from fish-hunt happy Alaska. "That's Appalachia," a friend of Karen's said, "not the whole country."

That's wrong. Twenty-five years ago, my father and I attended a trapper's convention in Chaplin, Connecticut. Fifty people were there, most flannelled, bearded men. On the way out, we walked by a pickup. A bottle of Mr. Boston lay across an ammo box and stack of blue leaflets, a particularly psychotic Hitler photo on display, captioned, "Next Time, No More Mr. Nice Guy." This was Connecticut. Rhode Island has its Swamp Yankees, most of Pennsylvania is known as Pennsyltucky, the Adirondacks have their brew, select Vermonters call bogs "nigger-heads," New Hampshire is Arkansas with snow, and the middle of Maine is no place for L.L.Beaners with their multi-cultural notions. That's just the Northeast. Old-line WASPs took three centuries to assimilate cultural disintegration, and we're still not thrilled. All around the country, then, many whites, WASP or no, fear the end of a life they think is theirs by right of Election, and the fear—if morally ungrounded—isn't unwarranted. If America is merging racially and ethnically, we're also urbanizing, growing distasteful of trot lines, fur sheds, deer stands, and even—Gasp!—wing-shooting ruffed grouse. Lifestyles and bloodlines will hang on, but like the Ramapough, oblivion can be sensed because it's there. White privilege is of course mixed into this, and that will go too, lost to Shannon's children if not to her, and to expect utter compliance throughout the KINGDOM is to expect of human beings too much. The arc has drifted well, and does still, but other forces array. From the Cro-Magnon to the Celts to the Mound People to the Jackson

Whites, our collective genetic memory knows cultural dissolution is no trick of paranoia. We're drifting indeed, and can only hope in the Hope of our better angels.

For my part, I've befriended Strangelove. Try to drive him out, he grows bigger. Ignore him, he'll ambush you. It's best to beguile him, make him feel important, allowing Olson Johnson to win every day, and how couldn't he?

With evening pressing, I skirted moored boats in the Wappingers Falls marina, and then those of Chelsea. The I-84 crossing—my only Hudson vantage until now—was in view. Across the water, on river-right, Newburgh's and Roseton's bankside factories—vacant and bricked—competed with revitalizing efforts. Visible chemicals and sewage long gone, condos and speedboats again appeal.

Tawana Brawley is from Wappingers Falls. As a teenager in 1987, she doused poor Al Sharpton with egg when she coaxed local cops into believing that multiple white men had raped her. They hadn't, but the fact that the trial made national news for three years revealed a shift in the country's power differential—if not an earthquake, then at least a frost heave. Previously, it was attention-hungry white women who falsified black rape. That Brawley's caper played out so effectively, however, only underscored the nation's racial anxieties, here exemplified in the mid-Hudson Valley.

Following his old man's public gusto, Robert Kennedy, Jr., has done much to restore the Hudson. In 1984, he probed Newburgh's efforts to reestablish river access, asking if it would be open to the public. He must have been speaking directly to *Merkwurdegliebe*. According to Kennedy, the private developer replied, "We are not going to have spades drinking and screwing and swimming around our *new* boat ramp, if that's what you mean by the public!"

What can we do but tend to ourselves? For race in America, the Hudson is where it began. Dutch came here, and English, and different German sects, rubbing shoulders with Indians, themselves gripped in aeonic ethnic angst. African slaves were imported, making a right-merry mess, but from that mess came a country where others poured in, mostly through the Hudson. That winter, I'd done a few jobs for a roofer, off-the-books stuff involving spreading tar and trying not to vomit off four-story ledges. One job was in Brooklyn Heights, with a clear shot of Ellis Island. If we no longer come through there, we still congregate in New York, and the stories never bore.

While Karen worked all summer, I'd toss Shannon in the Bjorn and walk the borough. Queens vies with the Bronx every year for the planet's most diverse community. Look for anyone here and you'll find them, most having fled the twentieth-century blood pool. Shannon's pediatrician was Romanian, as were many in the neighborhood, orphans of Nicolae Ceauşescu, and clipped African and Haitian French were all we heard passing the cab court on our way to the river. Turks and South Koreans run convenience stores, serving Irish, Hondurans, Salvadorans, Guatemalans, and Mexicans, along with every tint of Balkanite. They all mingle, they all date, they all breed, mixing as we always have. One day, heading to Central Park, we popped up on the 7 Train platform at Forty-Sixth/Bliss, passing the usual congeries. At the end hunched a wheelchaired Cambodian, graying, both legs gone. I'd lived in Cambodian-thick San Francisco. The square face, boxed jaw, and Beatle-wig hair were unmistakable. The guy might have had an accident, maybe something congenital, but I doubt it. Pol Pot likely crippled him, rifle, mine, or ax, and somehow he'd clawed to New York. What the hell do I know about the world? Prairie crud. Everybody.

I didn't make the bridge, but came close enough. A half mile above, eyeing a wooded peninsula choked round with river lettuce, I chatted up Strangelove, half dangling his shirtless five-inch frame off the bow. He'd had a good day. Plenty of sunshine, lots of exercise, jokes all around. We laughed at the way Karen falls into the American-Irish habit of droning on about Brits and rain and famine and everything people from New Rochelle have never known. We give her five minutes, then kick into the worst Irish accent I can muster, the Lucky Charms bit: "peenkk hharts, bloo doimonds, a'range stairz, green clohvairs . . ." She laughs too.

Unloading the boat, I dragged it into the cottonwoods, then paused.

"Go ahead, little buddy. Tell us the one about the priest, the rabbi, and the colored boy again."

He did, adding a paunchy *abuela* to keep current. A good time was had by all, then with the canoe buried in fern fronds, I cozied him back in his pouch and walked the tracks to Beacon.

The Wolf

Beacon is Pete Seeger's home, though that didn't pull me off the river. Mostly I hankered for another shower and bed with more Red Sox torture, but Seeger is something of a lion in Hudson lore as well as a hinge figure in how Americans view their environment. Not many know this, or this region's part in it, and if I could spend a little time at a nameless American shrine while finding out if the Yankees had taken the Pentagon, then another tentless night couldn't be bad.

The year before, Karen and I had spent an afternoon in Beacon, another Hudson revivalist town. Arts are the hope here, but from an afternoon's observation, the going was about level with Hudson's—a few nice restaurants sprinkled in with the boutiques, nothing to replace the past centuries' industrial roar.

Beacon made hats. In the nineteenth century, five hundred hat factories operated here, competing with nearby Danbury, Connecticut, for national hat capital. Bricks, too, a mid-Hudson bonanza, came from clays the glaciers put down. Drifting into the peninsula, peering through a silty ebb, red bricks appeared to be the region's natural rock, from decades, I imagined, of snapped crane cables and poorly loaded barges. For at least a half mile, this reef lines the east bank, the sun-baked blocks holding their shape for blue crab and juvenile shad up to a century after production. Oddly, the bricks seemed to be all that remained. Where was the factory? With the boat beached, I stepped out, footing the introduced cobble, green plants snaking through the cracks. Each brick was marked "Brockway." Muskrat pellets dotted a few half in, half out of the water, while above, drooped from an ash, an oriole nest loomed over the tide.

Further south, in the Tappan Zee, Haverstraw's blue clays fed New York's nineteenth-century boom with up to 325 million bricks a year, and Frank Baum, *The Wizard of Oz* inspiration, attended school in Peekskill, where the Dutch had built a yellow brick road. Granite, too, came from Peekskill, and marble from Ossining, the stuff with which Elam Lynds forced prisoners to build Sing Sing in 1825. Trap rock, slate rock, red rock. Brownstone, flagstone, limestone. Cement, cement, cement. Grit, grit, grit. From Glens Falls to the Palisades, Hudson mineral combined with Adirondack timber to nearly build New York. Before the modern mantra, then, New York was local before local was cool, largely because upriver brickies and quarrymen made it that way, though of course it didn't last. By the 1990s, eighty percent of Beacon's industrial sites alone were boarded up, making way for Dia:Beacon, a 300,000-square-foot art tabernacle, built from an old printing factory in 2003. As with Hudson and most other valley towns, Beacon has put its dreams elsewhere than grease and gears. While Storm King Mountain, not far to the south, may not be responsible, it is tangential, for what didn't happen there from 1963 to 1980 helped retool a national zeitgeist.

The peninsula was further out than I'd thought, maybe two miles, and by the time I'd hopped the train station fence and walked up Main Street, night had fallen. Not surprisingly, Beacon is built of brick. It has size, but not enough for lodging, which the ice cream parlor attendant told me, saying the closest hotel was in Fishkill. Thirteen miles later, a cab dumped me at the Quality Inn near the prisons we pass on our way to the Endless Mountains.

Karen was well, Shannon too. I told her it might be three days, no more. What she said I don't remember, just that air of relief, something I'd never heard. We'd had a brief, happy life as a distance couple, and I hoped that wasn't our best venue. "It's marriage," a friend had told me. "Don't think too much out there. Wake up every morning and make that day a good one. Look further out, and the trouble starts." It sounded like AA.

Flicking on the tube, the Red Sox were sunk. Of that alone I was sure. The river made me antsy. For months now I'd felt a stifling I'd never felt, and as much as I wanted to get back to Shannon and Karen, most of me would have rather met them on the bank, tossed them in the boat, and kept going, forever. The fatigue of the first nights had faded, the sun and constant paddling re-instilling that morning-thirst encouraged by thorough contentment. Lousy movies, lousy cop shows, lousy cable news—nothing worked, and I finally nodded off around 2:00 a.m., calling a cab a few hours later.

Dropped at the train station, I slipped around the "No Entry" signs and rewalked the tracks in the increasing light. This section is clear—no houses on the eastern hill, only river to the west. When the rails rang, I hopped into the brush, evading commuter trains. I picked a box turtle up and put him on the riverside where it was headed, then came upon a dying Monarch, whose Mexican migration had been thwarted by train draft. The black and salmon-flesh wings moved a bit, but death was certain. I lifted it from the gravel, then walked to the greenery, laying it in old oak leaves. Someone could live a hundred thousand years, and never satisfactorily answer whether humans exist inside or outside of nature.

Lately, we're all in. For most of our existence, we've done everything we could to leave nature, with survival as the reason. We ceaselessly mull whether amorality drives the world or if divine harmony is the engine. We do know this: we need to survive, and to do so within nature is brutal, as in its root, brutish. "Nature," Katharine Hepburn said to Bogey in *The African Queen*, "is what we were meant to rise above." That statement has many implications, most controversial, but to eke out the living we did for so long, to now thrive in the convenience we enjoy, we've had to remove from nature somewhat, providing Eden its pull—everyone, from the grungiest hippie down, senses that we were in nature once but left, now caught between our former home and wherever we might be headed. Currently, with our lifestyles affecting the earth as they are, growing numbers are shouting "Wait!"—scrambling to reclaim the home we've abandoned. This argument has tremendous theological import, but practically speaking, many feel it requires swifter resolution.

Energy is the topic. We forget that. Nature's essence, after all, is only matter robbing matter for energy, including us. We began rustling savannahs for meat and fruit in the manner of other creatures, before turning to fire, draft animals, and hydropower. A water wheel was one thing, but when internal combustion harnessed fossil fuels, the world changed. A dam alters a river's ecology. Coal plants and truck engines do more. How much more, of course, is how friendships are lost in the modern age.

Seeger's environmental story is typical. It just happened earlier than most. Born in 1919, he gained fame as a traveling singer, but yearned for the childhood country life he'd known in Patterson, New York, east of Fishkill. Accordingly, he moved to Beacon, where along with others he noticed the bilge the Hudson had become. In 1963, as the sixties were becoming what they became, Consolidated Edison, or ConEd, proposed blasting away a piece of Storm King Mountain north of West Point, where they'd suck water up, contain it, then generate energy as it tumbled down, all to feed the City-That-Never-Sleeps' neon lust. Mowton LeCompte Waring, fresh from completing the still-operating nuclear facility at Indian Point below Peekskill, designed Storm King. Permitting was perfunctory then, and neither Waring nor ConEd were prepared for the citizen glut that formed the Scenic Hudson Preservation Conference.

At that time, Henry Thoreau was an idyll of freshman lit, and "environment" meant little more than its origin—"surroundings." Rachel Carson, though, had published *Silent Spring* the year before, and America's industrial run had turned skies and water bodies into something even pro-industrialists couldn't stomach. Fishermen, shedding every political tie when the stripers run, became one of Scenic Hudson's stoutest blocs. As Fran Dunwell pointed out, the conglomerate launched a publicity campaign that "tapped a national consciousness." All it needed was a fight, and Storm King offered it.

Whether the American court system is just I can't say, only that it's slow. Finally, in 1980, threatened with law suit after law suit—including exposure of Indian Point as a horrific fish killer—ConEd conceded, dropping plans for Storm King and promising to address its nuclear fish kills. Seventeen years is long, and much else happened to shape the nation's environmental attitude during that time, but Storm King is the precedent, when courts first considered "the preservation of natural beauty and national historic shrines" while assessing public works. The decision inspired later Hudson mastiffs like Robert Kennedy, Jr., and John Cronin, *The Riverkeeper*'s first captain, a boat still patrolling potential Hudson polluters. Storm King also hatched environmental organizations across the country, and led Pete Seeger to his strange idea.

In 1961, before Storm King, Seeger wrote "Sailing Up My Dirty Stream":

> Sailing up my dirty stream
> Still I love it and I'll keep the dream
> That some day, though maybe not this year
> My Hudson River will once again run clear

Those engaged in Storm King legalities tap-danced around him. His Socialist ties were arsenic in those days, and to win the case, lawyers knew they needed John Birchers along with the beatniks and birdwatchers. The singer kept singing, though, and more importantly, thinking. Given a book detailing old Hudson sloops, he envisioned one's return, a ship teaching the curious both the marvel and importance of everyday estuary life. Not one for dreams unrealized, Seeger acted, and *The Clearwater*, built in Maine, first touched the Hudson in 1969, its flapped sails today more hope than relic, and a living symbol of both the river's and nation's remarkable forty-year ecological recovery.

What does this really mean though? From Henderson Lake to Beacon, I probably couldn't have filled the canoe with the trash I saw, and while PCBs and other toxins still haunt the water, to the eye everything runs clear, a marked improvement. Aldo Leopold, a Wisconsinite, published *A Sand County Almanac* in 1949, calling for a land ethic, something that treated wilderness with respect while allowing for the spiritual, physical, and economic interaction of human beings and landscape. Leopold was quite literally a voice in the wilderness, shunned by sixties environmentalists who favored cordoning natural places off to anyone but the Grateful Dead. Fortunately, things have matured, with many organizations merging the necessity of sixties spunk with Leopold's prudent wisdom.

The Open Space Institute (OSI), for instance, is responsible for Henderson Lake's access. OSI has purchased around a hundred thousand acres from Manhattan to the Adirondacks, including the ten thousand–acre Tahawus tract abandoned by NL Industries in the eighties. Joe Martens, OSI's 2009 president and now the head of the DEC, helped broker the 2003 deal. I asked if OSI was motivated by preservation alone.

"That camp still exists," he said by phone, "devoted exclusively to restrictive use, but important economic resentment comes with that. We try to do more than one thing at once, take a pragmatic approach to what works best sale to sale."

Such elastics made the Tahawus purchase agreeable to mountain residents who have enough difficulty without do-gooders buying up their environment to make private terrariums. OSI purchases acreage, but farms out the management to others, which for Tahawus mostly means New York State. The land lies within the park, leaving it subject to the garbled but effective patchwork of designated use.

"The McNaughton Cottage is one example," Martens went on. "It dates to 1829, the only original mining structure. Teddy Roosevelt was staying there when McKinley got shot. A quarter of a million dollars later, we've restored it, where it will be both a historic attraction as well as a conference center for dialogue about the future of the Northern Forest."

OSI has additionally restored a fire tower and old blast furnace, drawing tourists. Including Henderson Lake and the historic properties, seven thousand acres went as public land, while the remainder is a private in-holding for sustainable timber harvesting.

"There was pushback by organizations who oppose in-holdings," Martens said, "but I don't think it would have happened otherwise. Communities must be worked with." His voice lacked the silent regret of compromise, rather bearing a rectitude well earned by splitting the difference.

Northern Woodlands is another example, maybe the best of convergent redneck and hippie attitudes. Stephen Long, the organization's founder, explained to me that he wanted "a new way of looking at the forest as a means of distinguishing ourselves from older, less productive ways . . . one that has room for both preservation and use, botany and board feet." It operates out of Corinth, Vermont, but covers forests across New England and New York. *Northern Woodlands*, its magazine, might be unique, providing advice on how to sharpen mill blades alongside where to find nesting wood thrushes. Dave Mance, an editor, built on Long's thoughts: "We're trying to promote the notion of rural. This means songbirds and loggers. Our goal is to get people to see humankind as a part of nature, not separate from. In rural areas, this is status quo. In more urban areas it's being lost as people drift to either end of the spectrum, [which are] . . . the suburban alternative—strip malls and McMansions—or the gentrified alternative, where nature becomes faux-sacred and put behind a velvet rope. These two extremes seem antithetical but the result is the same—man and nature become divorced. I suspect that this is an evolved message, but at thirty-four don't feel comfortable saying if it is or not. I will say that our readers always surprise me. They're 'tree-huggers' who own chainsaws. They're loggers who actively support clean air/clean water initiatives, reaffirming my hunch that the world is a lot grayer than is often reported."

Mance's readers, then, are North Creek's greennecks, whose lineage lies with the first Adirondack hunters clamoring for nineteenth-century conservation. His assessment, too, negotiates the slick footing regarding humanity's place in nature, mostly by pointing out that the world is indeed gray, with our origin likely lost in that fog. His message, moreover, is, in fact, evolved, a comfort to pragmatists everywhere weary of the "growth overall versus no-humans-allowed" antipodes. Martens, Mance, and Long reflect the same burgeoning desire for practicality now pervading American agriculture through people like Sam Simon, a great encouragement. The trouble is, the country's—and by extension the world's—desire for energy runs unabated, and it's here where both our trickiest challenges lie and humanity most separates from nature.

Knowing how calamitous it would be to a future generation, Thomas Jefferson said of the slave economy, "It's like holding a wolf by the ears. You don't like it, but don't dare let go." A comparison of today's fossil fuel economy with America's 246-year reliance on slavery is too offensive to bear weight. That's a shame, for in Jefferson's analogy, the twenty-first century has a plum metaphor for an economic dilemma likely to bestow round-the-bend calamities of its own.

I've given up on global warming. It's happening, but whether humanity is the prime mover or not is a question too politically rancid to be of use. As far as whether the planet is getting warmer, it is. I was in Yakutat for ten years, zippo in glacier time. Still, the big ice retreated noticeably every year, though this is a suspect indicator of man's involvement. That the northern half of the lower forty-eight is habitable testifies to a warming trend that not only predates human industry, but on the whole has been beneficial to earthly life. Our problems, however, seem beyond natural cycles, and people far more studied than me see in the trend's recent spike an unfavorable future.

"The science is pretty dark," Bill McKibben said. He's an upbeat guy, but across the table his brow clouded when I asked about climate change. I wondered whether examples like the Hudson recovery provided hope. They did, but don't address carbon dioxide (CO_2), which McKibben said is the real boogeyman. John Elder, ever waiting his turn, did what poets do best, provided a comparison.

"It's like when you're office is a mess. It looks nicer when you neaten the books and papers, gather the trash, but the deep grunge is in the carpet. You need to vacuum."

McKibben's solution is simple. Less leads to more. Less population, less buying, less energy means stronger community ties, more control of your time, and a cleaner world. He's right, of course, in that less people buying less stuff would reduce carbon emissions, but as with most obvious solutions, human nature foils it. You can't tell people how many kids to have. You can't tell people how much stuff to buy. Reproduction and the accumulation of goods—*tchotchke* above all—are urges tattooed upon us from an evolution of scratch living. In America, combine this inheritance with our hypersensitivity to individual freedom and you're sunk. As with the problem of blaming GE for PCBs when your house is full of appliances, we're saddled with wanting a cleaner earth while surrendering none of the comforts that fossil fuels provide or in any way inhibiting our conception of free will. Joshua Lawrence Chamberlain commanded Maine's famous 20th Regiment at the Battle of Gettysburg. With few men, he held a position that would have lost the battle had the Confederates taken it. Shy on ammo, he ordered a bayonet charge, surprising the Alabamans below. Years later, reflecting on his thoughts to either retreat or charge, he wrote, "It can't be the former, but how can it be the latter?" He had his own wolf by the ears, then, but a global economy is not a spot decision on a battlefield, and to date we're showing few signs that we either have any idea what to do or the gumption to act if we did.

"Lobbying favors old ideas," McKibben said. "That's its true harm. Everyone points to the corruption and cronyism, and there is that, but mainly what it does is beat back innovation. You'll see it in the future. Wind power, or solar maybe, will get a foothold, and their lobbyists will crowd out tidal inventions, or whatever might be the next best thing. That's the trouble with our economic model. It's based on the morning's news, not the future. Take Vermont's governor with the dairy industry. He and the lobby keep jimmying the bottom line for an obsolescent economy."

I hate lobbying as much as the next voter, even when it favors me, and hated it more now. Fossil fuels, of course, aren't obsolete, and won't be for a time, but they're heading that way, and we do seem to wallow in the inertia their comforts provide. Wind, solar, tide, biofuels—who knows what combination of these might put oil derricks in the museum, but with the might of carbon lobbyists at play, it won't happen tomorrow.

As I came upon the stick I'd wedged in the gravel to mark the peninsula-turn, New York City was contemplating natural gas extraction around its aquifer. Natural gas is simply methane, much of it trapped in old sea floors. The largest currently known is the Marcellus, a six hundred–mile shale bed stretching through West Virginia, Ohio, Pennsylvania, and New York. The old seas trapped much, including uranium, mercury, arsenic, and lead, all useful in contained capacities, but not when bled into water tables or loam. When coal and oil stores seemed like they'd never end, not much attention was paid to natural gas, nor were profitable means available to release it. That's changed. Coal is still plentiful, but its dangers to both miners and ecologies are influencing public opinion. Oil, too, is on the run. Domestic supplies are thinning, and we create scads of America-haters a day with each bullying foray into countries like Niger, Iraq, and Yemen. Natural gas, then, is the new It Girl, and the means to unlock it are at hand in the form of high-volume, slick-water hydrofracturing, or "fracking."

To frack, a drill first bores the one-to-two miles down necessary to penetrate the shale, then angles horizontally. Next, a mix of water and some three hundred chemicals—including cancer-causing benzene—are flushed in with sand. The water fractures the rock, the sand keeps it open, and the chemicals ease friction and kill algae as the gas runs up the pipe along with a healthy portion of the fracking fluid and whatever native elements it releases. The rest stays in the ground, doing what fluid does, seeking other fissures, maybe into drinking water. Pennsylvania is shot-through with fracking, but while I paddled, New York was awaiting further study before hosing itself down with a three hundred–chemical cocktail from the Finger Lakes to the outer boroughs.

For the fossil fuel industry, fracking is great news. It's also great for anyone who likes to cook, take hot showers, and stay warm in winter, but this is the trick. What gives us all our comforts may kill us. Global warming might do it, but we've spewed enough carbon to keep temperatures rising for some time even if every human dropped dead tomorrow. It's the pollution—and all the disruptions it causes—that is the true fret, for we know that if something can go wrong it will. Put military bases and oil rigs in people's backyards, they'll object, sometimes violently. Haul oil around in ocean tankers and some of them will spill. Drilling in five thousand feet of water is a good way to eventually ruin that ecosystem. Blow mountain tops off and bury surrounding watersheds in coal slurry, the place becomes uninhabitable. Breathe smog, you'll get sick, maybe die. Pump carcinogens into the shadow of a water supply, and one day you'll drink your doom. We could dig up every potato in Idaho to find the one who couldn't tell us all this, but that would be one damned stupid spud, yet internal combustion persists, because for most of us most of the time, to have it otherwise is largely unthinkable.

The canoe lay where I left it, the sun nosing over the Fishkill Range. Earlier, I'd stumbled on the old Brockway factory, now a cement foundation, cracked further each spring by sumac shoots, the summer's goldenrod crop laying down more sediment every fall. *National Geographic* ran a program on what might happen should humans disappear, thinking not much would be left of us after five thousand years. Hard to say, but along this one river, nature's expedient iconoclasm flourishes. Still, though we rightly repeat that nature has the last laugh, humans have greater power than any species before. Our energy thirst has already crushed landscapes and the creatures that live on them, and will doubtlessly do much more before we find sufficient replacement for fossil fuels.

I knew it wouldn't be long to Indian Point, pictures of which I'd seen. Nuclear plants are unmistakable, the half-buried eggs resting in the earth like Grecian pots, and are a promising alternative to the coal/oil/gas grid. As many have pointed out, no one has yet died working a nuclear plant, and the emissions are zero. The only trouble is the waste, but if that can be handled, we should be off and running. The waste, however, isn't handled, and should a nuclear plant ever rupture, it will be nothing like an oil spill. A bartender in Yakutat took vacations to the cheapest places he could find, spending one winter in Chernobyl.

"What were the women like," we asked.

"Beautiful," he said, wiping down the bar. "Except their teeth. They all fall out, so everyone's are made of gold."

Another year, a new kid came to work for the Forest Service, a big guy, cocky but amiable. I worked a salmon weir that summer where brown bears are common. This guy was fishing a good stretch below us when a young bear came out of the brush thirty yards upstream of him. Three of us watched from the weir's catwalk. Bears nearly always shy from humans, so it wasn't surprising when this one ducked back in the willows when the kid stomped upstream, waving arms and shouting. We marveled at his greenness. An older guy, who'd worked the Alaskan bush for thirty years, shrugged his shoulders.

"You win that game until you don't," he said.

You win a lot of games until you don't. Some, like nukes, kill you fast, others, like oil, kill you slow. We dawdle with wind and dally in sun while pretending nothing bad would come from spent uranium, until a Pacific floor shudder outside Fukushima set us aright. Most of us worry, including me, but like most of us, I'm as culpable as Cain. When the Allman Brothers come on the radio—"Jessica," say, America's Ninth Symphony—the last thing I think of is blown-up mountain tops, oiled-down oysters, or Iranian mullahs. My only thought is, "Turn it up," which translated across six-billion-and-counting means, "You win that game until you don't."

Beacon's name wasn't happenstance. Continental soldiers lit fires atop the Fishkills to warn others of British troop movements. I stepped in the canoe, muscling through river lettuce, flushing a dozen mallards behind an up-turned stump. They lifted, frantic wings framed by the great hump past the interstate bridge, Storm King, the place that got us thinking about these things. A beacon indeed.

Such High Zest

Funny how little we know about our own country. I've lived in fair portions of it, driven across several times, soaked up its history where I can, but there's too much to ever say you understand this place. Hugging the rip-rap on river-left, I paddled beneath I-84, having spent most of my life within shouting distance of the Hudson, America's oldest storyteller. Yet until this trip, I'd scarcely considered the place other than to glance out the window as my parents ferried us across this bridge. In the Hudson watershed alone, partitions exist that are hardly breached. The Adirondacks didn't know much of the valley, and many in the valley wouldn't know for days if Manhattan sloughed into the river, and that island, of course, doesn't know that places like Queens and Hoboken exist. This is one river. To imagine the blindness across fifty states is heavy work. Every nook has stories, and from traveling salesmen to our most accomplished history profs, you'll never find someone who has burrowed into every backwater and hollow, every arroyo and bayou, heard every dialect from all the ridges, dunes, ex-urbs, hilltops, river towns, cornfields, soyfields, pastureland, buttes, knolls, high-rises, swamps, ghettos, prairies, tech dens, woodlands, and mill husks that we call a nation, who can honestly say, "This is America, and I know it."

Floating along Beacon's revived waterfront, I passed old men in chairs, fishing the tide. Who were they? The harbor was next, and there it was, *The Clearwater*, the stripped masts cutting the humidity, the wide, wooden aft a spark for Romantic imagining. Rigging laced the air above, while bustling young people prepared for the morning's pupils. I paddled within feet of it, this schooner, the likes of which once flooded the Hudson. Mountains rose ahead, Storm King to the west, and I knew West Point was cleft somewhere among them. Like any country, when approaching America you need to look at its wars, or more importantly how we perceive ourselves in war. This is no easy doing, for both the purpose and legacies of our many struggles are as complex as the people who fought them—us.

Twelve days in, the boat nearly paddled itself. After clearing Dening's Point, I eased into a wide bay, with a strange sight to the east. A red-brick castle thrusts out of a small island. The island, thought by Indians to contain evil spirits, is called Pollopel, and the structure is named for the Scotch dingbat who built it. Francis Bannerman VI, an eccentric, wanting America tabbed with bits of his homeland, bought ninety percent of the army surplus after the Spanish-American War, building the castle to store it. Even in decay, it's a pearl. An explosion wrecked a section in 1920, but it remained a Bannerman family retreat until 1967, when they sold it to New York State. Vandals had their say, fire blackened it, but there it stands, in glorious disrepair. Twenty minutes later I slipped between it and river-left, once again admiring what human hands can do, half-hoping William Wallace would pop up and chuck a spear at me from a soot-smeared rook: "Tay tha, ya Ainglish prrick, a' Goh bles whooze e'er poolin' yair nohb!"

This was the trip's hottest day. Sweat stung my eyes, and a couple times I slipped over the gunnels, treading, a bit awed by what I saw. I'd read of the Hudson Highlands, knew the inspirations they've caused, but wasn't prepared. The river is different here, confined, caulked by steep, densely forested slopes just then in the depth of summer green. After the patched-up grime of Poughkeepsie's and Newburgh's waterfronts, I thought I'd teleported north, drifting the Adirondacks again. Bathers swam a sandy beach above Cold Spring, once an east-bank iron and munitions forge, now a posh commuterville. Fathers barbecued brunch in the shade, while mothers built sandcastles with children. How peaceful it all seems, here in America, when you only ponder what's before you. Along Constitution Marsh, however, a bird preserve, I scraped a rocky outcrop to cross the estuary's narrowest cut, soon to pass a world that was not my own.

Someone gave a speech the year I floated—I forget who—addressing army officers. "America is at war," he said, to which a soldier stood. "No sir. The United States Army is at war. America is at the mall."

True enough. As I passed the West Point campus, the old stonework took in another day's sun, over two hundred years' worth now, the breeze rustling brown water. We'd been in Afghanistan for eight years and Iraq for six, roughly a fifth of my life. Still, each war had become what most of us—for or against—probably knew it would: living hell for those who fought, psychic hell for the families who sent them, and for the rest of us an occasional news glance, passing strange.

It's fitting that officers train here. Throughout the Revolution, the British couldn't take the Hudson, and the fortress designed by Thaddeus Kosciusko is largely the reason. The narrowest spot in the river, it's also the deepest, and one of few places where the estuary takes a noticeable turn—a quick eastward jag followed by a southerly. Brit man-of-wars were vulnerable here, and Kosciusko built the fort to command the river's breadth. It worked.

West Point is also where Benedict Arnold committed treason. Until 1780, he was the only soldier to rival Washington for rank-and-file inspiration. After his Saratoga wound and a two-year recovery in Philadelphia, Arnold commanded West Point, colluding with his young Philadelphian bride, Peggy Shippen, and a British major, John Andre, to sell the British diagrams on how to take his post. He met Andre near the fort. The major rode by horse downriver, but was picked up by three citizens, thieves by many counts, who found the plans. Arnold himself scarcely escaped to the British ship *The Vulture* in Haverstraw Bay, where he went on to serve the Crown. No one knows for sure why he turned, but if West Point remains a monument to American independence, it's also as fine a place as any to reflect on loyalty.

The year 1861 was another strain on loyalty. Every major Civil War battle fielded West Pointers on both sides, many of whom fought together in Mexico. One in ten died. Ulysses Grant and Robert Lee were graduates, but Michael Shaara featured the most touching case in *The Killer Angels*, where Winfield Hancock and Lewis Armistead—fast friends at their frontier Los Angeles post—said goodbye when Armistead joined the South. Hancock graduated West Point, while Armistead had been thrown out. Commanding the Union forces where Pickett's charge ended, Hancock feared his friend might be across the way. He was, dying near the peak of Southern penetration. Hancock helped kill him, then, being wounded in the process, one of ten thousand likenesses from that era. These stories move us, deeply. String them together, from Hector until now, and you have the Mythology of War, that institution's stealthiest agent.

Whether you've been or not, it's difficult to say why people go to war. Fistfights are easy. They're spontaneous and almost always involve beer and a cheap date, along with whatever genetic map refuses men the option of backing down. From this millstone we've chiseled honor, maybe the only connection between a brawl and a battlefield. Women, of course, have always fought in wars, but until recently it was mostly of necessity rather than choice. I can't guess why women take a walk in the park, so won't pretend to have any idea why they'd go to war, and while I've never been to war—and hope never to go—I was a young man once, and know very well the vulnerability that is.

It takes time, paddling by West Point, even at slack tide, but that's fine. It's impressive. Nothing but wilderness drapes the mountains, and the gray granite bulks from the ground like natural rock. If Francis Bannerman admired castles, he must have loved this place, and as with any good fort, you don't see much activity, just a stony breadth couching whatever goes on behind.

Most men don't go to war, but we all brood it. Like nations, landscapes, and species, however, thoughts evolve, changing as the physical world shapes them. Growing up, soldiers are scarcely human to boys, certainly ageless if not gods. To a ten-year-old, fifteen years seems all the experience you could ever know, so a forty-year-old you know to have been in war? A myth with flesh. My father attended football camp every summer through high school. No pads, lots of hitting, much blood. He speaks of it amusingly, but to this day, in his seventies, he acquires the aspect he had at sixteen when talking of the counselors fresh back from Korea. They were three, maybe five years older, but may as well have been Achilles. Sixteen is soft tissue, and the stamp these guys left on my pop never rubbed. All they had to do was breathe.

Boys fantasize of war, shooting one another with sticks as little kids, BB guns as teenagers, and in their private moments wondering please God, tell me how I'd hold up. The fear of fear drives boys to do much of what they do, usually peaking around twenty-one. Most snakebites happen to males in their late teens, early twenties, too afraid to shy from a stumbled-on rattler. If you grab a snake and don't get bit, people say, "Ooh!" If you go to war, people say more than that. Alive or dead, you'll be part of the Myth. It's no accident that West Point graduates call themselves "The Long Gray Line," stretching from Joseph Gardner Swift, the first to graduate in 1802, to the last called every year. This puts them within the Pantheon, the one separating those who have been to war—or are in line to go—from those who haven't. Whatever material interests may spur war's deciders—oil, gold, territory—whatever abstractions are necessary to motivate the populace—pride, loyalty, patriotism—without the hagiography accorded to those who fight, other means would usually settle the squabble. We've forgotten that, blinded by the aura recently surrounding the armed services, though it wasn't always so in America.

William Tecumseh Sherman's memoir is one of our culture's better outputs, detailing how he fought the war, but also saturated with fantastic understatement like, "We killed General Polk yesterday, and made good progress today." Michael Fellman's introduction to the Penguin edition serves Sherman well, framing what's to come in period background. Of extant attitudes toward soldiers, Fellman recounts what today would be heresy: "Life in the peace time army was apparently dull and insignificant, not in the least because professional soldiers were despised in nineteenth-century America as men on the sideline, parasites on the public dole, while the nation was being built by real men—pioneers and entrepreneurs." These views conveniently skipped the fact that such parasites were herding up Comanche and Sioux so that pioneers and entrepreneurs could do what they do, but the sentiment is not without either its point or historical follow-up. It's not those who volunteer for a few years, but the career men, "lifers," that have traditionally been frowned upon, and given other perennial American maxims, why not?

Like most boys, war fascinated me, and like most again, I hated complication. Vietnam was ending when I first became aware, and was anyway too complex to ponder. World War II wasn't. This was real white-hat/black-hat stuff, relieving youthful combat dreams of moral ambiguity. Japs pitched babies on bayonets and krauts threw them in ovens, and we appropriately kicked the crap out of each. My dad knew the war cold. I picked him clean while reading every book I could find, putting myself atop Audie Murphy's tank or on Iwo's black sands whenever the fear of fear had me by the throat. Combat has always provoked curiosity. It's the one place where sustained contact with violent death combines with a divestiture of civil restraint: where we kill—and are killed—without regard of consequence. Such release lies in the mulch of war's greatest appeal—the Romanticism to be sure, but further, impossible to reach precincts, involving humanity's taproot hatred of God. Combat levitates participants over every secular, religious, and commonsense law holding society together, teetering them in a different realm. We kill and maim there, and when the release is full, rape, torture, and exterminate, all the things that our every god has told us not to do.

You don't think about this at ten, even twenty, maybe ever, but it's there. After spending time with Marines in Afghanistan, Sebastian Junger excerpted a clip from his book *War* in *Newsweek*. "War is a lot of things," he wrote, "and it's useless to pretend that exciting isn't one of them. It's insanely exciting." Nevertheless, this has nothing to do with why career soldiers, until very recently, were scoffed by the American public. Guilt from Vietnam primed the change, and the Gulf War painted over its history.

Vietnam wasn't America's first dubiously waged war. The Mexican War, the Spanish-American War, and most Indian conflicts had similar public questionings, but they weren't broadcast in everyone's living room. In addition to television coverage, Vietnam came after World War II, when the country gulled itself into believing that everything it did was RIGHT. Here again, the nineteenth-century differed.

Though imbued with the Lordly sanction of its name, Manifest Destiny was grounded by the nineteenth-century Yankee mind, genocidal imperialism included. "We need to get from here to the Pacific, and after that get all the territory we can. To do it we kill red men and bust into other countries." World War II whitewashed what was left of that splendid if unadmirable candor, largely because World War II's material gains were incidental to liberating mankind. The Soviet Union extended this lease, as Stalin was no better than Hitler. Any inquiries into Korea's necessity were buried with inflated phobias of Mother Red, a jumpiness well paired with World War II righteousness, the combination possessing a sufficient enough half-life to sneak around Southeast Asia for a while, unmolested by the Great Why. Before most people knew it, then, five hundred thousand Americans were wiping out the Vietnamese DNA code under the

Gulf of Tonkin Resolution, the now infamous naval/politico charade. Midway through, to at least half the country, we weren't the white hats anymore, a shock registering in three ways—nationalist torpor, hyper-individuality, and the regrettable treatment of returning veterans. Like much indulgence, these reactions sprouted tumors, resulting in the need to purge the guilt of blaming nineteen-year-old boys for national sins. The Gulf War supplied that tonic.

More a battle than a war, the Gulf revamped the army's public perception. Remembering Vietnam's abused vets, the nation fell upon returning supply clerks and SEALs alike, fawning over every Yankee Doodle detail of their lives. Ever since, military people have been far from yesterday's parasites, though yesterday wasn't long ago.

World War II soldiers hated lifers. For all the Greatest Generation hoo-hah, we've put that out of mind. You see it in contemporary cartoons like *Willie and Joe* and movies from then through now. *Saving Private Ryan* is the latest, where Tom Hanks' underlings resent him until they learn he'd been a school teacher, not a lifelong bureaucrat. This is the most glaring of our unconscious American hypocrisies. We can't stand bureaucracy (even Euro-style liberals curse the DMV) but rarely call the armed services what they are—the most sprawling, inefficient, wasteful, tax-inhaling bureaucracies in the government roster, with everyone from privates to five-star generals doing as the manual instructs from 0001 to 2400, three squares and a federal pension to boot. Beetle Bailey had a long, storied funnies run, and not for the Impressionist brushstrokes. Vietnam changed this, briefly making Beetle a baby killer, then a forgotten eighties ward as the nation caught its breath. Along came Sadaam, and the Gulf War—amplified by 9/11 a decade later—turned every soldier into a selfless, sacrificial demigod, thinking of none but God and country. This needs prying.

My dad met a guy in Arizona, Bob Cecka, who's a book waiting for a movie deal. My pop introduced us along with another guy. Both were from Chicago's South Side, sixty-six and eighty-two respectively, and had never met. The next hour sounded like Saul Bellow reading *Augie March*, complete with neighborhood color, mob hits, and all the ethnic innuendo a good home needs. Decades before, Bob was a bored college kid, fumbling through a dentistry foray before a bout with Business Administration. This was 1965, two years before Vietnam became VIETNAM. Marine recruiters rushed campus, giving rides in a T-34 and spouting their canned come-be-a-hero shtick. They were looking specifically for pilots, and though *Top Gun* was a generation away, these guys could have written the script.

"I'm a romantic (spelled 'sucker') at heart," Bob said. His uncle had flown B-24s in World War II, which had become Bob's own childhood imprint of the Myth. "After scoring high on the aviation test, I signed up. Two summer boot camps were grinding, hot, and miserable, but exciting, and, yes, glamorous!—and the thought of flying the world's most sophisticated fighter jets was exhilarating. So I joined up not out of patriotism, but for the love and glamour of flying, a silly, youthful decision, but one of my best!"

He flew a hundred missions, getting shot down multiple times, then caught a break. "The Marines," he said, "are two hundred years of tradition unhampered by progress." They put him with the infantry as a forward observer, thinking pilots would exceed foot soldiers in pinpointing targets despite contrary evidence. "I wasn't happy about it, but it became one of the highlights of my combat experience."

I then asked if he thought eighteen to twenty-five-year-old soldiers—males—were driven more by a need to prove themselves than patriotism or the vagaries of "American interests," as it seemed with him. My hunch was yes. *The New Yorker*'s David Denby reviewed *Into the Wild*, Sean Penn's turn on Chris McCandless, who at twenty-two rejected his moneyed background for the Alaskan outback, dying soon after. Alaskans haven't made McCandless the profound, Romantic trope he's become elsewhere, but rather an artless wayward inspiring others to clown with death. They're right, and Denby saw it: "it may be hard for some of us to take [McCandless'] ambitions as seriously as Penn does. [He] didn't experience enough of life for his rejection of it to carry much weight, and Penn can't see the egocentricity in a revolt that was as naïve as it was self-destructive."

Ouch, but point scored. I implied to Bob that I didn't think guys that age knew enough of the world to understand things like patriotism and whatever the reasons given for a specific war are. I've never fought, but I was that age. At nineteen, prior to attending college, fresh from seeing *Platoon* twelve times, I called my parents aside for what I thought would please them. That week I'd been to a Marine recruiter, telling him I couldn't sign behind my parents' backs. The meeting with them, then, was a formality.

My mother promptly did the He's-Your-Goddamned-Son Two-Step out of the room, while my dad sat, even-keeled.

"Why do you want to join the Marines?"

"I want to see what war's like, and serve my country."

"We're not at war, and there are plenty of ways to serve your country."

"The recruiter said I was just what they were looking for."

"What? Blond, blue-eyed, all-American boy, something like that?"

Crap, I thought, that's exactly what he'd said.

"Let me tell you something. I've never been to war, but I've sold all my life. That guy is a salesman. Some five-foot-two Mexican came in behind you and the guy said, 'You're exactly what we're looking for. The new face of the Corps.' "

He gave time for a response, but I had none.

"Look, go to college, not for any job, but because that's where you get exposed to the greatest thinkers in history. If you want to join the Marines after a year, do it, but let me tell you what you'll do there, you're going to paint fences and dig latrines for four years then get out and not know what to do when nobody's telling you what to do."

This was my first exposure to that earlier disdain for army life. *Raising Arizona* came out the same year, supplying a line that serves up clean this sentiment's parentage, the American hatred of conformity. This is H-I McDonough again, a recovering robber adjusting to domesticity when his outlaw buddies show up. It's a hoot. H-I says no, I've got a steady job, to which one crook droops with sympathy, saying, "You're young, Hi, you got your health, what you want with a job?" We all need to make money, and jobs get us there, yet whether it's the frontier mind-set, the Preamble, or the Declaration I'm not sure, but the American spirit detests a boss, of being told what to do while the creative impulse is dulled by framework, even if that impulse leads to banditry. Nothing, then, squelches individual rigor like armed service. My father had it close—you serve out your term having someone tell you how to tie your shoes all day, and why would you forfeit youth for that?

This, though, is the peacetime army. Many people behind that gray granite were certain to go to war. They were McCandless' age. Cecka didn't quite agree that they weren't experienced enough to understand what they were getting into, just not informed. "Younger men romanticize war," he said, "but if they were required to read Remarque's *All Quiet on the Western Front*, the exposed realities of war would have a significant impact on enlistment." That hit close. I'd read Remarque's book early, but it had a split effect. It made me see the hogwash with which older men coerce younger ones to fight, but made me doubly eager to see what people see in war. This could be said of the ten million teenagers pouring through standard fare everyday such as *Apocalypse Now*, *For Whom the Bell Tolls*, or *Full Metal Jacket*, antiwar works that can't help being pro-war in the hands of young males. Exposure to the Horror is the Myth's chief draw. We want the experience the Chosen have had.

Cecka did think that ego and pride—children of the fear of fear—played a significant role in male recruitment, though he didn't discount patriotism and other abstractions. "I believe they're intertwined. Patriotism, honor, pride—I would say all of the above, along with it's sometimes a guy's best option in life." Everyone, then, has their own reasons, a distant point from the sacrifice incarnate that soldiers have become.

Forty-one isn't nineteen. I have no beef with soldiers, but do resent the starry-eyed persistence that people in Iraq and Afghanistan are fighting for "us," which I take to mean me. Mostly on gut instinct, I don't think we should be in either country, and therefore wince whenever I hear the words "they're fighting for you." Maybe we should be there, and there are undoubtedly a hundred thousand things I don't know about why we went, but each case seemed to me just another generational yearn to contribute to the Myth. Cecka agreed. Like a number of Vietnam soldiers, he values the combat experience while remaining outraged that older men beguiled his generation to war. Disillusioned, he stayed out of politics for thirty years, until it looked like Iraq was inevitable, when he threw in with the antiwar set. "Lessons taught are one thing," he said, "lessons learned another, and therein lies the greatest tragedy of our Vietnam experience: we didn't learn a thing."

My own reasons for not wanting either war lie in both camps, liberal and conservative. Mostly I'm fairly liberal, envying conservatives in one critical way. If you're unsure whether folks are left or right, ask them ten questions, any ten. If they answer directly, they're conservative. If they start most answers with, "Hmm, that's tricky. On the one hand . . . ," they're liberal. To liberals, everything is complicated. That's why conservatives attend church in disproportionate numbers. Liberals believe, they just don't know what to believe, whereas if you ask a conservative what God is, they say, "It's this," with "this" being whatever they've been preached to since childhood. Such clarity must be soothing.

I privately opposed both Afghanistan and Iraq on the usual humanitarian grounds, along with a sense that the invasions made us less secure, but wasn't blind to the other side. We were attacked, and the human need for vengeance never wants. Besides, self-defense is certainly a justifiable cause for war, and though I didn't think we approached ours the right way, something had to be done. In other words, it was complicated. My other reasons, however, have everything to do with our own soldiers. My Lai doesn't shock me, Abu Ghraib either, or any of the hundred billion other soldier outbursts in history. Put young people far from family without civilized constraint and underfoot of constant death—particularly with popular disinterest back home—what else do you think they're going to do? When people come back from such doings, or even war's grim regularity, it affects them, and neither is it surprising when young veterans kill themselves, get divorced, go homeless, or drown in booze, as ten thousands do. It's grotesquely sad, but with a hundred thousand generations of Shell Shock behind us, how can it amaze?

I sat next to a guy on a flight from Yakutat to Seattle, three hours. He was two weeks out of his third Iraq tour, coming down from Fort Wainwright. A big, white South Carolinian, heavily tattooed and friendly as can be, he had that southern way of talking through you without it being offensive. Mostly he was anxious to find a Seattle motel and get drunk. By the stench, he'd barely sobered from the night before, and his hands jiggled the whole flight. Having zero idea what this guy had been through, I realized that I barely thought of these people, the soldiers, and that I felt no guilt or shame because of it was both a confusion and a liberation. Each went for their private reasons—ego, fear, bloodlust, and money mixed in with the good stuff—and had enough of them stayed put, we wouldn't be fighting wars in my name that I didn't think needed fighting. I liked this guy, though, and knew I had nothing sincere to say. Toward the end, he paused in a series of drinking stories set in Fairbanks, the last involving friends who were returning to Baghdad.

"Well, maybe they'll get you guys out soon," was all I could drum up.

"Aw, man, I don't even think about it. I just know I'm out on August 11, 2011. That and my next beer are all I think about."

That flight was in 2007. Guys like this are why Bob Cecka became political. The young are susceptible to dreamwork. The old are supposed to protect them. That guy and thousands like him will come home for good, maybe grow old, be our neighbors, and ten million miles couldn't divide us further. It didn't have to be that way.

Ironically, one of the few areas where I have a conservative's gift for snap-decision is warfare, a place I've never been. If you're going to send people to war, make it total. This winning-of-hearts-and-minds bit is as preposterous as it is criminal. Of all the mistakes made in Iraq, I couldn't believe they dredged up that phrase, or worse the strategy. While I have no experience in this stuff, I do understand that counter-insurgency strategies are both well studied and occasionally effective. In terms of Iraq and Afghanistan, now that we're there, I hope they work as much as anyone, but to me it will always be asking too much of soldiers. To train twenty-year-olds to kill, then send them to a country with a predominantly irregular army blended into a tense populace loathsome of interloping, there to play patty-cake by day trying to figure out who to shoot at night is cruelty beyond description. War should be all in, not grenade launchers in one hand and teddy bears in the other. We killed untold Japanese and German civilians, and in 1945 the Russians raped two hundred thousand German women. We feign concern now, but not terribly deep down we have a better sense of balance. The Axis went all in and got it back in trade. The Vietnamese were cruel to each other, but did nothing to us, and even a handful of dead Afghan and Iraqi civilians put us off because we know only a clutch of very strange people enacted 9/11. We have that better balance, then, and when sending the young to war, those scales should read "total." Achieving that state requires patience, something Americans fancy only episodically. Since World II, our wars have been wars for war's sake. Pushed by shadowy commercial octopi? Assuredly. A demanding consumer base wanting cheaper stuff? Probably. Mostly, though, it's because the Myth's tug makes mobilizing the young so easy, and such manipulation is too shabby a treatment for one generation to enact upon another.

With the sun noon-high, an osprey caught an upstream breeze, scanning the eastern shore where the ebb might tempt a young carp. I was close enough to the west bank to hear a gray squirrel bark from an oak, while further down, near the campus' southern edge, a burnt-orange wing-patch gave a redstart away, its otherwise black form hunting duns up in a willow bower.

Envy for soldiers has largely left me, though the curiosity remains. It's not what those cadets will see, but what they'll feel that tampers with human magnetics, warfare's spiritual pull. That close to dying, inflicting and sustaining the worst that humans can do, must push the soul tight against the border we all cross—death—and the answers that in life lie beyond us. Rational beings wouldn't fiddle with such knowledge before its time, but passions have always known their way in and out of logic, like mice in a farmhouse. How does it feel, we wonder, to be set free, weapon in hand, stripped of every civilized propriety, the tedium of even the most titillating peacetime life vaporized by twenty minutes of combat? Chaos and violence, death and mangling, just as it might have been at Creation, when neither god nor man had yet to speak? To the young, figures that have been to this realm shine like what they nearly possess—immortality. Shrines are raised in the smallest towns along with the Washington Mall for every conflict, with the names of the dead distinguished from those who've returned, elevated to Valhalla. We think we know why, but are never entirely sure.

Data tells us much. It's useful for everything from marketing campaigns to political strategies to fisheries management to which corner a hooker struts. Inventors and science types have reached the moon and cured polio with data, but like everything, it has limits. Sometimes we live by hunch.

I heard Edward O. Wilson, an ant specialist, on Charlie Rose's show. Wilson has gained late-in-life fame by lamenting the fading interest in nature among young people, along with fearsome harangues about Industrial Man's afterclaps, particularly mass extinctions. A scientist with a Southerner's love of prose, Wilson had written his first novel, somehow about ants. Rose asked if there's a link between the warfare of ants and of people, for both of whom it's constant. "I'm afraid it's congenital," Wilson said, and he's right. Ten thousand years of reasoning, moreover, hasn't told us why, leaving us with hunch.

We make war for the obvious reasons—land, resources—but these alone could never produce such bewildering animus. People—noncriminals anyway—don't get peeved enough over gold or oil to rape, murder, and torture. Silence gives us our highest angst, and as such may be the ignition. Somehow life came about. Out of that swamp came us, and we wonder, constantly, why. Is there meaning, or does consciousness simply extinguish upon death and will the sun one day cool or the universe revert or an asteroid strike, obliterating all we've done? Churches have endured for thousands of years in the hope that they've answered these questions, and our greatest art has been wrought in their pursuit. Still, we need answers from the source, and all we've ever heard is silence. No one questions their existence more than the young, and none have more rage at the unrequiting air. Unable to fight what they can't see, the young exorcise themselves on the visible—other people. Wars are fought for territory, kingships, and oil, freedom, liberty, and dignity, but they all might share the hatred threaded into our love of God, our only way of saying, "You put us here, you son-of-a-bitch, and we don't know why. Speak."

As I've aged, the Myth still has pull, but the young—the soldiers—are less an interest than a redundancy. They join an army and do what they're told, too afraid to stand down from potential violence. Most act with courage, but war puts people in situations that demand it. What the war does to them afterward has become more moving, what it does to others—to whom soldiers bring war—even more so. Norman Rush wrote *Mortals*, a novel set in Africa. In it he coins "hell-mouth," described as "the opening up of the mouth of hell right in front of you, without warning, through no fault of your own." We all know faces blanched by hell-mouth. I worked with a guy in San Francisco, Ben, a floor manager in a warehouse. He was Filipino, a great baseball fan. In Tagalog, "yes" is "*o-o*," "no," "*hin'di*." An older guy, his kind face squished whenever he told me to do something and I said, "*Hin'di!*" Because of his accent, I called him "Meestir Behnsir." It stuck. He left the Philippines at twelve, when MacArthur returned. Two years before, the Japanese found his village, taking most of his family. He never saw them again, though a neighboring village heard the shots.

In Yakutat, an old Swiss guy, "Swiss Max," fishes sockeye every summer. He'd stop by the river cabin where I often worked, bringing chocolate from home. We made him meals. One day, my friend Nicole peeled garlic. "No," he said. "Please. No garlic." During World War II, his family nearly starved, and much of what they ate was wild garlic he picked in the mountains. He was eight.

Nicole came from Salem, Oregon. Her grandfather, John, was a Hollander, around sixteen when the Nazi's brought hell-mouth. After helping some Jews, he was thrown in a concentration camp, tortured and beaten. On his way to another one, certain to die, John jumped the train, unscathed. He served the British, then made his way to Dutch Indonesia, met a woman, and found sanctuary in the Catholic Church, who landed him in Salem. He had eleven kids and became a farmer, which along with drink distracted him from what he knew of the human soul.

My old boss Gordie was named for his uncle, his mother's youngest brother, who died in the last days of World War II as a tail-gunner. Gordie's grandfather fought in World War I, breathing mustard gas. He came home long enough to sire seven kids, but eventually died in a heap of clotted lung. Gordie's mom was highly intelligent, magna cum laude at Colby College, but detested Germans until she died, unable to span the hell-mouth that killed her pop and baby brother. Shrines aren't erected for these people, but they're who I think of now when I think of Wilfred Owen, a Brit killed days before the 1918 armistice. Owen fought a long time, writing poetry throughout, with his most famous piece, "Dulce et Decorum Est," a cutting plea to pause before sending young men to war:

> If in some smothering dreams you too could pace
> Behind the wagon that we flung him in,
> And watch the white eyes writhing in his face,
> His hanging face, like a devil's sick of sin;
> If you could hear, at every jolt, the blood
> Come gargling from the froth-corrupted lungs,
> Obscene as cancer, bitter as cud
> Of vile, incurable sores on innocent tongues,—
> My friend, you would not tell with such high zest
> To children ardent for some desperate glory,
> The old lie: Dulce et decorum est
> Pro patria mori.* [*How sweet and fitting it is to die for
>   one's country]

At seventeen, the same verse made me want to see what Owen had seen. At forty-one, I only thought of Ben and Max and John and Gordie's mom, for whom the high zest of others had opened up the mouth of hell, right in front of them, through no fault of their own. The Myth still had allure, but the gravity shifted, and as I cleared the last of West Point, I realized that I couldn't have been further from the people behind that wall if I'd been paddling a river on Neptune.

The Wide Water

It doesn't happen every time you go to the woods, or even frequently. When it does, the break is clean, like shears slicing cable. It might happen after five minutes in the field or five weeks, though it's never planned. Snap, the cable is gone, and you're on your own, no more informed of what God might be than a chicken dumpling. You live by impression out here, intuition, and no place exhilarates or terrifies more. Somewhere in the Highlands, I didn't know where, the cable snapped, and that broad river—in the last of its great mountains—couldn't have been a fitter setting.

I've never understood loneliness, something I couldn't articulate to at least a few girlfriends. There's too much to think about in the world, too much wonder, and our lives infused by too much culture for lack of company to be more than an ankle-bite. Out in the woods, moreover, you're in it, Creation, where life's nuts-and-bolts dissipate, leaving How and Why.

Below West Point there was hardly a boat, maybe one passing train, and only an occasional second home. There's a town or two, but not much fronts the river. The mountains are steep, healed from past timber cuts, bruised by old quarry blasts. Stony outcrops punctuate the deciduous canopy, tumbling off peaks like vinery. Working inside-bend to inside-bend, warped in heat, I looked ahead, close to river-right, where a snapping turtle's rawhide head peered near the bow. I drifted over, glimpsing meaty legs kick toward bottom. Looking up, two Baltimore orioles—males, midnight/sunrise/midnight—broke out of the greenery, one chasing the other. They vanished, and that was it. The woods cut me loose.

You're never actually alone. That's the joy. Everyone you know, everything you've read, all the movies you've seen and stories you've heard and experiences you've had are always with you. French vintners use a word, *terroir*, to describe the effect soils and atmospheres have upon grapes. High calcium on one slope won't taste the same as low nitrogen on another, with what the winds bring from various shores equally influential. The same seeds, then, produce different tastes, dependent on where they're grown. People are the same, with *littoir*—what we read, what we view, the way ambient cultures worm into us—every bit the creative agency as genetics. Nature/Nurture we always say, but how foolish to believe it's not both.

I was born in 1968 in the American Northeast. TV and movies are as critical to my litography as Plath, Picasso, or St. Augustine. This terrain exists in our heads, the denizens constantly swaying our opinions and therefore our lives. From my surroundings, I've absorbed Elmer Fudd along with Emily Brontë. Eugene O'Neill shares a bunk with Clark Griswold. Ralph Malph is as likely to be around the next corner as William Butler Yeats, laid out in a park, picnicking with Leo Tolstoy, Carla Tortelli, and Jesus Christ, haggling everything from the merit of the GNP to the designated hitter to what the saying "Sam Cunningham did more for Civil Rights than Martin Luther King" really means. How and Why, too, are knocked around *littoir* like billiard balls, with the minerals therein whispering what they know of God, flavoring our personal theologies as much as your mother, your church, or that starburst of starling down you found when you were five, at the edge of the lawn, a pindrop of blood the only sign of the sharp-shinned passing through. You're never on your own, then, yet when it comes to God, you are, for in terms of what you believe, as Jimmy Markham said to the hapless Dave before executing him in *Mystic River*, "This part you do alone."

That was the intent in America, at least as Roger Williams gifted it. Williams left the dour, state-imposed church of Massachusetts in the 1630s for what is now Rhode Island. Founding his own church, he created the concept of religious freedom, at least on paper, the first to use the phrase "wall of separation" for the relationship of church and state. Only a person's conscience, Williams declared, can lead them to salvation. Even this leap, though, was a bit too New England–dreary for many, and two centuries later, the Hudson Highlands registered an equally pivotal shift in American religion, this in the way wilderness influences belief.

Thomas Cole is thought to have commenced it, but going back to Henry Hudson's *Halv Maen*, a distinction can be made from the Puritan view of the woods to that in the less bricked-in mind of New Amsterdam. Adumbrating the ecstasies of Adriaen van der Donck in his *A Description of the New Netherlands*, Robert Juet, Hudson's first mate, kept a journal. The river valley, he wrote, "is a very good Land to fall with and a very pleasant Land to see," whereas in New England, according to Roderick Nash—whose *Wilderness and the American Mind* historicizes our manic effort to define nature—"Seventeenth-century [Puritan] writing is permeated with the idea of wild country as the environment of evil." The one exception was Thomas Morton, who described his 1622 Massachusetts arrival in *New English Canaan* (1637): "I did endeavor to take a survey of the country: The more I looked, the more I liked it. And when I had more seriously considered of the beauty of the place, with all her fair endowments, I did not think in all the knowne world it could be paralleled . . . in my eye t'was nature's Masterpiece; her chiefest magazine of all where lives her store: if this land be not rich, then is the whole world poor."

Morton also thought well of the various Algonquin tribes, inviting them around a Maypole for festivals and dancing, a pacific merger. His gloomy kith, however, weren't amused, booting him back to England, retrenching their convictions that the woods were a wild place peopled by Satan's own. While the Dutch and their increasingly diverse colony mates held similar views of Natives to the Puritans'—loosening only when it came to commerce—they didn't view the Hudson wilds as dismally as the English saw Massachusetts. Thomas Cole, then—himself an English immigrant—was a natural progression from Juet and Van der Donck, with one difference. If Europeans saw the Iroquois and Algonquin as primitive savages, Cole's generation faced an infant savagery, industrialism, which tore through Creation with far harsher hands than anything Lucifer might imagine.

Cole's own *littoir* was heavy in English Romanticism, supplying a dowry of Wordsworth and Coleridge, Blake and Keats, and the idea that Nature is divine language. Carrying this to America at seventeen, traveling up the Hudson, the deeply religious Cole must have believed that he had truly come unto the Kingdom of God. Europe couldn't compete. Cultivated for millennia—forests razed, mountainsides leveled—the Old World's Godspeak had been overlain with that of Man's. In the American wilderness, however, of which the High-lands were his favorite, Cole saw God unblemished. The Hudson view, therefore, differed from New England's only by conclusion—while the supernatural flooded both, the Hudsonites traded God's Light for the Puritanical Devil-Dark. Cole did two things new. He initiated the idea that Americans should take pride in their land, along with calls that presaged our own for wilderness preservation and industrial restraint. In his 1836 "Essay on American Landscapes"—after extolling that history's greatest religious minds sank themselves in wilderness—Cole rhapsodizes the American landscape before predicting its demise:

> The river scenery of the United States is a rich and boundless theme. The Hudson for natural magnificence is unsurpassed. What can be more beautiful than the lake-like expanses of Tappan and Haverstraw, as seen from the rich orchards of the surrounding hills. . . . [W]hat can be more imposing than the precipitous Highlands; whose dark foundations have been rent to make a passage for the deep-flowing river? And, ascending still, where can be found scenes more enchanting? The lofty Catskills stand afar off—the green hills gently rising from the flood, recede like steps by which we may ascend to a great temple, whose pillars are those everlasting hills, and whose dome is the blue boundless vault of heaven. . . . [Y]et I cannot but express my sorrow that the beauty of such landscapes are quickly passing away—the ravages of the axe are daily increasing—the most noble scenes are made desolate, and oftentimes with a wantonness and barbarism scarcely cred-ible in a civilized nation.

At this time, Europe belittled many Americans, being a far more cultured place. Cole's adoration of American wilderness, then, the New World's chief distinction, was embraced. The Hudson and the Adirondacks and everywhere else continued to be pillaged, but a fresh ethic had been sown, largely because Thomas Cole is far from the only person to sense that God's intent lies just beneath the leaf litter.

Prior to floating, Tarrytown was one of few Hudson places whose fame I knew. Washington Irving lived there. Even if we've never read the stories, Ichabod Crane and Rip Van Winkle seem like neighborhood chums. Ichabod was a Connecticut man, seeing in the Dutch Hudson wilds all the devilry of his ancestors, and what husband doesn't side with Rip, the man who fled a nagging wife for the woods, stumbled on the Boys, got hammered, then slept off the next twenty years? Irving, though, bequeathed more than loveable characters. Like Cole, he distinguished the American landscape—again the Hudson—making it as much a character as the people he put there. While not the first to use nature for purposes beyond setting, he began a trend that American writers have developed through the present day. The woods were where the mind detached from civilization, blending imagination with the original world. After describing Tarrytown in *The Legend of Sleepy Hollow*, Irving writes:

> Not far from this village, perhaps about two miles, there is a little valley, or rather lap of land, among the hills, which is one of the quietest places in the whole world. A small brook glides through it, with just murmur enough to lull one to repose; and the occasional whistle of a quail, or tapping of a woodpecker, is almost the only sound that ever breaks in upon the uniform tranquility. . . . If ever I should wish for a retreat, whither I might steal from the world and its distractions, and dream quietly away the remnant of a troubled life, I know of none more promising than this little valley.

Ever since, submersion in the natural world has suffused American letters, extending to Thoreau and Emerson, Dickinson and Whitman, Hemingway and Hurston, Faulkner and Frost, and on through to Annie Proulx and Toni Morrison. One of Irving's first descendants, Nathaniel Hawthorne, described the merger of wilderness and mind as a "neutral territory, somewhere between the real-world and fairy-land, where the Actual and the Imaginary may meet, and each imbue itself with the nature of the other." In other words, where God-on-the-hoof and humanity's cured version of it combine, creating something new.

Prior to Irving, American literature moralized in dull, predictable ways. After Irving, writing reflected the new nation's individual drive to shuck conformity and make its own stamp. Irving was offered an editorship from Sir Walter Scott, which would have required a boss, which would have required framework. Though he could have used the money, he turned the popular European down, stating in a letter that "[I am] peculiarly unfitted for the situation offered to me . . . by the very constitution and habits of my mind . . . I am unfitted for any periodically recurring task, or any stipulated labor of body or mind. . . . [P]ractice and training may bring me more into rule; but at present I am as useless for regular service as one of my own country Indians . . . [I] must therefore keep on pretty much as I have begun." In brief, "I'm young. I've got my health. I'm going to the woods. Shove it."

For every American, then, our *littoir* is steeped in this Irving-born, Hudson-inspired tradition, where our most sensitive minds engaged the wilderness in pursuit of original theology, and none dove deeper than Melville. Scarcely a theme is left out of *Moby Dick*, with much of that lattice concerned with what wilderness—the wild ocean—does to orthodox faith.

One hundred and fourteen chapters in, we come to *The Gilder*, long-absorbed in the horrors that people enact upon the natural world just to live, and the dread and wonder that world injects into us. We're sure what this has done to Ahab. We have no idea what it's done to Ishmael, only that it's engendered a curiosity equal to Ahab's conviction. In *The Gilder*, after a four hundred–page bath in whale gore, shark massacres, and the mad captain, we learn how it affects the mates—Starbuck and Stubb. The South Seas have quieted, steaming the crews in tranquil swells as they hunt their quarry, lulling them to reverie, where everything "mixes with your most mystic mood; so that fact and fancy, half-way meeting, interpenetrate, and form one seamless whole," a rephrasing of Irving's Highlands mysticism. Adrift in a whaleboat, seduced by the sea, Ishmael ruminates:

> Where lies the final harbor, whence we unmoor no more?
> In what rapt ether sails the world, of which the weariest
> will never weary? Where is the foundling's father hidden?
> Our souls are like those orphans whose unwedded mothers
> die in bearing them: the secret of our paternity lies in their
> grave, and we must there to learn it.

Perhaps at ease with his uncertainty, perhaps not, Ishmael watches Starbuck peer over the same gunwale, the mate's traditional faith affirmed by the "kidnapping cannibal" wild rather than wrecked by it. "Let faith oust fact; let fancy oust memory. I look deep down and do believe." Stubb is next, The Pequod's happy-go-luck. Despite its simplicity, his consideration runs deepest:

"And Stubb, fish-like, with sparkling scales, leaped up in that same golden light: —'I am Stubb, and Stubb has his history; but here Stubb takes oaths that he has always been jolly!' "

Stubb's history is that of the others—aware of the world's horrors and mystery—but he refuses to bow to speculation, rage, or orthodoxy, fixing only on life's joy. I'd like to say I envy him, but I don't, Starbuck either. Ignoring How and Why for optimum joy sounds nice, as does sincere belief in one true God, but Ishmael has it. Untiring doubt and inquisitiveness, combined with amorphous belief, leads to endless seeking, and seeking might just be Why we're here, particularly if you consult the American literary tradition, the members of which seem to think that our souls are like those orphans whose unwedded mothers die in bearing them.

I believe in God. For much of my life, I've been nearly embarrassed by that, but no more. The Northeast isn't devoid of belief as many think, but church-goers don't promote their creeds outwardly as they do elsewhere. Roger Williams' ghost may linger in the region, I don't know, but there seems to be a genuine desire here to leave people to their own conscience when it comes to God. Unfortunately, I grew up when Charles Darwin, Neil Armstrong, and the 1960s affirmed that divinity was a childish relic, concluding a trend that started with the Industrial Age, when it seemed that people had mastered both Nature and God. Thomas Cole, Frederic Church, Asher Durand, and the rest are known as the Hudson River School, but that term arrived only after canvases of untouched Creation had been derided by a new aesthetic, beaming over human technology. John Ferguson Weir, for instance, painted The Gun Foundry in 1867, finding within the forges of a Cold Spring munitions plant the same charge as Cole found in the Catskills, only this one anthropogenic. Internal combustion came next, and air travel, then space flight. Simultaneously, science did much to overturn the myths of the Abrahamic religions, and by the last quarter of the twentieth century, all this made belief a predicament rather than a delivery. Souped-up political divisions, moreover, from the 1992 elections onward, have made God the either/or simplicity that reflects nothing of the complex bloom it spawns in every mind. This won't do.

Riled by the religious faults of the twenty-first-century geopolitical sphere, recent atheists have been candid, describing belief as "stupid," "idiotic," and "delusional." Sam Harris, Richard Dawkins, Christopher Hitchens, and others have concluded that God can't exist anymore than Santa Claus, and that it's time to snuff this fantasy once and for all. On the other hand, the loudest believing voices are those of stout conviction, thinking their creed the only creed. In America, Evangelical Christians seem to make the most noise these days, which is too bad, as the feel-good, all-forgiving atmosphere of these multiplying churches is a far cry from Christianities of old.

I talked religion a bit with John Elder and Bill McKibben, both of whom maintain their Christian upbringings. I've never been to church, but certainly understand the quest, while the current science/ religion divide is an enigma to me. Each side often reaches the same destination, simply using different maps. Creation tells us that at some point we fell out of God's favor—Original Sin, the idea that human beings are at heart vicious, cunning, and cruel. Evolution tells us that all life descends from a common ancestor, with nature at best amoral, and every creature vicious, cunning, and cruel, humans included. There're differences obviously, but if you arrive at the same party, why quibble over how to get there? I asked McKibben and Elder this. McKibben looked across the table as if I were Rip himself, emerged from a primitive world.

"I don't think there are six Christians left in America who think about Original Sin," he said. This was horrific news, for if there's one thing I've always admired about churches, they were places people went to feel absolutely horrible about themselves.

Humility is one of religion's better effects. Cohesion and abstract thought two others. While the New Atheism is certainly spunky, its members cripple it at every turn. Claiming to be fact-based and science-oriented, they seem little interested in determining why religion—or the concept of god—may have begun and endured so long, as evolution quickly sheds mistakes. In this light, whether there's a God or not is irrelevant, only in how the concept has fortified human survival. We're a social creature, pooling the skills of various individuals to romp through evolution at a confounding pace, maybe even to God. To do this, cohesion was necessary, and as humanity is a species of competing tribes, the more cohesive a group the better its chances. People convinced that the Almighty approves their every move, then, would have a far better chance in wars than loose-knit hippie packs wandering circles and saying, "Hey, man. We're just like all energy man, and when you die, that's it, you just die, so why don't you relax, man?"

In addition, for people who call themselves "The Brights," neo-atheists don't want to throw much credit religion's way for human intelligence. Even if a Creator doesn't exist, even if we are just all energy man, some human-like creature first looked around and said, "Holy Mother of God! We're not alone!" giving birth to theology and probably abstract thought. Myth came out of this, sharpening storytelling, and as these cohesive gels developed speculative powers, intelligence doubtlessly ratcheted up. As we grew smarter and more powerful, we needed humility. God does that. Jews wear head cover to remind them that there's something higher. Catholics dangle their savior's corpse to recall human frailty. Muslims kneel five times a day. Protestants—back in the day, at any rate—needed no reminders, being disgusted with their filthy selves from one end of the day to the next. We're slipping from that—an extension, I believe, of the thoughts John Weir had when he saw more power in technology than in God.

For insight, there's never a wrong place to look. I lived in Juneau for a winter, working a wolverine project outside the city. Some entertainment magazine mailed a promotional issue, which I'd normally toss, but Bill Murray was on the cover dolled up like Elvis, so why fight it? An article covered an anniversary of *Tommy*, The Who's rock opera. While conceding its unwitting silliness, the author mourned that such endeavors today would never happen. No one would understand. *Tommy* signified the times, when people wanted to belong to something greater than themselves, be it the Vietnam divide, Civil Rights, Vince Lombardi, or Janis Joplin. That's changed. Today, sucked into our egos, further still by pixels and apps, we want smaller things to become part of us, the age of the Great I Am. While churches still provide a diminishing effect, it's more through the institutions' massive social structures than a higher power. McKibben was right. Many churches now promote the secular self, places your kid plays Xbox while you learn how to improve your portfolio, maybe score a platter of waffle fries. Humility in the face of a greater thing—penitence—is fast fading. Who knows what this means, but it's unsettling, and that this trend parallels our ever-widening distance from Nature is doubtful a coincidence.

My pop took me grouse hunting too early. He knew it as soon as he put the bird in my hands. I knew it too. I was seven, following him through the brush for the first time after imagining this day forever. He may as well have been St. Peter. Ruffed grouse like secondary growth, thick stuff where forest steadily reclaims old farmland. Moments from the car, I watched the backs of his knees while dodging rebounded hackberry rods and cutting around multifloral rose tangles peppering the derelict orchard. Hemlocks lined an old beaver swamp fifty yards away, its replenishing rot thatching the autumn air. Thunder cracked twice, and my dad was gone, back before I knew what happened. Excitement shortened his breath, and I looked down. Mottled feathers—so much like a forest floor—were in my hands, shaking, and a custard-colored membrane half-covered the glassy eye. I pulled a palm away, registering the rilled blood and the tresses a dozen feathers had left. The bird's wings pumped a few times, and throughout its body muscle trembled as something gave way. My dad took it, then tucked it in his game pouch.

"That's a grouse," he said.

He put a hand to my head, and I followed him around for another ten minutes before we left. Years later, I'd learn that was a two-hour hunt.

Maybe you're born with belief, maybe it's instilled, and it may be revealed. No one knows, but most of us, by some combination, believe. If a grouse shaking out the last of itself was too much at that age, it also left a brand for which I'll always be grateful. A thousand scientists could present a thousand studies proving that bird was not shucking its soul, but I'd laugh them off, and if we believe in spirit we believe in God.

When people say they know God, get suspicious. The humbling comes from feel, not knowledge, penitence from the unattainable, not assuredness, and despite taxonomy, marine biology, silviculture, herpetology, lepidoptery, genetics, geophysics, the Hubble telescope, and all the rest, even deep ecology, we still don't understand Nature, any better than Ishmael did a sperm whale. We know more than we have, with information compiling daily, but in terms of what made Nature or what might happen when we die, these perplex us as they did Job, with poetry and religion our only solace.

Annie Dillard called religion and literature the only "grammar" for articulating certain questions—love, life, death, war, and beyond. She's right. Science is our friend. It cures us, heats us, gets us around, explains more of the world than we ever dreamt, but for the biggies, mana and iambic pentameter crush the eggheads every time, and we must render unto Einstein what is Einstein's, leaving Shakespeare to the rest.

The words themselves say it. "Book" is of Germanic origin, from "beech," or beech tree, upon which pagan cultures scrawled runes, trying to extract meaning from Nature. "Religion" is from the Latin *religare*, "to bind fast, tie back," or gather up what you can of life to make it make sense. "Worship," too, is from proto-German, "worth + shape," or to shape from Nature something of worth. We've been at this a long time, then, and have come no further than Gilgamesh or Homer. This part we do alone, though we feed off our surroundings—Nature and the people who have interpreted it.

It's damning being turned loose, and a blessing. So close to God, you feel you're drifting right for it, yet equally sense that nothing is there, and that death will, in fact, bring only oblivion. The scariest words in literature come from its scariest mind, Dickinson:

> Behind Me—dips Eternity—
> Before Me—Immortality—
> Myself—the Term between—
>
> . . .
>
> 'Tis Miracle before Me—then—
> 'Tis Miracle behind—between—
> A Crescent in the Sea—
> With Midnight to the North of Her—
> And Midnight to the South of Her—
> And Maelstrom—in the Sky—

Groomed by hopes of Christian reward, the speaker touts its promises, only to be seized by the thought of nothingness as the narrative heads into sea and sky, or Nature. Midnight is oblivion, absent of time, which replaces "eternity" and "immortality" on either side of life, while "maelstrom," or chaos, consumes constructed order. The labor to resolve such questions never wanes, the answers just out of reach. Reconciling with uncertainty, then, is the last hope, the equanimity between the elation and terror that oscillates in the search.

The tide sucked me through the Highlands, a pace belying the heat. Even the high peaks weren't enough for the afternoon sun, with the only shade beneath overhanging branches. Breeding season long over, just an occasional warbler chipped in the forest, while a half-dozen turkey vultures bent circles tight to one ridge, fingery wing-tips manipulating humid air. Other than that, the day was still.

Even without orthodox faith beneath you, it's tough to grow up in America and not have a sense of Heaven and Hell, of a single human god passing judgment in the sky. If I don't call myself Christian, the scaffolding is there, though what I've experienced of the natural world has kept this frame unfurnished. Many people—likely all—struggle with this to varying degrees: the world couldn't exist without a god, yet everything is so still, so silent. From Olympus to Jerusalem, our myths hold societies together, but out in the woods, the pulse of something different loosens bonds, liberating and imprisoning at once. We have the sensations, but lack the words, so turn to verse.

Through no fault of his, I never thought of Wallace Stevens. Something awful happened to literature around his time. World War I left the world in doubt of everything from itself to its gods. Modern literature came out of this, detaching from such whimsies as narrative, theme, and character, leading to the great atrocity of Theory, where for decades the only worth fiction and poetry seemed to have was for professors to prove it had no worth. Happily, this is ending, but simply because Stevens wrote at the tragedy's onset, I dismissed him, only stumbling over his work shortly before I floated.

Karen has a book called *100 Great Poets of the English Language*. Her bookshelf was near the bed, and one day Shannon fell asleep across my left bicep in such a way that I was terrified to move. She'd be down for an hour, I knew, so I looked at the shelf. Yoga how-to's and Irish travel guides sandwiched *100 Great Poets*, leaving no choice. I reached, prying it loose with a finger tip. By chance, I opened to Stevens, and will never be the same.

He's a great curiosity. Like Dylan Thomas, Stevens' drunks were legendary, starting fistfights with Ernest Hemingway and arguments with Robert Frost. Most strange, though, was his occupation. Among the greats, poetry for Stevens was a moonlight affair. He spent his professional life at the Hartford Accident and Indemnity Company, an insurance man, for Christ's sake. This is quite a scandal, for poets usually leave such earthly matters to simpler minds, inhabiting the ether that few besides Stevens articulated so fruitfully. How he did this while examining claims is beyond me, but he did, and we're that much closer to easing our uncertainty because of it. Stevens also knew the Hudson. Living in New York for a time, desperate for the Nature that took him out of his unwanted career into more cherished realms, he headed north from the Bronx many days, walking up to thirty miles, absorbing the scapes that inspired so many others.

Thomas Cole's favored word for what the Highlands provoked was "subliminal," where Nature oozes meaning just beyond the conscious mind. Poets breach this barrier, slipping beneath the border, grabbing what contraband they can and beating it back against that same wall, making verse, bumps that read like Braille. We run our fingers across them, happy at last for expression. Bound-up in his Hartford high-rise, Stevens infiltrated that region longer than most.

With Shannon over my arm, it didn't take more than a few lines of "Sunday Morning" to produce the sensation that Dickinson marked as a great poem, the feeling that you're being scalped. By the end of the first stanza, I was flayed:

> Complacencies of the peignoir, and late
> Coffee and oranges in a sunny chair,
> And the green freedom of a cockatoo
> Upon a rug mingle to dissipate
> The holy hush of ancient sacrifice.
> She dreams a little, and she feels the dark
> Encroachment of that old catastrophe,
> As a calm darkens among water-lights.
> The pungent oranges and bright, green wings
> Seem things in some procession of the dead,
> Winding across wide water, without sound.
> The day is like wide water, without sound,
> Stilled for the passing of her dreaming feet
> Over the seas, to silent Palestine,
> Dominion of the blood and sepulchre.

If this isn't Everywoman, it's pretty close, with the narrator as Every-man, both struggling with the relinquishment of Christianity for an uncertain alternative. She's spent all of her Sunday mornings in church, but modern life and the natural world have eroded the old faith, leaving her unaffiliated, abandoning her to the search, or the wide water, without sound.

Like many in his generation, Stevens' own Christian upbringing was badly whittled by evolutionary theory, scientific discovery, and the carnage devised in French trenches. What, then, when the old structures give way? He knew framework was necessary to balance life, and imagination was where it grew, hewn from the natural world. He called this the "supreme fiction," the constant reimagining of story and structure from the mystery of the cosmos. In eight stanzas, "Sunday Morning" leads back and forth from the woman's letting go to the human history of religious conjuring to the narrator concluding that only Nature and mystery are constant, along with our ceaseless hunt for origin and what lies ahead when we die. Shannon heard more of it than she probably needed. Asleep or awake, I read it to her until I could recite it, murmuring it low in the Highlands as well, quite literally on wide water, without sound.

There was sound, of course, but not much. The tide sloshed shoreline gravel, while its ripples lapped the canoe. Everything else was quiet. Standing on the mountains looking down, Cole found rap-ture here, structure. Sitting in the river looking up, I saw something else—confusion, though no less convinced than Cole that something had created it. After speculating upon the birth of orthodoxy in eight eloquent lines, Stevens considers what future might exist in its decay:

> Shall our blood fail? Or shall it come to be
> The blood of paradise? And shall the earth
> Seem all of paradise that we shall know?
> The sky will be much friendlier then than now,
> A part of labor and a part of pain,
> And next in glory to enduring love,
> Not this dividing and indifferent blue.

He had foresight. With both orthodox extremism and indifference to it symptomatic of structured religion's slow rot, growing numbers today feel that earth is heaven, or at least all the evidence we need of

God's existence. Notions like Gaia—a Greek-derived concept of earth as goddess—have enjoyed revival, and Druids even dance in England again. I nearly envy these people as well, as the sky must be as friendly to them as it is to Starbuck and Stubb. Yet as much as I can sense the divine in Nature, I looked up from that boat—past Iona Island, under the Bear Mountain Bridge, and even through Peekskill to Indian Point on into Haverstraw Bay—at a dividing and indifferent blue.

Haverstraw heads the Tappan Zee. *Zee* is Dutch for "sea," and the Hudson here is nearly that, the three-mile width flushed with salt twice daily. Its shipping lanes dredged regularly, the Tappan is the estuary's shallowest reach, two feet deep in spots, and was a favorite of shad netters not long ago. Despite the shipping, despite pollution, despite development along its banks, you still, without effort, feel presence in natural rhythms here.

I wanted to make Croton-on-Hudson by nightfall, and after clearing a point in Verplanck, knew I would, though only after a long, dead-calm paddle in tide-swell. A mile from each shore, no wind, with Croton's moored boats growing bigger by the stroke, all I heard was "Sunday Morning," the summation:

> She hears, upon that water without sound,
> A voice that cries, "The tomb in Palestine
> Is not the porch of spirits lingering,
> It is the grave of Jesus, where he lay."
> We live in an old chaos of the sun,
> Or old dependency of day and night,
> Or island solitude, unsponsored, free,
> Of that wide water, inescapable.
> Deer walk upon our mountains, and the quail
> Whistle about us their spontaneous cries;
> Sweet berries ripen in the wilderness;
> And, in isolation of the sky,
> At evening, casual flocks of pigeons make
> Ambiguous undulations as they sink,
> Downward to darkness, on extended wings.

In among the boats, having picked out a woodsy spot above Croton's condo-crowded shore, I paddled through water made milk-like by the dropping sun over the Palisades, cliff-face rock walling the western bank. In that water, juvenile shad schooled in eel grass, stripers too, smolting up for their years at sea. Oyster spat—on the mend—fastened to stone and old factory iron, while blue crab scuttled up all manner of dead flesh. Sturgeon were down there, ancient, whiskering for ancient invertebrates, and in the air and on the water gulls awaited what the river might turn up.

Orthodox religion may be dying, I don't know, but it's certainly weakened. What's left? Are we unsponsored? Is there nothing hereafter? This is the wide water. Just as Stevens said, we're in paradox out there, at once bonded and free—condemned to ponder, free to sculpt our own myths. The patterns of nature, of process, are the only constant. From them, imagination resurrects anew, out of spontaneous cries and ambiguous undulations, from sweet smells, ripe tastes, and extended wings.

The tide evened. Fifty yards from shore, the sun gone, I drew a deep stroke, propelled in still water, Starbuck after all. "I look deep down, and do believe," though I'll never be quite able to say why, only knowing that I could barely stand were it otherwise.

Loomings

That was it really. I camped a couple miles above Croton, ditching the canoe in bankside briers, erecting the tent on a wooded slope between the rails and Route 9. Having only eaten a couple energy bars, I was starved, walking to Croton in darkness.

Greek diners set the Northeast apart. The rest of the country eats dog food. The Greeks even out-Italian the Italians. Three milk shakes washed the linguini with white clam sauce, and back up the tracks I went, hoping one last time to be chased by a MetroNorth man. Who doesn't have a little hobo in them? The tracks held the day's heat, and night creatures—cicadas maybe—nearly outdid the highway traffic. One song was appropriate to the moment, "Big Rock Candy Mountain":

> Well one evening as the sun went down
> And the jungle fires were burning,
> Down the tracks came a hobo hiking,
> And he said "Boys, I'm not turning,
> I'm going to a land that's far away,
> Beneath the crystal fountain.
> So come with me, we'll go and see
> The big rock candy mountain."

It's "The Star-Spangled Banner's" B-side, and I sang it freely.

I'd called my brother-in-law outside the diner. This was it. Sneaking onto a Yonkers easement or crossing what's close to ocean in the hope of not getting stabbed beneath the Palisades didn't appeal. It was Manhattan or bust. I thought it might be twenty-five miles, maybe thirty, and by afternoon the tide would be against me. No matter. I woke before dawn to get a jump on it.

New York City is proud of its water system and should be, with Croton as the jewel. Along with aqueducts from the Catskills, the Croton River—more a creek—has been dammed, supplying clean water through a gravity-fed system. Green, Green, Green. Pollutants still abound, sewage overflows, and non-point source stuff—leaky oil pans, fertilizer, gas-station run-off, and the like—does treachery to water everywhere, but New York's system is more efficient than most, cleaner too. *Aqua Dulce*, then, or thereabouts. With the day-gloam killing off the last stars, I cut a line south-southwest through anchored sailboats to get around Croton Point, looking for—but never seeing—the Croton River's mouth.

As the evening before, all was calm. I passed the park, the same land where I'd watch Bob Adams' crew purse young shad up a few weeks later. This jut cost at least an hour, as it thrusts into the river aways. Rounding it, the Tappan Zee Bridge was in full view, with commuters heading east at that hour. A few cars, though, drove west, and I wondered how many would keep going, barreling through the Appalachians to the prairies, further to the Rockies, across the Sierras, maybe the Cascades, and on to the coast, starting a new life. What joy. Flick through the static, hoping, until at last, crystal clear, Dobie Gray comes through. *Give me the beat, Boys, and free my soul*, you sing, with miles to drive and no particular destination in mind, as near to heaven as anyone deserves to be.

Something else was around the corner. A ton of water. Croton Point puts you close to the Tappan's middle, and I lined up with Tarrytown, hoping to be out of the shipping lane before the barge below the bridge passed. Once, in Alaska, my friend Nicole and I needed to survey a remote river, accessible by foot after jetboating a glacial lake. The lake's drainage is the aptly named Dangerous River, and off the launch we had to boat its first mile. Life is funny. Gas-feed bearings rarely crack, but when they do, there's no quick fix. Just before we hit the lake, fuel spewed everywhere, killing the motor. We drifted back down, twirling, ice bergs all around and a bridge abutment ahead. Had it happened thirty yards later, we would have been in the lake, no problem. It didn't, and we were now in the middle of a wide, near-frozen river, with old oars and busted locks for salvation. Nicole looked at me.

"What now? Paddle for Jesus?"

I handed her an oar, taking the other.

"Paddle for Jesus." We did, and made it, securing the alders fifty yards above the bridge.

I paddled for Jesus as well, maybe two miles' worth, having made it worse by misreading the buoys, too excited by the osprey nest atop the nearest to figure that barge would go further east than I'd thought. It was never close, maybe a quarter mile, but as far as barges go, that was the nearest I came to danger. With the big boat headed to Albany, I eased under the long bridge, a few hours since Croton. On a clear day, you can see Manhattan from here, but the August haze obscured it. The first breeze drew up, straight from the Atlantic, then more, until a steady, twenty-knot wind blew upriver. Prior to the trip, I counted wind as the chief impediment, but had been fortunate. One day of wind, though, still counts as luck, and I stuck tight to the east bank, paddling. Slow going, but going nonetheless.

So much on a boat seems insignificant, even laughable. The same is true of being on a mountain, in a desert, or walking a forest. Eventually, though, you come back, where life meets you with its own smile. I was a stay-at-home father. A lot of water pollution, including the Hudson's, contains molecular things called "endocrine-inhibitors," shown to toy with male mechanics enough to move them toward female. It's happening in fish, alligators, and possibly humans. Was I finished? Was menopause around the corner? I didn't know, only that in one important way, tending a kid is a job like any other—it's yours, and must be done. Perhaps in keeping with my endocrine blockage, I looked more to my mother for inspiration than my dad—her choices had inhibited her beloved freedom, but she did what they required and did it well. Shut up and do it, and do the best you can.

As for Karen, who knew? Who ever does? Buddy Holly is gone. We'll never replace him:

> Well alright so I've been foolish,
> Well alright let people say
> That the foolish kids can't be ready yet,
> For the love that comes their way.

I'd hummed this tune the whole trip, and for months before that. It was my daughter's favorite, rarely failing to set her down quietly. I'm sure people exist who are ready for the love, but I'd count them as dull. For most of us, it comes like a bag of bricks—something to beat yourselves to death with or the material to build things. Karen and I are wanderers, seekers. Unpacked bags and unchanged company don't suit this ilk, yet the urge to build has its own verve.

Communication wasn't our strength, at least to start. This was natural. We'd been together a few days prior to Shannon's conception. We never said it, but knew our greatest angst was mutual. Relationships are built on memories, experiences, not the need to have kids. Throughout her pregnancy, we both knew that if one of us died, the other would tremble at an uncertain future rather than mourn a shared, hard-earned past. Love, though, is a bit like paddling tricky water. Just load up and go. You'll either make it or you won't. We had some memories now, and a child, and as I passed seawalls along Tarrytown and Irvington, I thought of a few. I once told her she reminded me of every character in *One Flew Over the Cuckoo's Nest* except R. P. McMurphy, which she thought was funny, even flattering, until I was dumb enough to rent the movie. Birth and the ensuing weeks, of course, contain a blur of memories for any couple, mostly of exhaustion. Her Catholic upbringing has reserved in Karen a nodule of belief in Adam and Eve as humanity's genesis, but having met my family she's now certain all are descended from apes. I had to tell her how to bake a potato when I left for a night. For her part, she hasn't come to terms with the fact that I'm barely kidding when I say that before her, laundry was a quarterly nuisance. Such things make us laugh. Not everything does. You live in tight quarters, sometimes pleased, sometimes not, with thoughts of greener pastures never far away. You stay, though, building, working eddies, dodging boulders, fighting through it, eventually shaping something of worth. Freedoms are lost, they're bound to be, but what do we gain when we lose? I supposed that was decided along the way, knowing it was already taking shape. Still, silly to deny you don't miss the old life.

Other things, too, seemed laughable, until now. There was a recession, with things lined up for a depression. Through the haze, Manhattan's sky line grew clearer, the peach-fuzz-vapor thinning with each stroke. Wall Street was down there, the proper name for America's financial district. If the Dutch didn't invent capitalism, they certainly refined it, largely creating what we now call the stock market. In New Amsterdam, Wall Street was literally a wall, meant to turn back invasion. It was never needed. The Dutch didn't have the manpower to resist England, and when the Crown took over, in went a street, where Dutch-style capitalism flourished.

I understand capitalism. I understand the wheel. One is round and rolls, and hasn't needed improvement since conception. The other is genius. Someone—Bill Gates maybe—has an idea, with the smarts to make it work. He just needs money. Responsible people look over his plan, then solicit investors. Gates builds his stuff, people are better off, and the investors make some dough, with the responsible people analyzing Gates' efforts all the while. It's round and it rolls, and doesn't need improvement. Money types, though, are pesky. They label as improvement any prevarication that funnels them reams of cash without benefiting others, bamboozling the public that everything is fine. Chimpanzees would see the need for reform, but life is more complicated than that, and the people who might reform—the government types—think everything is fine too, having two-hundred-plus years of history in support.

Like most people, I can't explain what a hedge fund does or what a credit-default swap might be, but know several people in finance. They can't either, nor can anyone on television without a top hat and white rabbit. I pushed past the Dobbs Ferry train stop, noticing the first urban birds—house sparrows and starlings—crumbing on the platform. Across the river, a little to the south in Weehawken, New Jersey, Alexander Hamilton had been shot 205 years before. He largely designed our economic model, where government and big business are cozily wed. Like any marriage, he knew, they'd have their feuds, maybe a few infidelities, but saw the union as the path to the greatest growth, and it's difficult to argue he wasn't right.

Manhattan has few graveyards, most historical. Walking Shannon downtown near Wall Street, I passed one, and looking up, there he was, Alex Himself, or at least his headstone. What he'd think today is impossible to know, but we'd hope he'd apply a little marriage counseling. "Maybe you've taken it a bit far," he'd say, and we'd rejoice.

The wind grew stiffer, the waves steeper. The last two weeks had been kind. When I reached those tall buildings, stepped ashore and went back to life, I knew that might not last. Money-changers don't like regulation any more than Adirondack timber-rollers did, nor, for that matter, do I. My father and I never took a mink or muskrat out of season, but by God we trapped people's land without permission. There's a feel to such poaching that the law, not the act, is wrong, that we knew the woods and animals better than the people who held the deed—knew them and loved them—and the land was more ours because of it. Right or wrong, I still feel that way, and if I don't understand short-selling or how market algorithms have anything to do with a company's business status, I certainly understand the mind-set that leads to such chicanery. A few dead muskrats though, are probably shy of global despair, a metric I do understand.

We're an odd country, built on three pillars—religious, economic, constitutional. All are predicated on the belief that human nature is wicked if left unchecked. The Constitution is glutted with enough fail-safes to plug nearly all action for precisely that reason. Religions—pick one—are dedicated to the same belief, having been arranged to save human nature from itself. Our economy, too, acknowledges fundamental human cupidity. Whereas religious and Constitutional mechanisms, however, throttle human nature, our financial system embraces its most sordid aspects, wishing them set free. Maybe this mix provides our dynamism, I don't know, but it's awfully strange.

Around Hastings-on-Hudson, where Karen was born, the industrial decay starts and never stops. Parks have sprung up, segmenting the dilapidation, but if you want further proof that America is no longer a place of great manufacture, come here. The tombs are replete. One park, half an acre, shaded by willow and sycamore, must have been put atop another brick site. At river's edge, a tree has overturned, the roots taking up soil. As in Beacon, bricks were everywhere, studding the upturned dirt like rubies. Four cormorants stood on a jetty off the tree, oiling feathers, while a half-dozen gadwall dabbled bottom. Gerard Hopkins, an Englishman turned Irish priest, never let his religious dread obscure more hopeful sensibilities. In nineteenth-century England, he saw what we now see on the Hudson—a generational human stamp unable to entirely blot Creation:

Generations have trod, have trod, have trod;
And all is seared with trade; bleared, smeared with toil;
And wears man's smudge and shares man's smell; the soil
Is bare now, nor can foot feel, being shod.

And for all this, nature is never spent;
There lives the dearest freshness deep down things;

I'd never realized it before, but with factories rotting on shore like boats run aground, old bricks turned up in seventy-year roots, cormorants and gadwall enduring it, making what living they can in the archeology, America was no longer a young country, but one caught in middle age, its once secure future adrift in a drudge of remembered success, bodily change, and sudden uncertainty. This may have been the country I was born into, but no longer felt like it.

In Yonkers, the wind grew mean, but equally fun for that. I hid where I could, ducking behind jetties, dipping under old factories built over the water, but mostly had to grind through troughs and whitecaps as the tide poured in, feeling like a buckaroo, driving herd.

To the west, the Palisades stood sheer against the water, another landmark conservation moment, as well as one for women. Unable to vote, the region's well-to-do females organized behind such people as Elizabeth Vermilye to preserve the great cliffs from quarry blasts and other depredations. In 1900, not long after the Adirondack Park passage, New York and New Jersey formed an interstate commission, protecting the Palisades. Now they stand untouched, healed, a massive block of Creation directly across from Manhattan's chilly commercial-scape, one more symbol of America's dichotomous land lust. Four barges held position just ahead of the George Washington Bridge, loaded down, awaiting the upriver chug to Albany.

Passing the Bronx, I smelled the sulphur, quite certain of the human sacrifice still practiced here. Late at night, by full moon, middle relievers pitch helpless waifs off a certain mezzanine, down to the cloven-hoofed goat-man clattering about the infield, its face very like a certain shortstop's, who may or may not wear Number 2. It's only baseball, they say, but won't they be surprised when the Prince of Darkness reveals himself.

The river here is simple, though place-names foul it up. Manhattan is a Hudson island, but we call the lace carving it from the east bank the Harlem and East rivers, both of which are the Hudson. Out in front of the Harlem is Spuyten Duyvel, Dutch for "Spitting Devil," where even today, whirlpools and water-spits can mar the surface. I thought this might be a problem, but it wasn't. The island, too, blocked the wind, leaving only the tide to fight.

Elk lived on Manhattan, and beaver, and every creature that inhabited the region when Henry Hudson arrived. Today, Inwood Park makes the island's northern tip. It's steep, deeply wooded. Milk snakes live there, and raccoons, screech owls, maybe a great-horned, just taste enough from the river to make you see it, wish for it, dream it all back to truth. As I cleared the Harlem, paddling a couple yards off the park's shore, props floated by that brought back Columbia County and all the promise it holds. Thirty or more crab apple cores drifted past, freshly gnawed. My God, I thought. They're eating feral apples in Washington Heights again. We're gaining.

A hundred yards later, I could hear my brother-in-law before I saw him, yapping on his cell. Then he was there, waving away in his pink Izod, standing on a defunct boat launch. I beached, or at least concreted, and we slipped canoe and gear through a hole in the fence, an odd sight to the Dominican revelers and ball players, who looked at us as such. We tossed the bags in the minivan, roped the canoe to the roof and were off, finding I-95 for Connecticut.

I can't say what the trip meant, or what the Hudson might mean to America's past, present, or future, only that like any waterway, its banks are littered with rune. We live in a big, beautiful country, with many rivers running through it. Any of them—from the Mississippi to the Hudson to all the hop-across trout streams you see—can tell their piece. Take some time. Put your hands on them. Listen.

Notes

৯

"The Maturity of Idols"

Quote taken from *Spirit of Change*, Winter, 2009, "Mohawk Vision of Sacred Land," Steven McFadden

"Quiet Is the Word"

Quote taken from *The New Yorker*, 11/24/03, "Current Cinema," David Denby

"Purging Strangelove"

Quote taken from *Newsweek*, March 12, 2010, "Prime-Time Supremacy," Joshua Alston

Quote taken from *The Washington Monthly*, June, 2002, "In a Snob-Free Zone," Joseph Epstein

Quote taken from *The Future of Liberty: Illiberal Democracy at Home and Abroad*; W. W. Norton and Company, New York, 2003

"Such High Zest"

Quote taken from *The New Yorker*, 10/15/07, "Current Cinema," Anthony Lane

Suggested Reading

ॐ

Hudson

Dunwell, Frances F. *The Hudson: America's River*; Columbia UP, New York, 2008

Lewis, Tom *The Hudson: A History*; Yale UP, New Haven, CT, 2005

Adirondacks

Randorf, Gary A. *The Adirondacks: Wild Island of Hope*; Johns Hopkins UP, Baltimore, MD, 2002

Saunders, Andrew D. *Adirondack Mammals*; State University of New York College of Environmental Science and Forestry, Syracuse UP, 1989

Schneider, Paul *The Adirondacks: A History of America's First Wilderness*; Henry Holt and Company, New York, 1997

Erie Canal

Bernstein, Peter L. *Wedding of the Waters: The Erie Canal and the Making of a Great Nation*; W.W. Norton and Company, New York, 2005

Hudson Valley General Interest

Flad, Harvey K. and Griffin Clyde *main street to MAIN FRAMES: Landscape and Social Change in Poughkeepsie*; SUNY Press, Albany, NY, 2009

Philip, Leila *A Family Place: A Hudson Valley Farm, Three Centuries, Five Wars, One Family*; SUNY Press, Albany, NY, 2009

Patrick, William B. *Saving Troy: A Year with Firefighters and Paramedics in a Battered City*; SUNY Press, Albany, NY, 2005

General Interest

Elder, John *Imagining the Earth: Poetry and the Vision of Nature*; UP of Georgia, Athens, GA, 1996

Lepore, Jill *The Name of War: King Philip's War and the Origins of American Identity*; Knopf, New York, 1998

McKibben, Bill *Eaarth: Making a Life on a Tough New Planet*; Times Books, New York, 2010

Stamets, Paul *Mycelium Running: How Mushrooms Can Save the World*; Ten Speed Press, Berkeley, CA, 2005

Strand, Ginger *Inventing Niagra: Beauty, Power, andLies*; Simon and Schuster, New York, 2009

de Tocqueville, Alexis *Democracy in America*; Bantam/Random House, New York, 2000

Vendler, Helen *On Extended Wings: Wallace Stevens' Longer Poems*; Harvard UP, Cambridge, MA, 1969

Vendler, Helen *The Odes of John Keats*; Belknap Press/Harvard UP, Cambridge, MA, 1985

Zakaria, Fareed *The Future of Freedom: Illiberal Democracy at Home and Abroad*; W.W. Norton and Company, New York, 2003

Nearly anything by Herman Melville, Robert Frost, and Emily Dickinson. They've shaped us, and not many know it.